Beer Blast

Beer Blast

THE INSIDE STORY OF THE BREWING INDUSTRY'S BIZARRE BATTLES FOR YOUR MONEY

Philip Van Munching

TIMES BUSINESS

RANDOM HOUSE

 Published in the United States by Times Books, a division of Random House, Inc., New York, and simultaneously in Canada by Random House of Canada Limited, Toronto.

Library of Congress Cataloging-in-Publication Data
Van Munching, Philip.
Beer blast : the inside story of the brewing industry's bizarre battles for your money / Philip Van Munching.
p. cm.
ISBN 0-8129-6391-1
1. Beer industry—United States—History—20th century.
2. Brewing industry—United States—History—20th century.
3. Advertising—Beer—United States—History—20th century.
4. Competition—United States—History—20th century. I. Title.
HD9397.U52V36 1997
338.4'766342'0973—dc21 96-37514

Manufactured in the United States of America on acid-free paper
2 4 6 8 9 7 5 3
First Edition
Random House website address: http://www.randomhouse.com

Book design by Deborah Kerner

For my mother

(and favorite writer),

Margaret Patricia Van Munching

ACKNOWLEDGMENTS

I cannot recommend more highly chucking the nine-to-five in favor of the writing life, for three reasons: You get to burn all but one or two of your neckties, you get to go to the movies in the middle of the day (unless you're on deadline), and most important, you really learn who your friends are. They're the ones who'll read and reread material for you, and who will endure endless phone calls where you list and describe your mounting insecurities. Most of the folks below deserve the friendship Medal of Honor. I cannot thank them enough.

Terri Allan, Gerry Khermouch, and especially my brother, Leo Van Munching III, helped shape the manuscript with their insight and common sense, and my friend Giulio Martini lent invaluable business perspective. Terri was extremely kind in making *Impact Databank* resources available to me early and often; similarly, Peter V. K. Reid, the terrific editor of *Modern Brewery Age,* provided reams of information by phone, fax, and mail.

Sharon Buckley, Barbara Fiore, Bob Fiore, Tony Hooper, Bob

Keane, and Allison Smythe each read some or all of the chapters as they came out of the Mac, and (gently) suggested ways of improving them.

Tanya Anne Crosby, Steve Laico, and Anne Sanger, through the miracle of e-mail, lent their guidance, support, and friendship from the moment I started outlining.

Though many of the sources for the book asked that I not quote them by name, I'd like to thank them for their patient answering of questions. Among those who did not need to remain anonymous, I'd especially like to thank Pete Fearon, George Kahl, Marvin Kimmel, Bob Maxwell, and Joe Tighe for sharing their time and experience.

I'd also like to thank Pete Coors and Joe Fuentes of Coors Brewing; Neil Harrison, Susan Henderson, Jack MacDonough, and Jerome Schmutte of Miller Brewing; the staff of *Impact;* and all the employees of Van Munching & Company and Heineken USA who provided information and insight.

Should you ever have the good fortune of selling a book, do your best to get an editor like Karl Weber at *Times Business.* Karl gave shape to the subject matter, managed to make the rewriting process fun (!), and if you find this book enjoyable, it's mostly his doing. Thanks also to Gordon Rafajac and Steve Weissman, who conspired to get the original book proposal into Karl's hands, and to my agent, Ginger Knowlton, who sold it to him. Sona Vogel and Nancy Inglis have my gratitude for their keen (and sensitive) copy editing, as does Eleanor Wickland, for her graciousness and good cheer in the face of my constant phone queries. (And God bless my patient and ceaselessly optimistic friends Christina Meyers, Christine Pepe, and Shelly Poulton, who talked me through the entire publishing process.)

I would like to express my love and thanks to my sister Anne, my brother Christopher, and my friends Jennifer Bill and Dave Spalthoff for support above and beyond the call over the last two years. And finally, I look forward to spending the rest of my life repaying an awesome debt of gratitude to three extraordinary people; my daughters Anna and Maggie, and my best friend and great love, Christina.

CONTENTS

Part Three: Border Skirmishes

Part Four: A Soldier's Story

Part Five: Dispatches from the Front

Beer Blast

Introduction

PRISONERS OF WAR

In business schools around the country, they teach something called "the Prisoner's Dilemma." It's one of those children's one-paragraph mysteries ("There's a fatally stabbed man in a room locked from the inside, and the only other thing in the room is a puddle of water . . ."), with a notable difference: there is no real solution. There is no moment when one says, "Got it! He locked himself in and stabbed *himself* with an icicle!"

Rather, "the Prisoner's Dilemma" is a bite-size version of what philosophers call rational decision theory. It is about dealing with a set of options in which your own deliberations have to take into consideration what someone else might do. It is about the art of second-guessing.

It goes like this: You and an accomplice commit a crime and are picked up by the police. You are put in separate rooms and have no opportunity to get your stories straight. Four things can happen. Maybe you cooperate with the police and he doesn't. You might clam up while he sings like a canary. Perhaps you both keep your mouths shut, perhaps you both talk. The possible outcomes are: you talk and your accomplice doesn't; you get a year in jail while he gets ten (or vice versa); neither of you talks and you both get two years; or both of you talk and you both get five.

Simple, right? You keep quiet, hope your accomplice does the same, and you're out in less than half the time you'd do if both of you confessed. Of course, your accomplice doesn't know what you're thinking. He might reason that you're gambling on his coming to the same conclusion and that you're going to double-cross him to cut your two years to one. You fear he might double-cross *you.* The point, according to the average business professor, is that there's just no way to know. There's no right answer, and what's worse, there's every likelihood that by acting in your own rational self-interest, you might wind up with the second-worst of the four options: five years of making license plates.

See, that's what's wrong with business school. Of *course* there's a right answer, and it's this: You and your accomplice should commit your crime in Los Angeles, where they almost never convict *anyone,* no matter how compelling the evidence.

I'm not completely kidding.

There is one course that's missing from the curriculum of most business schools: Abnormal Psychology 101. Business, after all, is the story of good ideas mistreated by the vagaries of the human psyche. It is the constant battle against a thousand unknown and unknowable enemies. It is the clash of intelligence and breathtaking stupidity, the point at which even the slightest desire to serve the common good inevitably crashes into voracious personal greed. It is a war in which each army is composed of equal parts Rhodes scholars, average Joes, and asylum inmates. It's no wonder that cynics deride the workings of Congress thusly: "It's just business as usual."

More than anything, though, business is a game, albeit one with deliriously high stakes. It involves strategy and intuition, mental flexibility and poise. Perhaps that's why most business schools broaden their philosophical scope beyond "the Prisoner's Dilemma" to teach overall game theory, which looks at what happens when the goal is a common one but the contestants come in infinite numbers and temperaments. In game theory, the road to success is paved with cooperation. Applied to business, it works something like this: You sell widgets, and you charge roughly the same price as your competition. The issue of price increases comes up. In the best-case scenario for you, all your competitors raise their prices in unison and your price stays the same, which leaves your widgets the least expensive and boosts your sales. You win, they lose. The mutually beneficial scenario is that you all raise prices at the same time, so no one gets the clear advantage. The scenario in which *you* lose, of course, is the one in which you are the only widget seller raising prices. This is known in philosophical circles as "the chump position."

Stay with the game analogy for a moment: if most businesses are Monopoly or Stratego, the beer business is Twister. It's goofier than any board game, and it's more ecumenical in its appeal, because the rules are simple. It demands odd, often comical, often sexy contortions. And everyone who plays it ends up falling on their ass from time to time.

I played the beer game for just under ten years, though as the son and grandson of very successful players, I've been around it my whole life. I got into the game to get to know my father better; I stayed in because the beer game turned out to be a great deal of fun, in much the same way the demolition derby is fun. Or professional wrestling. What other endeavor involves billions of dollars in sales, a staggering amount of image-based advertising, virulent public debate . . . and a *legally* mood-altering substance? What other industry uses animals, rock stars, jocks, and bikini-clad women to sell its wares?

And what other industry has botched "the Prisoner's Dilemma" so thoroughly? There is a reason you cannot turn on your television, go to a concert or a ball game, or even take a drive without being assaulted by beer commercial messages, and it is this: Big brewers, desperately afraid of what the other guy might do next, have advertised, promoted, and generally spent themselves into the frenzied overkill that is today's beer business. In 1975, according to *Impact Databank,* the leading publisher of alcoholic beverage data in the country, America's breweries spent $140 million dollars to advertise the 147 million barrels of beer they produced. Some nineteen years later, while total beer production had increased just under 37 percent, ad spending had climbed *500 percent,* to a whopping $700 million. It's no wonder "Bud Bowl" seems inescapable.

In their efforts to get into your wallet, some of the best-known names in beer have, over the last two decades, traded any stake in common sense for permanent residence in the "chump position." Here's how it happened.

Part One

Preparing for Battle

THE PHILLY KEG PARTY, BILLY CARTER'S NEAR MISS, AND AL CAPONE'S BATHTUB:

A BRIEF HISTORY OF BEER IN THE U.S.

Historically speaking, Freud was wrong and my college roommates were right: sex is not the dominant motivation in life . . . beer is. As a nation, America has been shaped more by brewing than by any other single business endeavor, from the laws that govern us to the technological innovations that propel our industries. Our history is soaking in malted barley.

When the *Mayflower* set sail in 1620, it carried a large supply of beer, one of the only foodstuffs that resisted contamination and that could, when needed, be fortified with vitamins to help fight scurvy. In fact, the *Mayflower* cut its voyage short, landing on Plymouth Rock rather than the intended Virginia, because the beer supply was running low. (John Alden, who would be made famous by Longfellow as the first American to steal someone else's girl, was on the ship not as a passenger but in his capacity as a cooper—he'd come to look after the barrels the beer was transported in.)

Though brewing was going on nearby at the time of the Pilgrims' arrival—Dutch settlers had been brewing in New Amsterdam (New York) since 1612—the only brewing happening in Plymouth was Native American in origin and consisted of adding black birch sap to corn and water and letting natural fermentation do its thing. The Pilgrims weren't *that* thirsty, however, and they quickly built brewhouses capable of making the English-style ale they favored. Far from being a sore spot for the Puritans to come, ale was actually encouraged as an aid to temperance; it was seen as a moderate alternative to the distilled liquor that could be all too easily made from the local corn.

Brewing spread quickly throughout the established colonies, aided not only by strong feelings about temperance, but also because it was seen by the Founding Fathers as providing a foot in the door of international trade—in this case, supplying the West Indies with sought-after ales. The first commercial brewery was opened in New Amsterdam in 1632, just about the same time America got its first paved road, Stone Street, created with cobblestones by a Dutch brewer near Wall Street who wanted to smooth the path from his brewery to the local taverns.

As the colonies expanded, breweries stayed local in nature; that is, a brewery in Brooklyn brewed beer consumed in Brooklyn. Though the completion of the Erie Canal and the start of the railroad system would eventually ease the transportation problems brewers faced, it was the types of beer favored by European settlers that proved most problematic. Ale and stout, like the porter that would be introduced early in the eighteenth century, are made with a yeast that rises during fermentation, giving them their dark color and cloudy look. Early American brews, with their short fermentation time and lack of adequate filtration, were especially prone to the bacterias that spoil beer and therefore had to be handled carefully. Paved roads made for quicker deliveries to local taverns.

The thirst for English-style beer meant a thriving import business continued throughout the first three-quarters of the eighteenth century, for two reasons: New England breweries didn't flourish because barley couldn't be grown locally, and most of the early cities were seaports, which made imported beer readily accessible. George Washington, an amateur brewer whose own beer recipe is still on display in the New York Public Library, was an avid porter drinker whose taste for the newer, sweeter beer couldn't be quenched domestically until a scant two years before the Declaration of Independence. By that time, Washington's nationalist fervor had prompted him (in 1770) to join with Patrick Henry and others in a call to boycott English beer imports and thereby bolster the (untaxed) efforts of domestic brewers. Had they gotten as rowdy in their efforts as the tea dumpers in Boston would get three years later, the touchstone of the American Revolution might well have been the Philadelphia Keg Party.

Revolution would end the importation of English ale and prompt the Founding Fathers to bolster domestic brewing legislatively. By 1789 future president James Madison convinced the House of Representatives to limit the tax on beer in the hopes of expanding commercial brewing. It worked. In fact, even Thomas Jefferson seems to have played at professional brewer for a time; with the help of an English brewer displaced by the war, Jefferson made and bottled his own beer at Monticello. (The quantity of bottles ordered by Jefferson suggests he was selling his home brew; that, or he was throwing *very* good parties at his estate.)

And he damned near changed Billy Carter's life.

Jefferson championed the plan of one Joseph Coppinger, a British entrepreneur, to create a government agency to brew beer. More specifically, better beer. Recognizing the sorry state of American brewing following the break with England—imports had dried up, and domestic breweries were too small and underdeveloped to handle the demand—Coppinger played on the government's fear that drinkers would turn to harder stuff when he proposed to now President Madison in 1810 that a national brewery be created, which Coppinger would run, as secretary of the brewery. Though Madison didn't act on the proposal, he did share it with former president (and continued brewing enthusiast) Jefferson, who became an advocate. Unfortunately, the War of 1812 proved a bit more pressing on the president's time, and the idea was dropped. Had Coppinger gotten his act together two years earlier, while Jefferson was still the occupant of the White House, our thirty-ninth president's brother, Billy, might very well have had a suitable post waiting for him in the cabinet. Of course, then the rest of us would have been deprived of Billy Beer.

While Coppinger was pushing unsuccessfully for a government job—brewmaster general?—what would ultimately be one of the last great English-style breweries in America was being rebuilt, in Poughkeepsie, New York. James Vassar's Eagle Brewery, ravaged by fire in 1810, would reopen three years later under the guidance of Vassar's son, Matthew. The subsequent fortune Matthew made brewing ale, porter, and stout would serve as the bankroll for Vassar College in 1861. Though college students historically try to sneak alcohol references into their school songs, it must be noted that the women (and men, the school having recently gone coed) of Vassar proudly and *officially* still sing the following:

And so you see, for old V.C.
Our love shall never fail.
Full well we know
That all we owe
To Matthew Vassar's Ale!

Vassar's brewery closed in 1896, the victim of a reluctance to adapt to the country's changing tastes. Neither Vassar nor those who followed him at the Eagle Brewery would accept that by midcentury a new type of beer was completely redefining—and wildly expanding—the beer business.

As early as the fifteenth century, Bavarians had known of a yeast that believed in gravity—it sank during the brewing process. Unlike dark, cloudy ales, beers made with sinking yeast were clearer and lighter and didn't spoil as easily. As with all good things, there was a catch: this new brewing technique, named "lagering" from the German *lagern* (to store), could be done only in areas that provided natural, cool storage . . . places like the foothills of the Bavarian Alps. Lager was an impossibility in the U.S. until nearly the middle of the nineteenth century for two reasons: the yeast cultures needed were short-lived and couldn't be counted on to last the long ocean voyage until much faster clipper ships were in use, and cold storage was all but impossible in the large brewing markets until the invention of industrial refrigeration.

In 1840 lager made its first appearance on our shores, fittingly in the hands of a Bavarian brewer, Johann Wagner. Wagner landed (though probably not by clipper ship; those wouldn't be common until five years later) in Philadelphia with bottom-fermenting yeast from Munich. Though this newcomer didn't recognize the potential of what he'd brought, local Philadelphian brewer George Manger did, and after purchasing some of Wagner's yeast, he set up Philly's (and America's) first commercial lager brewery. Exactly thirty years after Joseph Coppinger suggested to President Madison that beer of more consistent quality would revive a moribund brewing industry, he was proven right.

Next time some beer snob tries to tell you that ale, porter, and stout are somehow more authentic than lager, tell him he's right, if one considers authenticity to be measurable by age. Then, just before lifting your glass to take a long pull of cold, smooth lager, tell him that by his definition, cave dwelling is authentic, too. Lager may be a latecomer to the beer party, but it is unquestionably the most important guest. Without it, the brewing revolution that would eventually launch America past Germany as the world's largest producer of beer might never have happened.

Revolutions are rarely made overnight, though. It took two years after Manger's initial success with it for lager to make the trip north to

New York City, in the hands of the Prussian Schaefer brothers, Frederick and Maximillian. The Schaefers set up shop on what is now the tony location of Park Avenue and Fifty-first Street.

In that same year, 1842, what would eventually become the most common type of lager in America was unveiled in Bohemia (now the Czech Republic): pilsener. Named for its hometown of Pilsen, pilsener urquell was the lightest, clearest lager made. Pilsener had a clean taste that won over Europeans—okay, not the thick, room-temperature top-fermented beer-loving Brits, but everyone else—immediately. In this instance, what Europeans loved meant a great deal to America, as so many Europeans were about to head our way.

A wave of German immigration in the mid-nineteenth century brought not only vastly increased demand for this new brew, but also brewers eager to satisfy that demand. Many of the new German brewers worked in breweries up and down the eastern seaboard, searching for the best location to start their own. Most of them found brewing heaven not far from shore . . . the shore of Lake Michigan.

With its harbor, freshwater supply, and proximity to grain, Milwaukee was lager mecca. Of course, its large German immigrant population didn't hurt. Though the first German to brew in Milwaukee was Herman Reuthlisberger in 1841, he was soon followed by Jacob Best, whose daughter would marry a steamboat captain named Frederick Pabst; August Krug, whose widow would marry his bookkeeper, Joseph Schlitz; and Jacob Best's sons, Charles and Lorenz, who would establish the Plank Road Brewery, eventually selling to a fellow German by the name of Miller. Perhaps because neither brewery wants to admit to their common lineage, both Pabst and Miller have, for over a century, ignored their shared claim on a name that fellow brewers would kill for: the Best Brewing Company.

While the first government tally of American breweries, taken in 1810, could come up with only 132, forty years later that number had grown steadily to 431. Only ten years after that, there were 1,269, most of them lager brewers. Milwaukee's explosive growth as a brewing center meant unheard-of competition for customers, and shipping to other markets became crucial to a brewery's survival. While other big cities had brewers who were content to stay in their own backyards, Milwaukee started peering over fences.

On October 8, 1871, Mrs. O'Leary's cow lent a hoof. By mythologically starting the Great Chicago Fire with a single kick, the crispy bovine gave Milwaukee a chance not only to raid a major city's thirst, but to look heroic in doing so. While many of Chicago's breweries perished in the blaze, it was the damage to the water supply that necessitated a long-term infusion of Milwaukee beer. Milwaukee came, saw, conquered, and never left. Its newfound renown would cause one brewer to gush of itself: "Schlitz . . . the Beer That Made Milwaukee Famous."

Two years later America would reach its peak in terms of sheer number of breweries: 4,131, which produced some nine million barrels of beer. One of those was the newly founded Golden Brewery, a Colorado concern built by Adolph Coors and Jacob Schueler. Coors, a Prussian who'd stowed away on a transatlantic voyage in 1868, had followed the immigrant stream west, spending a few years as a brewery foreman in Illinois before settling in Denver as a bottler. Seven years after persuading Schueler to use his candy and ice-cream fortune to bankroll the brewery, Coors bought him out.

Another German immigrant would make it as far west as St. Louis and have the insight to marry the daughter of a prosperous local brewer, Eberhard Anheuser. Adolphus Busch wasn't even a brewer, but he was an incredible salesman. Because the beer Anheuser brewed was just plain lousy (*American Mercury* magazine described it as "so inferior [that] St. Louis rowdies were known to project mouthfuls of it back over the bar"), Busch offered lucrative incentives for tavern owners and barkeeps to sell his brand, often even bankrolling their places of business. Busch's deep pockets created a cutthroat selling atmosphere in which he and his competitors were often asked to bid against each other for exclusive placements in local bars. The excesses of Busch's business-building strategy helped prompt strong legislation that to this day forbids financial ties between brewers and bars.

In 1876 Busch got around to fixing the beer. His efforts led him to the work of French scientist Louis Pasteur, who that same year published *Études sur le Bière,* an examination of both the fermentation process and the damage to beer brought on by bacteria. Ironically, the patriotic Pasteur had meant his studies to boost French brewing efforts past those of Germany, but his countrymen largely ignored his work while German brewers embraced it. Pasteur's studies showed Busch how to apply heat to beer to kill bacteria and extend its shelf life, allowing him to ship it great distances without fear of spoilage.

Recognizing the popularity of pilsener, and dreaming of the first national brand of beer, Busch found the perfect recipe in České Budějovice, a town in Bohemia better known by its German name of Budweis. Budweiser was born. (Of course, Busch found a name *so* popular that it was used freely by other brewers—who argued it was a beer *type,* like pilsener—almost immediately. A Brooklynite went so far as to change his brewery's name to Budweiser less than a decade later, before backing down in the face of a lawsuit at the close of the century. Schlitz and Miller each brewed short-lived brands featuring the Budweiser name, though DuBois Brewing of DuBois, Pennsylvania, held on the longest. Their DuBois Budweiser lasted from 1905 until 1970, when a Pennsylvania Supreme Court judge made them stop.)

Anheuser-Busch's fortunes rose with the new brand, and Adolphus Busch, now packing a quite drinkable lager, could concentrate on his dream of expansion. Like John Molson, the Canadian brewer whose company built his country's first railroad in 1836, Busch saw the rails as his ticket out of his local market. He set up the Manufacturers Rail Company to transport his beer to the main St. Louis rail lines. Industrial refrigeration and the culmination of Louis Pasteur's bacteria-elimination efforts, pasteurization, meant that bottled Budweiser could be shipped considerable distances and keep for reasonable periods of time. In fact, even before Budweiser was introduced, Busch was shipping Anheuser's beer to thirsty German immigrants as far away as Texas.

Busch's territorial ambitions for Budweiser got a major boost in

1892, with the invention of the crown bottle cap. The new cap extended the shelf life of beer further still, allowing Busch to expand his thinking to a national scale.

As the regional brands got bigger, the smaller, local brewers consolidated—or went out of business. One of the chief problems for the little guys was the dawning popularity of bottled beer. A federal law, not repealed until 1890, prohibited the brewing and bottling of beer on the same premises, adding an extra labor step too costly for many small-volume brewers. Bottled beer was more profitable, so the rich got richer . . . and bigger. The math is simple: for a company like Anheuser-Busch, which had an advanced shipping system in place, bottled beer meant expansion into new territories, which meant sales increases. For the small local brewer lacking the wherewithal to expand, bottled beer meant new competition for existing customers, which meant a sales decline.

The shipping of bottled beer created the first real emphasis on brand identification, since shipping meant labeling, and labeling meant imagery. In 1882 Pabst decided to dress up its Select lager packaging by having lengths of blue ribbon tied around the top of each bottle. Spurred on by both the acceptance of the ribbon and gold medal victories at the Centennial Exposition and the Paris World's Fair, Pabst changed the name to Blue Ribbon in 1897.

By the end of the nineteenth century, pooling his resources was all the small brewer could do to survive. In Pittsburgh alone, scale economics pushed thirty-six brewers to merge into just two brewing companies: Pittsburgh Brewing and the ironically named Independent Brewing. By 1910 the national tally of breweries had fallen back to 1,568 from its high of over 4,000 just thirty-seven years earlier, though the combined output in 1910 was fifty-three million barrels, nearly six times as much volume from well under half the breweries. The days of the small-volume, local brewery were coming to an end, as much larger-capacity regional concerns sprang up.

By the start of the twentieth century, the United States had surpassed England in brewing volume and stood second only to Germany, though just one of Germany's breweries was anywhere near in size to America's big three: Anheuser-Busch, Pabst, and Schlitz.

Of the big boys, Adolphus Busch was perhaps the most well-known for letting his volume do the talking. While his competitive feelings for Captain Pabst were legendary—he once went as far as Europe to get an exposition taste-testing judge to reconsider his decision for Pabst—he was not above suggesting to Pabst and to the Jos. Schlitz Brewing Company that they use their stranglehold on the market to set prices. (Joseph Schlitz himself had drowned in an accident in 1875, only one year after renaming August Krug's operation.) Noticing that tavern owners were playing his brand off Pabst's and thereby driving prices down, Busch wrote to Pabst in 1889, suggesting a beer trust in the mold of other industrial trusts started by men like Rockefeller and Carnegie. Within a year the Sherman Anti-Trust Act would outlaw such arrangements. Not dissuaded by an extremely hard-to-enforce law, Busch became notorious for using his size to bully small local brewers into keeping their prices in line with his.

Massive European immigration, quickly expanding rail routes, and the ability to manufacture ice all contributed to the creation of the first truly national brands in the second half of the nineteenth century, making fortunes for the companies built by Busch, Pabst, and Schlitz. Yet the expansion of moral fervor, driven by the demonization of alcohol, and growing anti-German sentiment would nearly break them early in the twentieth century.

A number of states flirted with Prohibition as early as the 1840s; some went so far as to ask her to dance. Through the efforts of groups like the Congregational Church and the American Temperance Society, as many as thirteen states were dry by 1855. The first push toward national prohibition would be short-lived, however, thanks to the Civil War. Armed internal conflict made moral reform seem inconsequential, and as membership in temperance groups dwindled, most of the dry states repealed their antialcohol laws.

By 1912, though, attention returned to Prohibition as part of a debate on public decency, and nine states dried up again. This push toward an alcohol-free society was spearheaded by three new groups. The National Prohibition Party and the Woman's Christian Temperance Union were founded five years apart, in 1869 and 1874. Though both were successful to a point, it was the efforts of the Anti-Saloon League, founded in 1893, that bore the most fruit.

Unlike its predecessors, the Anti-Saloon League didn't field candidates for political office; it threw its sizable resources behind existing candidates who opposed alcohol. The league recognized that rural America, where political power still rested at the turn of the century, was deeply suspicious of the effects of rampant immigration. Wary of the millions of Catholics coming from eastern and southern Europe, xenophobic Protestant America worked to protect its values legislatively—even if those values were more wishful thinking than societal reality. One of the very first political action committees, the league was ready to take the lead role in rounding up the votes, once it could get the federal government to offer the legislation.

But the final nail in the brewing industry's coffin wasn't a nail at all: it was a torpedo.

Though the country was officially neutral when World War I broke out in 1914, the American mood quickly turned anti-German. Horrific accounts of the 1915 sinking of the British passenger ship *Lusitania* by a German submarine helped push President Woodrow Wilson to ask Congress for a declaration of war in April of 1917. He got it. As part of his war bill, Wilson (with the full support of the Anti-Saloon League) introduced the Food Control Act, ostensibly to save grain for the war effort. In fact, the act, thanks to tinkering by league-supported congressmen, was a thinly veiled attempt to kill the beer, wine, and liquor businesses, as it forbade the use of foodstuffs in the manufacture of alcohol. On top of this, Wilson used the powers granted him by the act to put limits on the alcoholic content of beer. For the German Americans running many of the nation's most successful breweries, the message was clear—anti-German feelings sounded the death knell for the alcoholic beverage industry. Those feelings, when coupled with Protestant moralism and its attendant fear of rampant immigration, would help the temperance movement achieve its ultimate goal: national prohibition.

With the organized help of the Anti-Saloon League, Congress ratified the Sheppard Resolution, proposing national Prohibition, in January of 1919. The resolution had stormed through state legislatures in just over a year. As of January 19, 1920, "the manufacture, sale, or transportation of intoxicating liquors within, the importation thereof into, or the exportation thereof from the United States and all territory subject to the jurisdiction thereof for beverage purposes" was prohibited. Though no self-respecting grammarian would ever use three "thereof's" in the same sentence, the words were clear enough. The country had dried out.

The year-long warning allowed some breweries to retool their physical plants for other uses. Some made industrial alcohol, others soft drinks; many others gave up and shut down. Nonalcoholic brew, or "near beer," gained some necessity-driven popularity, and the big breweries churned out dozens of nonalcoholic brands, from Anheuser-Busch's Bevo to Schlitz's Famo. Listed together, the brand names begin to sound like either a bad school fight song ("Vivo, Luxo, fight fight fight!") or character names from a low-rent children's show (Hoppy, Pablo, and Yip). Ironically, the near beers, which had been gaining in popularity as Prohibition approached, fell off in sales precipitously as Americans developed a taste for a different alternative to the beer they could no longer buy legally: bathtub gin.

The Puritans were right: beer *had* been the road to temperance, in more ways than they might have imagined. Without beer, liquor gained new prominence on the American palate, and a little growth industry called organized crime sprang up. What were once just ethnic gangs in the big cities became, thanks to Prohibition, structured companies, built around the importation and manufacture of liquor (dubbed "bathtub gin" for the less-than-sophisticated nature of its production). With public sentiment largely with them, and with much of the police force in their pocket, men like Al Capone made fortunes that would rival those of Pabst, Schlitz, and Busch.

Law and order suffered, as did the stomach linings of those brave or foolhardy enough to drink the stuff coming from mob distilleries. Oh, yes . . . the Republicans suffered, too. Tired of the effects of what Herbert Hoover called the "noble experiment," many who'd once fought for Prohibition switched sides in the twenties. The stock market crash of '29, and the unemployment that characterized the Depression, eventually underscored for everyone the foolishness of putting so many brewery workers out on the streets. It didn't take nearly that long, though, for the new lawlessness to put a scare into the Protestants who had so dearly wanted to impose order. Democrats were born.

The first casualty of political shifting occurred early in the thirteen-year run of Prohibition. Andrew J. Volstead, the U.S. representative who had actually authored the Eighteenth Amendment, was defeated in his bid for reelection in 1922, only two years after his words became law. By 1928 Democrats carried many of the major cities by running Alfred E. Smith for president. Though he was defeated, his strong anti-Prohibition stance remained a popular plank on the Democratic platform. Standing firmly on that plank, Franklin D. Roosevelt was elected in 1932. Even before he could be sworn in, Congress proposed the Twenty-first Amendment to the states, calling for the repeal of Prohibition. It took all of a month to get it ratified, and by December of 1933 Prohibition was a bad memory. Al Capone's bathtub was once again safe for bathing.

The brewers who had managed to keep their businesses afloat during the dry spell were ready, as were some new players. Among the latest wave of immigrants sailing past New York Harbor's Statue of Liberty that December was a Dutchman named Leo van Munching, who brought with him his family and fifty cases of beer from his homeland. While working as a bar manager aboard a Dutch luxury liner, van Munching had convinced an executive from the Heineken Brewery that he was the man to shepherd the brand through its first concerted effort to break into the American market. Pre-Prohibition efforts at exporting to the states, done directly through a New York distributorship and without the benefit of a brewery representative, hadn't gone particularly well, and Heineken was eager to have an advocate on American shores.

A workaholic with an ego the size of Manhattan, van Munching might well have fancied himself the next Adolphus Busch; he and Busch certainly shared an immigrant's belief in limitless opportunity. Bar owners in Manhattan never knew what hit them. Quickly dubbed "the baron" by those who didn't distinguish Dutchmen from Germans, my grandfather was known for high-pressure sales tactics, including a little playacting. His best-known gambit for selling an account on his more expensive imported beer involved multiple visits: he'd convince the manager during the day to take in a minimal amount of Heineken, he'd show up later that night, when a new man would be on the stick, and order a Heineken, pretending never to have heard of it. He'd slam his fist on the bar, loudly declaring the wonderful taste of his "new find" and goading his fellow drinkers into trying it. Finally he'd show up the next day, to be told by the bar manager how popular the beer had become—how quickly—and how much more the manager was prepared to order.

While Heineken enjoyed some *very* modest success in and around one major market, the national brands were having a hard time bouncing back from exile, thanks largely to the Depression. The one bright spot in a sluggish beer market was take-home packaging, which had been perfected by the soft-drink companies who had made it big during the country's dry spell. Bottled beer, a popular but not a major part of the market (volumewise) before Prohibition, would account for a quarter of all beer sold just a year after repeal. In 1935 the Continental Can Company introduced a metal can with a cap seal (so it resembled a stubby tin bottle), and the American Can Company came up with a flat-top version. Both offered greater protection from the harmful effects of light, and both dealt with the problem of glass breakage. Canned beer had arrived.

And it was big. By the start of the 1940s take-home packaging accounted for half of all beer sold. Beer had become part of grocery shopping, available packaged together in groups of six. Why six? No one is sure anymore, but it seems to have to do with the maximum weight convenient for the average housewife to load into the shopping cart. The decision-making powers of the American housewife figured in another beer industry innovation of the late thirties: the vitamin craze. With a nod toward health consciousness, breweries like Schlitz started adding vitamins to their beer, boasting in their advertising of the digestive benefits of the additives. Better digestion claims were too much for the government to swallow, however: the Federal Alcoholic Administration (FAA) banned the mention of vitamins in beer labeling in 1940, fearing that the public would get the notion that beer was actually good for them.

The 1940s brought a second world war and a much more prepared set of brewers. In fact, unlike the deadening effect the previous international conflict would have on domestic brewing, WWII managed to raise the industry to levels never before reached. For starters, the brewers with German names had finally been accepted as Americans, helped no doubt by the time that had elapsed since their arrival and the fact that the men now running the breweries were mostly Americans born and raised. (August Busch Jr., Adolphus's grandson, went so far as to accept a commission in the U.S. Army in 1942, one that would put him squarely in the middle of the action . . . in Washington, D.C. Hey, it's better than Dan Quayle did.) Second, and of much more importance, the troops wanted their beer, and no one wanted to hurt morale.

For their part, brewers had learned the lessons of the previous war and were only too eager to make 15 percent of their output available to the military. It was smart business for the big boys, as it exposed huge numbers of small-town Americans to their by now national brands and built intense loyalty among grateful soldiers. The upswing in brewing meant four more joined the million-barrel-a-year club that had been the sole domain of Anheuser-Busch, Pabst, and Schlitz: New York's Ballantine, Ruppert, Rheingold, and Schaefer.

The most colorful of the New York contingent was Jacob Ruppert, the brewer of Ruppert Beer. In addition to financially backing Admiral Byrd's second Antarctic expedition and spending three terms as his district's congressional representative, Ruppert was known for one of the twentieth century's most egregious acts of plunder—he went to Boston and bought much of the Red Sox baseball team—including Babe Ruth—for his own New York Yankees. Ruppert, an avid baseball fan, had purchased the struggling Yankees in 1915 when he found his beloved New York Giants were not for sale. Taking advantage of Red Sox owner Harry Frazee's problems with red ink, Ruppert bought a number of players in 1923, and built them a stadium that reflected their newfound stature. From the Sox came much of the Yankee strength throughout the twenties; Ruth, Carl Mays, Jumping Joe Dugan, Duffy Lewis, and Waite Hoyt among them. Erected right across the Harlem River from the Giants' Polo Grounds, Yankee Stadium was an elegant thumbed nose to the team Ruppert couldn't have.

Ruppert's brewery on Manhattan's Upper East Side, along with the Schaefer Brewery (now off of Park Avenue and relocated to Brooklyn) and the Ballantine Brewery in Newark, New Jersey, were all enjoying pieces of a very large New York pie. Quickly becoming the most populous city on earth, New York was big enough to support four separate million-barrel breweries all by itself, and therein lay the eventual demise of Rheingold, Schaefer, Ruppert, and Ballantine. They hadn't been hungry enough to expand into other markets, and they were about to be squeezed in their own backyard.

After the war, the troops went home. They went to the supermarket or to the local bar. If they lived outside the New York metropolitan area, they found Budweiser, Schlitz, and Pabst. The troops shrugged their shoulders and forgot all about Rheingold, Schaefer, Ruppert, and Ballantine. If they *did* live in the New York area, they found all seven brands, and the local brewers found that the field was getting crowded.

For the importers of European beers that had set up shop before WWII, the war was a mixed blessing. As an exhibitor at the 1939

World's Fair in New York, van Munching had just managed to expose great numbers of Americans to Heineken when the invasion of Holland by the Nazis cut off his supply. Quickly shifting gears, he managed to bring in beer from a Heineken brewery in Java, until the Japanese entered the war and left him completely dry for the duration. Instead of expanding into new markets and reaching consumers who'd had a taste of imported beer at the World's Fair, van Munching spent his time helping the Dutch war effort from his end of the Atlantic. The end of the war, rather than putting him right back to work, brought a PR problem that nearly kept him without product indefinitely.

The United States was sending grain to war-ravaged Europe, and it didn't look right for Europe to return some of that grain in the form of expensive imported beer, especially not when mothers across the country admonished picky eaters that "the children in Europe are starving!" The Dutch government forbade Heineken to resume shipments to the United States until August of 1946. By then van Munching was wondering openly if anyone would remember a beer that had been off the market for six years. But once again, the troops came through. Even though it had been long exiled from American soil, Heineken was very much on the minds of servicemen who had spent the end of the war in Europe and grown fond of the richer European lagers. When the beer in the green bottle returned to the States, veterans could boast of the sophisticated taste they had acquired overseas. A status symbol was born.

Heineken's image was largely dependent upon its point of origin, as Guinness would discover during an unsuccessful attempt at contracting the brewing of its stout to a concern in Long Island City, New York, around the time of the war. Though they did so on the correct assumption that a world war would halt their shipments, Guinness found that once the war was over, no one much cared about an "Irish" stout brewed near the East River. (The lesson would be lost on Miller Brewing some forty years later when they decided to brew Germany's Löwenbräu domestically.)

For the big brewers from St. Louis and Milwaukee, the postwar challenge was to expand their positions as national brews, which they did by becoming national brewers. Pabst would crack the New York market as early as 1946, by buying a Newark brewery. They were followed east by Schlitz, which bought a Brooklyn brewery in 1949, and Anheuser-Busch, which built a new brewery in Newark two years later. Pabst chose to stop its geographic spread there; its next major acquisition wasn't until 1958, when it bought out the once great Blatz Brewery in its home market of Milwaukee.

Schlitz and Anheuser-Busch were just getting started, however. One and two, respectively, in terms of sales, they turned their attentions to the West Coast and especially the state that was now the most populated in the country, California. Both built new breweries in Los Angeles in 1954, before racing back across the country to establish competing breweries in Tampa, Florida, in 1959. Though Schlitz had tweaked Anheuser-Busch in 1956 by buying a brewery in Kansas City, Missouri—not all that far from the Busch family's home base—the brewers of Budweiser had the last laugh. Anheuser-Busch pulled ahead of Schlitz in terms of sales in 1957 and hasn't lost the top spot since.

New York City, once the brewing capital of America, watched the rapid expansion of Anheuser-Busch and Schlitz from the sidelines, no longer economically attractive—or even geographically necessary—as a brewing site. Not counting Brooklyn, there were only five breweries left in the city by 1950, and none by 1973. By 1976 even the last Brooklyn brewery, a Schaefer operation, shut its doors for good.

Where consolidation had been the buzzword at the end of the nineteenth century, by the third quarter of the twentieth it was merger. In the sixties and early seventies following the American beer business was like going to a ball game. To keep track of the players, you needed a scorecard. G. Heileman Brewing, a small regional player in Wisconsin founded in the 1850s by a man frustrated at his inability to reach master brewer status in his German homeland, achieved national prominence a century later by buying up other small regional players. It became the first national concern made up of regional brands, with familiar names like Old Style, Blatz, Schmidt, Rainier, and Lone Star in its portfolio. St. Paul, Minnesota's Hamm's beer, a regional giant, was bought by Olympia, another regional survivor of Prohibition and national brand carpetbagging, in 1975. Just eight years later Olympia would be bought out by Pabst. Pabst itself would eventually become part of California millionaire Paul Kalmanovitz's portfolio of brands, which already included the once great Ballantine name. You getting dizzy yet?

Don't panic. That last paragraph was written simply to make the point that, as had happened three-quarters of a century earlier, brewers were bowing down to the great god Scale Economies. For the purposes of this book, there's only one pre-1975 buyout that counts: the purchase, completed in 1970, of Miller Brewing.

For tobacco giant Philip Morris, Miller Brewing's arrival on the proverbial auction block couldn't have come at a better time. While Philip Morris's overseas business had been booming during the 1960s, its forays into nontobacco domestic ventures were less than successful. Its American Safety Razor product couldn't seem to pull market share from entrenched brands like Gillette and Schick. Philip Morris's purchase of Clark chewing gum in 1963 was done with the thought of injecting candy into their wholesale distribution system; again, with giants like Wrigley as competitors, the company couldn't seem to make inroads, and the Clark products languished.

With television advertising by cigarettes about to be legally banned, Philip Morris ended the sixties with the knowledge that they'd soon have lots of cash to spend. They cast around for a new industry to enter, one that—unlike razor blades and chewing gum—had enough profit potential to justify the time and money spent on it. Their search was interrupted by a call from shipping magnate Peter Grace in 1969, looking for a suitor willing to better PepsiCo's $120 million offer on Grace's controlling interest in Miller Brewing. Grace, not happy with the terms of PepsiCo's offer, gave Philip Morris one day to come up with a better one. They did. It was quickly apparent to them that beer was a category they could work with. Like cigarettes, it was an agriculturally based product, it was somewhat immune to economic recession (as it was considered a low-cost pleasure item), and it was advertising dependent. Having toiled for decades in a business where competitive products had very little real differentiation, Philip Morris understood the power of product imagery. After shelling out $127 million to Grace, and another $100 million to buy out the remaining Miller shares, held by a Catholic foundation, the Marlboro men were now in the beer business.

The emergence of truly national brewers like Anheuser-Busch, Schlitz, and the newly purchased Miller signaled the end of an era in the brewing industry: the end of skirmishes fought on a strictly regional scale, often with different contestants in each of the regions. Now, one battlefield was brought into sharp focus, and it was the whole enchilada; the whole U.S. of A. The list of contestants was still a fluid thing, but now it was *one* list. Growth for the biggest brewers could no longer come from expanding distribution geographically. *Real growth,* the kind that stays ahead of overall category growth, would have to come at the expense of the competition. For a national brewer to keep score, he would have to focus on market share.

The Philip Morris buyout of Miller signaled the start of a new era in the brewing industry, one in which the marketer would play a role as large as that of the brewmaster or even the sales manager . . . and in most of the stories told in the chapters to follow, an even larger role. Decades of experience in the similarly competitive cigarette industry had proven to Miller's new owners that appealing to the taste buds of Joe Consumer wasn't enough, nor was appealing to his wallet, especially when so many products were similar in taste and price. Philip Morris made its fortunes on the image it gave to each of its brands: think of the Marlboro Man, macho personified, riding the range with his distinctive black-and-red pack of cigarettes. Think of the Virginia Slims flapper, stylish symbol of a brand of cigarettes created exclusively for women.

Now think of light beer, whose introduction by Philip Morris's Miller is detailed in the next chapter. Though it's hard to remember in this time of dry beers and ice beers and draft beers, of craft brews and microbrews and brew pubs, there was a time when introducing a new beer segment was a bold and risky act. Because this particular act was committed by a well-financed underdog, it was considered an act of war.

"Let There Be Lite"

Three years before Miller was even a twinkle in Philip Morris's eye, Rheingold introduced the first reduced-calorie beer. Named for the Swiss doctor who'd created it, Gablinger's beer was just spectacularly awful.

The taste was appalling. As one of Rheingold's own sales managers, George Kahl, described it, Gablinger's was "god-awful . . . so metallic it would set your teeth on edge." The packaging, a brown can bearing the doctor's countenance, was worse. The advertising—a moderation campaign that at one point even crowed with grammatical inaccuracy that Gablinger's had "less calories than skim milk"—was completely lost on beer's largely blue-collar constituency. No one wanted the stuff. The government added to the problems facing the new brew by putting the brewer in a regulatory catch-22; the FDA ruled that Rheingold must put the caloric content on the label, as Gablinger's was being marketed as a diet aid, but the Federal Alcoholic Administration Act—the same set of laws that killed the vitamin-enriched beer fad four or five pages ago—forbade the inclusion of the caloric count on the grounds that it constituted a health claim. It would take two years for Rheingold to win the right to put their caloric count (99) on their packaging.

Shortly thereafter, any thought of growing the brand by improving the recipe/packaging/advertising would become academic: Rheingold closed the doors of their Brooklyn Brewery for good. It was a sad ending for one of New York's legendary brewers, an ending caused largely by two things: family ownership that never looked far enough into the future to actually invest in it by upgrading their technology or expanding their markets, and a persistent whispering campaign Rheingold workers were convinced was the work of crosstown rival Schaefer. For over a decade rumors were circulated that the Jewish-owned Rheingold was a heavy contributor to the Congress of Racial Equality. For the anti-Semitic, racist owners of many of New York's watering holes, it was a double whammy. "You'd walk into a bar [as a Rheingold salesman] and hear one of two things: 'Here comes the Jew beer' or 'Here comes the nigger beer,' " said Kahl.

Just after Gablinger's was introduced in 1967, Chicago-based Meister Brau began marketing their own low-calorie beer locally, based on a formula they'd obtained when they bought out Toledo, Ohio's Buckeye Brewing a year earlier. Though much better tasting than the Rheingold product, Meister Brau Lite had only limited success, probably because the beer-drinking public had no idea what to make of a "health-conscious" beer.

Miller gobbled up Meister Brau in 1972, and with it the rights to the fledgling Lite. Their brewers tinkered with the process and reintroduced the product in regional markets a year later, with a new moniker.

Not quite comfortable with a tie as direct as Miller Lite, they christened it Lite Beer from Miller. The Beer Wars were about to begin.

In 1973, the year Lite was introduced, Schlitz was the number two brewer in the land, with about a third less volume than Anheuser-Busch. Schlitz was actually number one in many states and was telling the press that it was about to embark on a major expansion program, with an eye toward regaining its best-seller status. Coors, in forty-ninth place only twenty-five years before, was the number four brewer, hard on the heels of Pabst. Amazingly, Coors had managed the climb up the charts without ever building or buying even a second brewery. In 1973 all of Coors's nearly eleven million barrels of beer were brewed in Golden, Colorado. About half of Coors's volume was sold in California, where it had nearly a 40 percent market share.

Miller had climbed from number seven to number five, with the help of its new management. The Philip Morris folks brought some marketer's skills to what had always been essentially a street salesman's industry; they understood targeting advertising and promotion to the most likely consumer, and perhaps more important, they understood the power of brand imagery in a category where actual product differences were often minute. They immediately set about to reinvigorate the brewery's flagship brand, Miller High Life, with an aggressive pitch to younger drinkers and blue-collar workers bearing the tag line "Miller Time." As they saw it, one of the chief problems High Life faced was the slightly effete, largely snobby image the brand had as a result of decades of calling itself "The Champagne of Bottled Beers." That tag line and the little-girl-sitting-on-the-moon logo had no relevance to the average middle-class beer drinker, to whom champagne was a luxury for the rich.

So the image of the brand was rebuilt, in a way that avoided the generic "we sell great beer" approach taken by most of the competition. Miller High Life was suddenly all about five P.M., the workingman's favorite hour. Miller became the reward you gave yourself at the end of the day . . . the very masculine reward you could share with your buddies. Though the competition would eventually appropriate the positioning ("For all you do, this Bud's for you"), Miller pioneered a very targeted pitch to the average Joe, and Miller High Life's slump ended spectacularly. The usefulness of macho imagery was not lost on the men planning to roll out Lite Beer over the next few years.

Miller recognized the folly of Gablinger's disastrous advertising. Going after beer drinkers with a stern and scolding message of moderation and calorie consciousness was the very definition of wrong: not only are you talking to people who like the idea of multiple beers in one sitting, you're basically accusing them of being overweight as a result of their love for beer. Forget for a minute whether it was right or not in what it preached; Gablinger's was incredibly impolitic in communicating its product benefits. By making its sales message so accusatory, it had managed to stigmatize light beer conceptually: this is a product intended for slobs who don't know where to draw the line. And by being so god-awful, Gablinger's created an even harder obstacle for Miller to surmount—the idea that whatever took those calories out made the beer taste just plain terrible.

When McCann-Erickson, Miller's advertising agency at the time, got the call to create ads for a light beer, they were only too aware of the problems created by Gablinger's. They knew that their campaign, whatever it ended up being, had to deal with two issues: the wimpy imagery of reduced calories and the question of taste. A tag line was quickly born: "Everything you always wanted in a beer . . . and less." Spokesmen were needed. Spokesmen who could confirm that it was indeed manly to drink Lite Beer. Spokesmen who reeked of masculinity. Spokesmen who could beat the crap out of you.

In July 1973 former New York Jet Matt Snell became the first in an endless line of ex-jocks who would tout the virtues of Lite. In a cheaply shot commercial, Snell uttered the tag line and discussed the benefits of the brand, including its reduced carbohydrates. No one knew quite what was good about reduced carbohydrates, but if a Super Bowl hero thought it merited a mention, who was the average beer drinker to argue? The Snell spot went into test markets and seemed to play well.

Not yet concentrating on jocks, McCann turned to a different kind of macho for the next Lite ad. Two kinds of macho, in fact. Writer Mickey Spillane, creator of tough-guy extraordinaire Mike Hammer, appeared in the ad, once again talking about carbohydrates. For anyone missing the macho imagery being bestowed upon Lite, sexy actress Lee Meredith came into view long enough for Mickey to toss off a double entendre. In the interest of full and complete *reportage,* I'm compelled to add that, thanks to an excess of air-conditioning, Miss Meredith's nipples nearly made a cameo. Though they knew full well that that particular bit of imagery might boost sales even further (anyone remember a little poster of Farrah Fawcett-Majors that sold like fifty gazillion copies?), the ad guys realized that prime-time wasn't ready for it. According to sportswriter Frank Deford, an eventual Lite advertising star, Band-Aids solved the problem.

Eventually in the Lite campaign, the ad agency would jettison the carbohydrate discussion in favor of a far more effective sell: the "tastes great . . . less filling" debate. While a bit on the obvious side in terms of selling strategy—can you get any more direct than "tastes great"?—the first part of the equation at least spoke directly to the fears of drinkers in the post-Gablinger era. The "less filling" bit, though, was sheer genius. Not only was the idea of reduced calories being put across in a less offensive way, it was actually being turned into a winking bonus: where Gablinger had suggested that maybe you should drink less beer, Miller was telling you that its brand wouldn't fill you up . . . so go ahead and have another. Hell, have a few more. (Though even the suggestion of heavy drinking is strictly verboten by law in advertising these days, it's worth noting that the mood of the country was sufficiently different in 1973 for Schaefer beer to field the memorable "the one beer to have when you're having more than one" campaign.)

Within a year Lite was available in enough markets to total 30 percent of the country, and Miller was speeding up its projections for going national, which it did the next year, 1975. Now completely hip to the usefulness of macho imagery, the brewery continued to pitch Miller High Life squarely at the workingman with its "If you've got the time, we've got the beer" jingle (including the not-so-subtle "beer after beer" nod to the Schaefer strategy). Climbing past Coors to the number four spot, Miller ended 1975 just beneath crosstown rival Pabst in terms of sales. By the end of the same year it had gone national, Lite accounted for some 20 percent of Miller's total volume. Though still roughly a third of Anheuser-Busch's size, it quickly became clear that Miller was plotting a course to dethrone the self-professed "King of Beers." What was not clear was what Anheuser-Busch was prepared to do about it.

On the surface, it didn't seem A-B was willing to do much. Hit hard by industrywide cost increases in raw ingredients, packaging, and freight, August A. "Gussie" Busch Jr.—Adolphus's grandson—had slashed the marketing department to almost nothing in the early seventies. Unlike many of his competitors, Gussie was not willing to make cost-saving changes to either the recipe of the brand or its brewing process, so he sought to keep up his profits by cutting the size of the company, with a special emphasis on the marketing department. Gussie "didn't understand long-range planning," groused one A-B executive.

Gussie Busch was a legend, which was a good thing and a bad thing. The good thing was that Gussie knew the power of personality in the marketplace, being old enough to have attended meetings between his grandfather Adolphus and Budweiser wholesalers. If nothing else, Gussie was a four-times-married, hard-drinking, loud-talking, Clydesdale-riding personality. He was a proud show-off, constantly demonstrating proper beer-pouring technique and charging traveling companions $2 each time they accidentally asked for a "beer" instead of a "Budweiser." According to A-B executive Edward Vogel, Gussie actually bet one of the owners of New York's famed "21" Club his restaurant that the beer Gussie had been served wasn't the Michelob he'd ordered. When a visit to the cold box proved Gussie right, he let the owner off the hook—but not before bellowing at the frightened man, "I don't want to hear your goddamn excuses. This is my restaurant now! What in the hell are you doing in my restaurant?"

Gussie knew that strength of personality counted for a lot in the beer trade; it was a source of strength for his brands that he was the stuff of legend. He also knew the power of ownership, inasmuch as he controlled some 13 percent of Anheuser-Busch stock, which could be used as a very large club. Gussie liked to club people. That was the bad thing.

A large, well-established company that does only one thing but does it well and consistently can usually manage to thrive for an extended period of time. When companies fail, it's often from an ill-conceived management change or a grab for profits that compromises the quality of whatever the company produces. Indeed, Anheuser-Busch had its share of management types who suggested to Gussie that if only the brewing process were made more economical, if only the ingredients were a bit cheaper or the aging cycle shortened, Budweiser could be even more profitable. Gussie would have none of it. Unfortunately, along with such ill-conceived cost-saving plans, most other ideas for doing things differently—many of them good ideas—fell on the same deaf ears. The last new product introduction from Anheuser-Busch, a popular-priced brand named Busch Bavarian, had come in 1955, and then only as a means to fill production gaps and keep breweries running at close to capacity. Under Gussie, one of his executives would later grouse, the company held steadfastly to a lack of operational sophistication: "Anheuser-Busch was a $700 million company that was run like a corner grocery store."

Gussie's narrow-mindedness would bypass his son, August Busch III. In 1957 August began his career in the family business in the most respectable way possible: he became a Teamster and spent long days shoveling malt in the malthouse. It was hard, unpleasant work, but it was myth making. No immediate board membership here; this guy worked in each department and went to the Siebel Institute of Technology in Chicago to earn a brewmaster's diploma. August seemed to know instinctively that this way, every story written about him in the years to come would mention his humble beginnings and bear some macho quote from him about life in the malthouse, like "When you finished a shift there, you knew you were a man." Though much of his early career may sound like grist for the personal myth mill, his quick ascent within Anheuser-Busch was not unearned.

Though he was a college dropout, August got himself an MBA of sorts when he hired Wharton School of Economics professor Russell Ackoff as a personal consultant. The A-B board of directors watched quietly while, under Ackoff's tutelage (and under his father's nose), August brought a number of MBAs into the company. Though August's taste for business philosophy impressed some board members, most didn't like his brash style and probably feared the sea change in management style August seemed to be planning. Where would Gussie's handpicked board members be once the college boys had the reins?

August parked his fresh hires in a new planning department and set them on the tasks of rethinking the way the brewery did things and wringing every last drop of profitability from Budweiser. (One of the planning department's eventual successes would be the integration of packaging into the Anheuser-Busch operation. Though Coors was already making its own packaging, Anheuser-Busch had lost a potential fortune in profit over the years by buying its bottles and cartons from outside suppliers and paying their markups. August, unlike his father, didn't care where good ideas came from.)

In the trade, August was by reputation a shark. With his incessant questioning and his brusque manner, he terrified his wholesalers when he came to town. He wore them down with the frequency of his visits and the length of his workday. It seemed to Budweiser wholesalers that if August ever stopped moving, he'd die. If his brands weren't growing so swiftly, and making them all so much money, they might have wished it. But more than anything, his wholesalers were in awe of the man they called "Three-Sticks," after the Roman numerals that followed his name. The nickname may have been meant derisively at first—a way, perhaps, of deflating the grandeur of his name. Eventually, though, the Three-Sticks tag would take on an almost romanticized gangster connotation. You could almost see his face on the front page of the paper with the legend "August 'Three-Sticks' Busch III" underneath it. Three-Sticks—more than his old man had ever been—was *capo di tutti capi:* boss of all bosses. He was a man you feared and a man you respected. Three-Sticks never asked anyone to do things he hadn't done or wasn't willing to do himself, and no one worked harder in the trade. He was notorious for spot-checking the beer inventory of even the smallest accounts, and heaven help the Budweiser salesman who hadn't come in and pulled old product from the shelves. And, like Michael Corleone in *The Godfather,* cautioning his brother Fredo, Three-Sticks—August—believed in never taking sides against the family.

Though August played the good son in the eyes of his wholesalers, there wasn't much trust between himself and Gussie. Gussie's paranoia about family members wanting to usurp his power—he'd forced his own cousin, Adie von Gontard, out of the company in 1955 out of fear that Adie was plotting to take his job—kept the thirty-four-year-old August waiting in the wings when Gussie left his role as company president in 1971. Naming one of his own trusted foot soldiers over his own son, Gussie shocked everyone by installing the first non-Busch president in the company's history. It was all the prompting August needed to work harder. If the old man wouldn't give him the reins, he'd simply take them.

August's loyalists, the young business school grads feared by the old guard, took to meeting secretly, often at August's farm, to plan for the day when they would run the company. They might have toiled in vain had the cost of doing business not skyrocketed during the early seventies.

Gussie may have controlled 13 percent of the company bearing his name, but the other 87 percent was in the hands of stockholders who were not at all happy that the price of their shares was swirling down the toilet. Though sales kept racing higher and higher, profit sank throughout the beer industry as the cost of making, packaging, and shipping beer climbed quickly. While some other brewers cut production costs (most disastrously Schlitz, as chronicled in the next chapter), Gussie took a different route to restore some of the company's fortunes. He cut overhead. He slashed well over one hundred white-collar jobs. His dictatorial approach to problem solving had two major effects: it caused his handpicked president to resign in protest, and it started to convince his board members that the old man was losing his grip. Maybe, they thought, the kid and his collection of workaholic MBAs weren't so bad after all.

For his part, August worked the board tirelessly, gaining their trust even as his father was losing it. When Gussie named August president of the company in 1974, the board approved his decision quickly, but this time not completely out of loyalty to Gussie. Within one year August would demonstrate to his father that he indeed had the leadership capabilities to run the company: he led a coup that would completely remove Gussie from the company. Using some of the same strong arm tactics Gussie had been famous for, August would prod, threaten, and cajole board members not already in his camp that it was in their best interest to take sides with Busch the Younger.

One key board member was August's second cousin, James Orthwein, who was president of D'Arcy Advertising. The rumor went around that August locked up Orthwein's loyalty by promising never to fire D'Arcy from the Anheuser-Busch account. He got Orthwein's vote against his father, just as he collected the votes of others with similar gambits. Reportedly, Gussie was told that if he didn't sign on to his own ouster, by issuing a statement agreeing with it, he would not only still be out, he'd no longer be allowed to run the St. Louis Cardinals, the baseball team he'd purchased in 1953. Gussie went quietly, though he reportedly seriously considered an offer from R. J. Reynolds to buy the company out from under his son's feet.

The final straw for Gussie, some board members felt, had been his lack of response to Miller's surge of growth under Philip Morris. August was not about to ignore the threat from Milwaukee, but before he could set his sights on Miller, he had one last major internal obstacle and his first major test as a leader: the Teamsters.

Gussie had avoided confrontation with Anheuser-Busch's largest union whenever possible because Gussie feared strikes: strikes limit capacity when they don't shut down production altogether, and limited capacity means retailers go without. That means reduced market share. Market share was Gussie's strength in the marketplace; it was his assurance that wholesalers who carried products from an assortment of brewers paid most of their attention to *his* brands. August, taking over with a dramatically depressed stock price and determined to increase profitability, knew that his first negotiations with the Teamsters were critical. His former malthouse compatriots were testing August and his business school brain trust. For ninety-five days in the spring of 1976, the bottlers' local unions struck at each Anheuser-Busch brewery across the country, over a new contract.

With production cut nearly in half, the costliest strike in Anheuser-Busch history would mean a 4 percent drop in market share and a further deflation of company stock. Tens of millions in income was lost. Labor relations suffered.

But no one would ever doubt August's resolve again. "It was the first time they had dealt with me on the front line," he would say later. "They wanted written into the contract that they would have the right to approve or disapprove any changes in production before we could implement them. They would manage our production, not us." In the end the union accepted the original financial package August had offered them. He'd essentially waited them out, and in the process he'd passed his first test.

It was a good thing, too, because August lacked an essential element in Gussie's reign at Anheuser-Busch: significant ownership. Where Gussie had controlled 13 percent of the company's stock, August would eventually control approximately 0.6 percent, the rest diluted a decade later among Gussie's surviving ex-wives and nine other children. Realizing his need to solidify his power quickly, August got himself named chairman of the board in 1977, at the age of forty. His house in order, August turned his considerable will toward battling the boys in Milwaukee.

3

Number Two Schlitz Its Wrists

In 1976 Milwaukee was still very much a three-horse town: Schlitz, Pabst, and the reinvigorated Miller. Numbers two, three, and four in sales, respectively, Milwaukee's Big Three smelled blood in the water during Anheuser-Busch's strike, though Pabst seemed content to let its hometown competition take on "the King" by themselves. Schlitz and Miller were only too happy to make a grab at Budweiser's dropping market share. For Schlitz, the newfound confidence that the top spot was again reachable would be short-lived.

The Uihleins were Milwaukee's Buschs. Robert Uihlein (pronounced E-line), the last in the clan to run the company that brewed "the beer that made Milwaukee famous," was Gussie Busch's fiercest competitor. Uihlein's Schlitz had been the last beer to hold the number one sales spot before Budweiser grabbed it for good in 1957. Thanks to the Teamsters strike on Anheuser-Busch in 1976, Uihlein's twenty-four million barrels in sales were only five million shy of August's, down from a twelve-million-barrel gap just one year before. To reach Budweiser, Schlitz needed to improve capacity, and it needed to do it quickly.

There are two ways to increase capacity in the brewing business. The first is to build more of it by expanding existing breweries or investing in new ones, as Budweiser was doing as quickly as possible. The second is to reduce the brewing cycle and get more beer from the same brewery in less time. The first, capital investment, is risky because it involves projecting volume needs well into the future; the second, shortcutting, is risky because, well, the quality of your product *matters.*

Bob Uihlein wasn't worried. He boasted openly about the cost-saving measures Schlitz would take during the early and mid-seventies, clearly insinuating that he had a better business head than all of August's MBAs put together. Though he'd cut back on the barley malt in Schlitz's recipe, and significantly cut back on the brewing cycle (where Budweiser's was nearly forty days, his was now *fifteen*), he insisted that Schlitz's quality was never in danger.

Uihlein's clever thinking and strict adherence to the laws of profitability—reduce costs to increase profits—just about killed his brand, however.

An executive from a rival brewer pointed to the methodical cheapening of the Schlitz brewing process and convincingly speculated that the thinking behind it went like this: Small differences in ingredients and the brewing process are undetectable to the average drinker. The shift from A to B is barely distinguishable tastewise, but quite meaningful profitwise. From B to C it's the same, and so on. Unfortunately, the eventual difference—the one between A and M—is huge, and though his brewers begged him to stop pushing for more cost-saving measures, he became too enamored of the extra cash.

The dumbest cost-cutting measure Uihlein insisted upon, it turned out, was the severe reduction of the brewing cycle. Another basic brewing lesson: For lager beer, age is everything. The aging (or lagering) process not only improves the flavor of the beer, it naturally—through the process of creating carbon dioxide—purges substances that cause beer to spoil more quickly. When lager beer isn't properly aged, carbon dioxide has to be added in, robbing the beer of the benefits of the natural process of its creation. Without those benefits, lager beer has to be artificially chill proofed. Chill proofing keeps beer from becoming cloudy at very low temperatures, or, to be technical, it helps keep the proteins in beer from bonding with tannin, a natural acid, and creating a solid matter that settles to the bottom. Solid matter is a nice way of putting it. In its advanced stages, the solid matter, or "haze," looks disconcertingly like mucus.

In 1976 Schlitz made a change in the foam stabilizer it was using to prolong the beer's shelf life. (This helped the brewer avoid a new labeling law that would have required it to list its previous stabilizer; the new one was made to filter out during brewing and would not have been considered an ingredient in the final product.) Unfortunately, the new stabilizer actually *sped up* the breaking down of the beer by bonding with proteins to create "haze" almost immediately. Suddenly Schlitz found itself shipping out a great deal of apparently snot-ridden beer. The brewery knew about it pretty quickly and made a command decision—to do nothing. Noting that haze isn't physically harmful, Uihlein declined a costly recall for months, wagering that not much of the beer would be subjected to the kinds of temperatures at which most haze forms. He lost the bet, sales plummeted as beer drinkers turned up their noses at this "green" (as in inadequately aged) beer, and Schlitz began a long, steady slide from the top three.

Ironically, while justifying the scrapping of plans to build a new Schlitz brewery in New Hampshire, Uihlein would take a successful if completely misleading swipe at Budweiser's quality. The public relations wars that characterize the beer business to this day would begin on the banks of a New England river.

During an earlier bout of keeping up with the Busches, Uihlein had taken out an option on a parcel of land just up the Merrimack River from a new Budweiser brewery. But rather than just dropping the plans and letting the option lapse, Uihlein couldn't resist a little staged drama. Schlitz called a press conference to announce that it was no longer planning on building its brewery, as it had found the waters on the Merrimack River too polluted to meet its quality requirements. Though they never said it outright, the message was clear: Schlitz cares about the water you drink, Anheuser-Busch doesn't.

Schlitz's press conference was misleading on two fronts. First, considering the financial straits they were in because of the rising cost of brewing and their own quickly declining sales volume, it is reasonable to assume that Schlitz scrapped the plans purely to save money. Their quality concerns couldn't have been more laughable at the time, as thousands of drinkers who found stuff floating in their bottle of Schlitz could attest. Second, the waters of the Merrimack never found their way into a Bud bottle; Anheuser-Busch used crystal-clear well water, as Schlitz surely knew.

But try explaining subtleties to scandalized beer drinkers. Shortly after the Schlitz press conference, Budweiser sales dropped 90 percent in nearby Boston. One liquor store in Cambridge actually went so far as to put a sign in their window announcing that they carried St. Louis–brewed Budweiser. To undo the damage, Anheuser-Busch started busing Boston drinkers to their Merrimack facility and, after a stop to show them the pristine wells, treated them to free Budweiser and Busch. It was the kind of quick and decisive response to a public relations problem that Schlitz was so desperately lacking.

The King of Beers recovered quickly, but the folks at Schlitz remained incapable of pulling themselves out of the slide started by their disastrous brewing decisions. Though by 1977 they'd finally admitted their folly, returned to quality brewing methods, and actually hired an Anheuser-Busch executive to run their company, consumers were not prepared to forgive them. It didn't help that their latest advertising campaign, "You want to take away my gusto?" was a steroid-enhanced spin on the macho offerings from Budweiser and Miller High Life. In the ads, tough guys were asked to switch from Schlitz to another brand. Glowering right into the lens, they would deliver the tag line. So aggressive was this approach, in fact, that advertising people took to calling it "Drink Schlitz or I'll kill you." Not only were beer drinkers wary of the quality of the brand, they found the new ads so "menacing [that the] approach was yanked off the air," according to *Fortune.*

What Schlitz needed was to refocus its leadership on fixing the problems with the brand and rebuilding what had been considerable brand loyalty. Unfortunately, Uihlein found the worst possible moment to make some abrupt management changes.

In the mid-seventies the newly created Bureau of Alcohol, Tobacco and Firearms (BATF) cracked down on the big brewing companies for illegal trade practices, largely using information supplied by the brewers themselves. Competing nationally, it seemed, now included ratting out the other guy with the feds. The BATF had been formed during the Nixon administration, according to one bureau insider, to give Nixon a law enforcement arm he could have some control over. (The FBI at the time was still under the all-powerful thumb of J. Edgar Hoover.) There was even some thought, before Watergate ended the political careers of both men, of Nixon installing G. Gordon Liddy as the head of the new bureau. The Federal Alcoholic Administration Act (FAA), which had been enforced by the Internal Revenue Service since the FAA itself was disbanded in the thirties, was now overseen by the BATF.

When complaints were brought by the bureau against the big brewers, they argued that they were being punished for doing things that were quite legal for, say, Coke and Pepsi. They were largely right: some of the "offenses" listed included providing promotional signs to retailers. Regardless, the bureau maintained that the law was clear on what brewing companies were and were not allowed to do in the course of selling their wares. Anheuser-Busch's settlement alone amounted to a whopping $750,000 and an admission that it had made "questionable payments" to retailers.

Though others followed along and settled up rather than having their business practices dissected in court, Schlitz was not among them. In fact, Schlitz's general counsel went to the regional BATF office in Chicago and told the regional director that not only would Schlitz not pay up its fines, but the bureau could "go to hell," according to Bob Maxwell, then a bureau director of field operations. The regional director, as soon as Schlitz counsel had left the office, turned to Maxwell and said, "Go make a case against Schlitz."

Whether he got some bad legal advice or simply thought getting rid of the men responsible would get rid of the problem, Uihlein's approach to BATF's complaints was to hold an internal investigation first and fire whole bunches of the people involved in making illegal payments. Fully half of Uihlein's top eight sales and marketing people were purged. Angry at the company for not taking the blame along with them, some of Uihlein's former employees turned state's evidence against Schlitz. A Milwaukee grand jury would launch its own three-year investigation into Schlitz's marketing practices, ultimately handing down an indictment listing more than seven hundred counts of alcohol-control law violations, including the falsifying of documents and tax evasion. Late in 1976 Uihlein passed away, leaving the company with a battered management roster and a flagship brand on the ropes.

Even in its weakened state, though, Schlitz managed to be the first one to jump on the light beer bandwagon Miller had created. Ironically, considering the horrid flavor of the cheapened Schlitz flagship, Schlitz Light was positioned in its advertising as a much better-tasting alternative to Lite. Anheuser-Busch would not climb aboard, though. Beginning a pattern they would follow again and again over the years (a pattern marketing writer Gerry Khermouch would puckishly label "denigrate, regulate, and replicate"), the folks who brewed Budweiser tried denial as their first concerted response to Miller. Derisive comments on the quality of light beer in general found their way into the press, often circuitously. At one point an industry analyst named Bob

Weinberg sniffed to a local St. Louis reporter, "The whole light beer thing is a fraud. It's people rationalizing. The beer tastes awful." What the reporter failed to note was that Weinberg was a former Anheuser-Busch executive who still did consulting for them. The "fraud," Weinberg forgot to mention, had moved Miller past Schlitz in 1977 and put them firmly in the number two spot. The "fraud" was also something Anheuser-Busch would finally jump into that same year—four years after Miller had first introduced it.

With a name that August Busch III would later concede was "too damn long," Anheuser-Busch Natural Light was rolled out nationally without any regional testing or introduction; in essence, Lite Beer had been the test-marketing guinea pig. Despite the name (which was quickly shortened to Natural Light), it was a hit. The sour grapes emanating from St. Louis was now no longer about light beer, it was about percentages. "A lot of people think Miller outsmarted us with Lite Beer," an Anheuser-Busch vice president would tell *Fortune,* "but that was one successful brand out of eight brands introduced or acquired. We've clicked on three out of three." Of the three introductions the VP alluded to, two—Natural Light and the also new Michelob Light—could trace their paternity to Miller, inasmuch as Miller was the first major force behind the light category. The third, a reformulated version of the Busch Bavarian brand introduced in 1955 now known simply as Busch, was aimed squarely at the younger drinkers who were making light beer so successful.

With a bit more candor than the A-B vice president quoted in *Fortune,* August conceded to *Forbes* in 1978 that "we were simply unsmarted." Unwilling to let Miller grow any bigger, he started a marketing spending war. In 1978, just three years after he took the presidency of the company, August raised the promotional budget at Anheuser-Busch from a prestrike $30 million to $100 million. It was bold, it was risky, and it was forward thinking. Unlike the "arrogant and complacent" leader *Forbes* made him out to be, August was the man who shook Anheuser-Busch out of the stupor Gussie's mass firings had produced. Where Gussie had protected his margins, August looked to grow the company. Where Gussie could play the capricious dictator while sitting on his 13 percent throne, August had to prove to the board that fortunes were changing. Though there *was* enough arrogance at Anheuser-Busch to refuse Philip Morris even the most grudging respect, there was no question whom the company was setting its sights on. "This business," August would say, "is now a two-horse race."

There were two contestants, to be sure, but the horse-race analogy was all wrong in that it conjured up images of grace and class. This was a barroom brawl.

With Schlitz dying a slow death, and Pabst lacking the size (read: funding) to go to war, Anheuser-Busch and Miller set their sights on each other and let fly. John Murphy, chairman and chief executive officer of Miller, had a rug made with the Anheuser-Busch seal on it, the better to roll his swivel chair on. He showed the press his August III voodoo doll and at one point in 1978 applied for a trademark for something called "Gussie Beer." Anheuser-Busch wouldn't rise to the bait except to hint around at a lawsuit should Miller actually introduce the stuff. It didn't. Over in St. Louis, workers took to wearing "Miller Killer" T-shirts and were unofficially banned from smoking Philip Morris cigarette brands.

The fight spilled over to the regulatory commissions, with Miller leading the way. Perhaps as a way of underscoring their introduction of the segment, Miller went after G. Heileman Brewing of Wisconsin for using the "light" designation. They lost, because the courts, in a bout of common sense, decreed that light is a generic term, like lager.

Miller then went to the Federal Trade Commission to file a complaint against Anheuser-Busch for making all-natural ingredient claims. Anheuser-Busch, Miller claimed, used chemicals in their process, including their famed beechwood aging. "We seriously doubt," their complaint said, "that consumers understand that beechwood aging consists of dumping chemically treated lumber into glass-lined or stainless-steel storage tanks." Though Miller lost again, the damage to

Anheuser-Busch's pride was done—beechwood aging was considered sacred at A-B headquarters—and the giant was more angry than ever.

Of course, the giant was also a bit smug, and rightly so. Anheuser-Busch had been successful in the regulatory phase of the Beer Wars by going after Miller's new Löwenbräu.

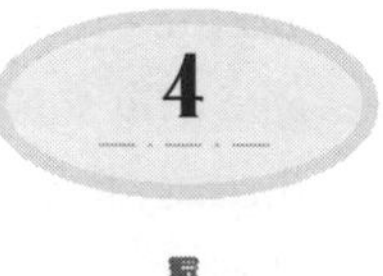

4 The Regulatory Waltz

Germany's Löwenbräu had been neck and neck with Holland's Heineken for years in the then tiny (at less than 1 percent beer market share) import segment when Miller bought it in the early seventies. The thinking was that producing a brand with an import cachet would allow Miller to compete with Anheuser-Busch's superpremium offering, Michelob. (Superpremiums are priced higher than so-called premium beers, like Budweiser, but not as high as imports.) Up to that point, Michelob had had the segment for its own. Rather than becoming an importer and trying to pull consumers up in price to import levels, Miller thought it could split the difference and charge a superpremium price for a locally brewed version of a German beer.

Only Miller didn't go out of its way to make it clear that Löwenbräu was locally brewed. With the same bottle and label as the German stuff, and ads that featured the European brewing awards won by the German stuff, it was no wonder that many restaurants still listed Löwenbräu as an import. With the extra profit from charging a super-premium price for a domestically brewed beer, it was no wonder Miller didn't correct anybody.

The inevitable complaint Anheuser-Busch filed with the Federal Trade Commission (FTC) was the first real indication that the Beer Wars was a take-no-prisoners affair. Miller's shots at beechwood aging must have seemed niggling sour grapes to the FTC's consumer protection staff, coming as they did on the heels of Anheuser-Busch's thirty-two-page Löwenbräu complaint. Aside from the obvious objection to the Germanic advertising, the complaint called into question the legitimacy of the brand—not only are they lying to consumers about where Löwenbräu comes from, A-B was saying, they're not even making a good copy of the original—and by doing so exposed to the world the brewing industry's odd little regulatory secret.

You, *Madame et Monsieur Consumer,* are allowed to know what's in your cornflakes. The Food and Drug Administration mandates it. You are allowed to know if there are chemicals in your fruit punch; you are guaranteed the right to know what's in that frozen entrée. Our government says that you have the right to be made aware of what's in everything you ingest. Well, almost everything. You are *not* privy to what's in your beer, wine, or booze. You have no legal right to know. The BATF ruled long ago that it will not reveal the contents of any alcohol beverage brand because it considers those contents to be company secrets. Because the FDA doesn't have labeling jurisdiction over alcoholic products—one attempt to wrest it away from the BATF was successfully blocked by distiller Brown Forman—you don't have any legal right to know what it is you're drinking. Neat, huh?

The fact that Miller didn't publish the ingredients or process behind the domestically brewed Löwenbräu didn't stop Anheuser-Busch from figuring them out. Or from telling the world what it found.

The most damaging for Miller was Anheuser-Busch's charge that the Löwenbräu brewed here wouldn't even pass for beer in the Fatherland. Instead of using European-grown two-row barley malt in its recipe, the complaint charged, Miller was cutting its costs by using the significantly cheaper (and of lesser quality) domestic six-row malt and cutting even that with 28 percent corn grits. Because of the corn, and the three additional additives alleged in the complaint, Löwenbräu wouldn't have passed the German beer purity law, which at the time mandated that only four ingredients could be used in brewing: malt, water, yeast, and hops. To further embarrass Miller, Anheuser-Busch charged that the domestic Löwenbräu wasn't even fermented like its namesake: rather than the six-week natural carbonization process known as krausening, the complaint said, Löwenbräu was injected with carbon dioxide and aged a whopping nine days. And, just in case Miller wasn't blushing deeply enough, Anheuser-Busch claimed that the difference between the light and dark versions of domestic Löwenbräu was food coloring and packaging. Miller wouldn't comment on the charges.

Though the consumer protection staffers at the FTC agreed with Anheuser-Busch and officially recommended that some action be taken against Miller, the four seated commissioners split on the recommendation. That initial split, while a hopeful sign for Miller, had an unforeseen side effect on Miller's parent.

Miller was never really Miller, not when it came to the perception of the company among competitors and legislators. Miller was Philip Morris. Philip Morris was huge. So huge, in fact, that two of the people instrumental in the FTC's decision-making process had once represented Philip Morris while in private legal practice. Michael Sohn, the FTC's chief counsel, and Alfred Kramer, the chief of the consumer protection bureau, both fought any action against Miller. Eyebrows were raised. Though the FTC would eventually agree with Anheuser-Busch about the misleading nature of Löwenbräu advertising and packaging, the initial split among the commissioners had effectively raised questions about the strength of Philip Morris's political influence, and in post-Watergate Washington, D.C., no less. Perhaps, the whispers went in the corridors of regulatory agencies, the big boys have gotten too big. Perhaps, the wags said, the Justice Department should have listened when it was warned about letting a huge tobacco company buy its way into an industry populated largely by small, family-run concerns.

Such talk wasn't helped by the fact that while the FTC agreed with Anheuser-Busch in principle, it didn't actually *do* anything to Miller, arguing that the whole thing was really under the jurisdiction of the BATF. That put the bureau in a bind; having already (over strenuous internal objections) given label approval to Löwenbräu, it couldn't attack the most serious part of A-B's charge. It got some help on that score from a disgruntled former Löwenbräu drinker.

Former Watergate prosecutor Richard Davis, made an assistant secretary of the Treasury Department during the Carter administration, had stopped drinking Löwenbräu when it became a domestic. According to one BATF official, it offended Davis's sensibilities that Miller was so blatantly misleading consumers about the brand's current origin, and when the FTC passed the buck to the bureau, he found himself in a position to do something about it. The BATF was an arm of the Treasury Department and, as such, had to listen when Davis made the strong suggestion that it put pressure on Miller to come clean with consumers.

The BATF made a very concise offer to Miller: "Make changes to your label and ads for Löwenbräu, or the Treasury Department (our boss, over whom we have no control) will go out of its way to find new and interesting methods of screwing you." Miller chose the former option, and suddenly Löwenbräu's label carried the words "Product of USA," and its television advertising added the phrase "a fine American beer."

The King of Beers had plenty to celebrate. With Heineken cheering on the sidelines (it being too small, at something under 1 percent of U.S. market share, to take on Philip Morris itself), Anheuser-Busch had humiliated the formerly imported Löwenbräu and scored the first (roundabout) regulatory victory. A-B also scored the first clear victory in the court of public opinion. As *The New Republic* would write during the FTC's deliberations, Miller's campaign for Löwenbräu "shows how a large manufacturer, if it wishes to get ahead quickly, learns to shade the truth, wriggle around federal regulators who stand in its way and manipulate popular images to fit its plan."

Miller kept swinging, though, and its next jab was aimed squarely at Michelob Light. Having lost the right to claim light beer as a trademark, Miller found a subtler approach to its attacks: it pointedly asked, "What constitutes light beer?" Surely not Michelob Light, Miller argued to the BATF. That version of Anheuser-Busch's superpremium had 134 calories, Miller pointed out, just a few less than a Budweiser, so it could hardly be light. Though Miller would lose this game, too, at least with the bureau, it managed to score a few points where it counted.

With its most recent BATF complaint, Miller scored some public relations points against not only its competition, but also detractors of the light beer category. Miller, like Budweiser, knew the inherent weaknesses in slugging it out with competitors through the medium of advertising. Not only do ads rarely provide enough time or space to make a cogent argument, they just aren't trusted by consumers. Claims in ads, especially competitive ones, aren't always taken that seriously. But news stories are. The brilliance of the regulatory complaints flying back and forth between Milwaukee and St. Louis were that they guaranteed not only that the claims within them would be taken more seriously, but also that they would often be given adequate explanation by the press.

In this case, Miller tipped off the consumer to the fast and loose way imitators could use the word "light." It also found a way to explain just what light beer is in the first place. And what it isn't.

A fellow named Joseph Ortleib, who owned Henry F. Ortleib Brewing of Philadelphia, ran a very clever little commercial in the late seventies entitled "Drink Joe's Beer." In the spot, Ortleib himself holds a pitcher of water and a bottle of the beer he produced. "This," Ortleib says to the camera, "is how we would make light beer." He pours some of the water into a half-filled glass of beer. Looking at the resulting liquid, he adds, "Now, that's why we don't make it." Very clever, and very misleading.

Ortleib never said that adding water was how Miller made Lite. If he had, they'd have destroyed him with a lawsuit. But he didn't have to say it; it's what people assumed. Miller had avoided talking about their brewing process in advertising, possibly for the same reason they dropped the carbohydrate discussion from early Lite ads. Thirty-second ads are not the place for complex concepts—especially when those concepts involved words like "enzyme" and "dextrin." In yet another complaint to the BATF in 1979, Miller not only discussed the shortcomings of its competition—Michelob Light really was made from regular beer and carbonated water, Miller charged it laid the groundwork for the press to find out and publicize just how Lite was brewed. Miller again banked on the knowledge that people are more willing to believe claims made in legal briefs than they are claims made in advertising.

Another quick lesson in brewing: In 1964, brewers discovered an enzyme that during the brewing process could convert all dextrins (nonfermentable sugars) into fermentable sugars. Because sugar is caloric, and fermentation of sugar converts it to alcohol, when the enzyme (amyloglucosidase, for those scientists in the audience) is added, the beer produced is lower in caloric content and higher in alcoholic content. That's right: under natural conditions, light beer has more alcohol. Only it doesn't, because the people who brew it a) can reduce calories even further by removing some of the alcohol, b) realize that those who want light beer are probably not the people who want to get tanked as quickly as possible, and c) don't need the hassle of higher alcoholic content from a legal standpoint. That hassle can come from two directions: states that mandate that any brew containing more than 5.5 percent alcohol by volume be called malt liquor rather than beer, and distillers who point to higher-alcohol beer products as proof that the higher taxes on wine and spirits are unfair. (More on that latter argument in chapter 8.) Mostly, though, brewers remove the extra alcohol and a smidge more for good measure, so that light beer is not as intoxicating as regular beer. That way, you can drink more of it. That way, you can buy more of it.

Though Anheuser-Busch was on the receiving end of Miller's bit of litigious grandstanding, they appreciated the value of being victorious in the court of public opinion and found new and interesting ways to stick it back to the Miller folks. When the United States Brewers Association (whose president at the time was one August Busch III) considered a proposal to pressure brewers into voluntary ingredient labeling (sponsored by one August Busch III), Miller withdrew from the group, still smarting from the Löwenbräu debacle. Though John Murphy denied that he pulled out his company over labeling, no one quite believed him. His morning chair roll over the Anheuser-Busch rug suddenly seemed more like sour grapes than bravado.

Of course, in the waging of war, nothing is more effective than a little well-placed disinformation about the enemy. Schlitz suffered for years because of a lack of public understanding about what caused beer cloudiness. Wild stories about insect eggs and strange chemicals would surface from time to time, in much the same way they'd haunt the makers of Bubble Yum bubble gum a decade later. Miller faced a similar fate, in that High Life's clear glass bottling made even the slightest haze easy to see. The *St. Louis Post-Dispatch* would report that competing distributors were known to go into stores, posing as customers, hold a cloudy bottle of High Life, and shout, "What's wrong with this beer?"

The most damaging rumor came at the expense of Anheuser-Busch and Pabst. Somehow the story circulated that the leadership of both companies were "hysterically anti-gun, giving substantial donations to firearms control causes." The *Post-Dispatch* pointed out the irony of the rumor, especially concerning A-B, considering August III's fame as "a marksman and an avid hunter." The same clubs and lodges where August would have felt right at home began throwing out his brands left and right, convinced that he'd donated money to gun control groups. Though it was untrue, it was a hard rumor to battle, as both companies realized the even greater potential danger of appearing to be too pro-gun. "Hey, c'mon, we *love* weaponry!" didn't seem an appropriate response, especially from any company that produced mood-altering substances. August made a concerted effort to find the source of the rumor but never did. Eventually it died down.

More dangerous than the burgeoning rumor mill, though, was the scrutiny the beer industry was bringing down on itself through all the very public mudslinging and litigation. Fraud claims and alcohol-content discussions, not to mention the huge settlements brewers had paid for illegal business practices, caused the public spotlight to shine brighter on the major brewers than it had since the temperance movement. And for the first time since Prohibition, alcohol industry foes—from religious groups to government officials—were getting organized for action.

Anheuser-Busch was the first to get slapped. Strangely enough, it would be for its first nonbeer product since the repeal.

Looking for a category to call its own, Anheuser-Busch introduced Chelsea in 1978. Called an "adult soft drink," Chelsea was a blend of fruit juices that had no preservatives and boasted a third less sugar and calories than conventional soda. What made it "adult" was the head of foam that formed when you poured it, its amber coloring, and packaging clearly intended to resemble that of a superpremium beer. It was advertised as the "not-so-soft drink," which, of course, was all critics needed. Convinced that this was a nefarious attempt to lead children down the path to beer, the folks August would dub "neoprohibitionists" pointed to the fact that Chelsea contained traces of alcohol (actually, less than 0.5 percent). Ignoring the fact that Chelsea had about as much alcohol as just about any other soft drink (because of the slight natural fermentation that takes place in any sugar-containing beverage), folks from Utah senator Orrin Hatch to Secretary of Health, Education, and Welfare Joseph Califano, from the Seventh-Day Adventists to the Virginia Nurses Association, called for its swift demise. They won. Chelsea was pulled from the market and reformulated; gone were the head, even more of the alcohol, and the "not-so-soft drink" advertising. Unfortunately, so was Anheuser-Busch's enthusiasm for the product. No one, of course, found the irony in the fact that the brewers of Budweiser had been slapped down for trying to give drinkers a socially acceptable substitute for beer.

Philip Morris would take the easier approach to the soft-drink business and simply buy 7UP, spending over $500 million. Apparently Senator Hatch was not quite as concerned about a *cigarette* company peddling soft drinks with trace amounts of alcohol to children.

The reaction to Chelsea made it clear that Anheuser-Busch and Miller had created a competitive atmosphere that they could not completely control. To continue the war that was making them both bigger and richer, they'd have to find new battlegrounds. Which they did. On every motor speedway, baseball diamond, football field, and basketball court in America. And in bowling alleys, on tennis courts . . .

Part Two

Hand-to-Hand Combat

5

TAKE ME OUT TO THE BEER GAME

Research is a wonderful thing. As any marketer knows, it can be used to bolster almost any opinion or justify nearly any move. It can be inverted, subverted, perverted, and contraverted as the needs arise. It is often shapeless, and therefore easily shaped. Corporate vice presidents love research, because very rarely can they be held accountable for actions they've taken "resulting from" research.

Once in a great while, though, research is used for its truest purpose: to reiterate what anyone with the slightest business experience could recognize as common sense. So it was that the Miller Brewing Company seized upon the earth-shattering notion that televised sporting events were wonderful places to advertise beer.

The statistics go something like this: The years in which men drink the most beer fall between ages eighteen and twenty-nine. The years in which men get the most involved in sports—as participants *and* spectators—fall at the same time. By adding five years to the tail end, and looking at eighteen- to thirty-four-year-old men as a demographic, you find a 20 percent chunk of all beer drinkers that manages to drink about 70 percent of all beer sold. If you'd ever wondered why beer commercials are so universally aimed at young men, you don't anymore.

A quick read of marketing history will indicate that Miller started the sports-related media-buying frenzy that has made it impossible to turn on a game these days without encountering wall-to-wall beer ads. But Miller didn't create the marriage between sports and beer; it just had the bucks to try to corner the market. Beer and sports—especially beer and baseball—had been going steady for a very long time.

Long before Jacob Ruppert spent his brewing money to snag Babe Ruth for the New York Yankees, before the turn of the century, even, the Cincinnati Reds went so far as to drop out of the National League for a time because of a local ordinance that prohibited beer sales in the ballpark. At about the same time, a St. Louis brewer would foreshadow Gussie Busch's 1953 purchase of the Cardinals. Chris von der Ahe was a prosperous saloon owner who noticed an odd phenomenon: business was always better when the local baseball team, then the St. Louis Brown Stockings, was in town. Figuring to fish a little closer to the deep end of the pond, von der Ahe tried to sell beer at the stadium, but he was rebuffed. In 1881 he would get into the ballpark with his beer the old-fashioned way: by buying part of the team. Seventy-two years later, Gussie's purchase, for $3.75 million, of essentially the same franchise would net him the chance not only to sell his beer to thousands of thirsty fans at each and every game, but also to plaster the stadium with Budweiser signs—signs that would be seen on every television tuned to a Cardinals game, for as long as his family owned the team. This, marketing students, is what the folks who purchase advertising space call "an efficient buy."

So strong is the bond between baseball and beer—and so influential is Anheuser-Busch—that during a special election in 1983 St. Louis would actually change a law prohibiting alcoholic beverage sales while the polls were open rather than allow a "dry" opening day at Busch Stadium. So strong was the bond between Gussie and the Cardinals that the most remembered image from the 1987 World Series was Gussie's triumphant ride around the outfield of Busch Stadium aboard a wagon pulled by his beloved Clydesdales.

But a strong bond didn't translate into heavy advertising tie-ins on a regional or national basis in the days before Lite Beer; most previous sports sponsorships tended toward local broadcasts, sponsored by local brewers. Though Anheuser-Busch had used sports in its advertising from time to time, like the 1909 Budweiser ad touting the brand as "the proper drink for athletes in training," ad expenditures hadn't been a large part of the company's overhead. This was the luxurious problem faced by Anheuser-Busch for many years: it was growing too fast to spend much on advertising. Capacity was the first priority. The rapid growth of Anheuser-Busch in the mid-seventies meant that the company was worried about where the money was going to come from to build the next brewery. Lavish advertising would have been counterproductive, because it may very well have increased demand past capacity and pushed consumers to the competition in a snit. (Yes, scarcity can be a good thing from a PR standpoint, but almost solely when dealing with new products or when products are new to a specific market. Coors, anyone? But we'll get to that. . . .)

Meanwhile in Milwaukee, Philip Morris was willing to use the phenomenal access to credit it had as a huge multinational corporation to dominate beer marketing. Philip Morris didn't need revenue from its new beer operation right away, and it could afford to invest heavily on behalf of its brands. This was a luxury that its competitors—companies that couldn't spread their debt among other, more profitable pursuits—

didn't have. An economics professor from Wisconsin, doing some consulting for the Stroh Brewery Company, was amazed to find that between the years of 1971 and 1977 Philip Morris increased its debt to the tune of nearly $1 billion, most of which, he said, went to expanding Miller's operation. Miller didn't have to worry, as Anheuser-Busch did, about how to pay for the next brewery; Miller had to worry about creating enough awareness of and demand for its products to pull up volume to meet its brewing capacity.

As large as it was, Anheuser-Busch was still rooted in the tradition of a family-owned, single-venture company. It didn't have the deep pockets or the stomach for debt of a huge, publicly owned conglomerate. Gussie's trimming of the marketing department in the first part of the decade only exacerbated his problems, because it meant that not only could Anheuser-Busch not keep up with Miller's spending, it couldn't do a decent job of paying attention to what it was Miller was doing with all that green.

What Miller was doing was buying airtime. To push a product that held a great deal of appeal for athletic, fitness-conscious people, Miller bought sports. Any sports. If it was a major sporting event, Miller owned it. By the time Anheuser-Busch went looking for available sports airtime, Miller owned something like 70 percent of network television sports beer advertising. Even with the locally televised stuff figured in, Miller's share was over 50 percent. Perception being reality, Miller was on its way to becoming number one.

In 1976 the people most convinced that Anheuser-Busch would be overtaken in sales by Miller Brewing were Anheuser-Busch people. They'd watched Gussie fire much of the marketing department to cut back his overhead. They'd gone through an extremely unpleasant, and extremely secretive, management change. They'd lived through a hundred-day strike that had cost them millions of barrels in sales. They'd watched their shares of company stock sink to the basement: from $69 a share in 1972 to a low of $18 at one point during the Teamsters strike. What was there to indicate that things would get better?

Well, there was August. Though such a thought process is unheard of in business today, August basically decided, "The hell with my stock price, time to invest in the brands." Gussie hadn't had to answer to anyone, so the decision to keep up his own profits in the short term went unchallenged. August wanted to be around in the long term, and his 0.6 percent guaranteed nothing along those lines. He needed to meet Miller's challenge. It was time to step up efforts in the marketplace and to look like the leader again. It helped, of course, that around the same time August deepened Anheuser-Busch's pockets, Philip Morris decided to slow down investment spending so that they might show their shareholders the profitability of Lite.

In 1977 August decided that the first person he would impress would be the average beer-drinking television watcher. With so much more volume than Miller to spread his costs over, he was going to dominate his Milwaukee rival on the airwaves *right away*. Or so he thought.

On the day that Anheuser-Busch asked its ad agency how it was that Miller had exclusive rights to advertise in so many important sporting events, they got a four-word response: "We told you so." In 1975, it turned out, Anheuser-Busch's ad agency had pleaded with August's MBAs to take a look at Miller's spending habits. Particularly the contracts they were signing with the networks, contracts that had "exclusivity clauses" that locked out any competitive advertising and often gave Miller right of first refusal for years to come. The pleas were ignored and completely forgotten. By the time Anheuser-Busch was ready to start spending some serious money on sports, recalled Michael Roarty, its vice president of marketing at the time, the networks "looked at us like we had just come to town on a bus and they said, 'Where have you been? We've been sold out for years!' "

It was humiliating for August, but as with other defeats, it only strengthened his resolve. Russia may have been the first nation into space, but damned if the good ol' U. S. of A. wasn't going to put a man on the moon first . . . and so it was in the marketing race. If August couldn't break into the advertising time available on network sporting events, he'd own everything else.

He started with college sports. Staffers were asked to compile a book listing every college in the country with an athletic program. As one exec recalled to Peter Hernon and Terry Ganey, the authors of *Under the Influence: The Unauthorized Story of the Anheuser-Busch Dynasty,* "That book was about five or six inches thick. We got together and August said, 'Well, let's go. Read 'em.' We had a media guy reading them off . . . August would say, 'What about Albion? What do they do?' And we'd say, 'Naw, that's just a very small liberal arts college and they don't do anything.' August would say, 'Okay, what about Albuquerque A&M?' We'd say, 'Yeah, they play football.' And August would say, 'Buy 'em!' "

August would not be satisfied until he'd bought advertising time in every contest available; from the powerhouses of the Big Ten to the little colleges no one had ever heard of, Budweiser would be there at the station break. So-called alternative sports went the same way. These were the things not covered by the networks, from speedboat racing to hot-air ballooning. The fledgling cable industry was a major recipient of Anheuser-Busch's largess: the company spent well over a million dollars on the brand-new Entertainment & Sports Programming Network alone, sponsoring not-ready-for-prime-time events like the Moscow Spartacade. It didn't really matter to August if much of the programming Budweiser sponsored was crap, as long as it was *sports* crap.

So-called exclusivity clauses in network contracts would help ensure August's eventual domination. Though the Stroh Brewery Company would go to court in 1985 to test their validity, the networks and cable channels were offering the guys with the big bankrolls exclusive rights to their events and, in some cases, their entire coverage of a particular sport. ABC's popular *Monday Night Football* broadcast had been snatched up by Miller, as were events like the Indianapolis 500. August made it clear he was willing to buy everything Miller didn't want or deemed too pricey. And because he was willing to spend at exactly the time Miller was looking for a little profit, he didn't have to wait long to become the biggest sports advertiser in the land.

Exclusivity clauses in contracts didn't include just the rights to the current season's broadcasts; they guaranteed the right to renew contracts for years to come. In the case of ESPN, Anheuser-Busch's exclusivity contract would extend to everything the network covered. Though such a contract would seem like restraint of trade, the Justice Department rejected the 1985 challenge to exclusivity clauses brought by Stroh. The contracts didn't keep the networks or cable channels from seeking competitive advertising, Justice reasoned; they merely guaranteed the current advertiser the right of first refusal. Could justice help it if Anheuser-Busch and Miller almost never refused? The net effect, of course, was that just about everyone else was shut out of sports advertising indefinitely.

In the third phase of its "denigrate, regulate, replicate" attack on Lite, Anheuser-Busch would steal a page right out of the Miller playbook. August would buy some ball players of his own.

To push Natural Light, an advertising campaign was created that featured—drum roll, please—former jocks. Stealing the idea wasn't laziness, and it wasn't exactly a tip of the cap to the marketing guys at Miller. It was, whether by design or by accident, a moderately effective way of confusing the public. Keep in mind that Lite Beer wasn't so much a brand in the eyes of Joe Consumer as it was a segment. Except for Schlitz's crippled effort to steal some of the (forgive me) gusto, Lite had the market to itself, with a product that wasn't loved for its taste as much as it was for its benefits: lower calories, slightly less alcohol. By using the goofy spelling of light as its name, Miller may have erred on the side of making the first reduced-calorie brand sound like a generic. Anheuser-Busch's strategy was to capitalize on that mistake and convince beer drinkers that all lights were the same; that way, they wouldn't have to recruit more drinkers into the category—drinkers who would more than likely come from the ranks of Budweiser drinkers, anyhow—but could snatch the folks already drinking Lite.

So Natural Light ads looked like Lite ads. Some Natural Light ads actually featured players *from* Lite ads. It was typical of August's competitive nature that he was willing to pay big money to pull Mickey Mantle, Joe Frazier, and Nick Buoniconti away from Lite, in what one Anheuser-Busch executive would dub "the greatest defection since Solzhenitsyn." (Miller would lose an even more popular member of the team, Bubba Smith—who memorably tore the lid off an aluminum Lite can in one commercial—to a bout of conscience in 1985. While grand marshal in that year's Michigan State homecoming parade, Smith was "freaked out" to realize that the students along the parade route, many of whom were too young to drink legally, weren't shouting pro-State slogans, they were hectoring each other across the roadway with call-and-response chants of "Tastes great" and "Less filling.")

Miller, by the time Anheuser-Busch played copycat, had signed with a new ad agency, Backer & Spielvogel. Essentially a spin-off of the giant McCann-Erickson, Backer was built around the Miller account, so its fortunes were tied to a quick and decisive response to the Natural Light advertising. Scant months after the agency's birth, it found itself in a life-or-death situation.

The first impulse of most ad guys in a crisis situation is to change course, come up with something completely new—especially ad guys who can argue that it was a previous agency's work that's being challenged. Backer was smarter. Backer circled the wagons. Backer strengthened a campaign that was already working, by creating the Lite All-Stars program. New Lite ads grouped the jock-spokesmen, often throwing in guests like Spillane, Meredith, and comedian Rodney Dangerfield. Under Backer's guidance, Miller signed many of its all-stars to personal appearance contracts on behalf of the brewery. The Lite All-Stars comprised an eccentric family of big names, has-beens, and never-weres, a rotating sitcom cast almost as lovable as the folks from *The Mary Tyler Moore Show* or, later, *Cheers*. Lite advertising became more popular than ever, and Miller liked to rub in the fact that Anheuser-Busch's lame imitation of their marketing strategy spurred them on to even greater heights.

But Miller missed the point of Natural Light's mimicry. To an extent, the Natural Light ads worked at convincing drinkers that all light beers were the same. Maybe drinkers did feel, as Miller research would indicate, that they thought less of Anheuser-Busch for swiping the ad campaign. But so what? When they walked into a bar at night, would those drinkers choose Lite Beer to punish an unoriginal marketer? Not likely. Natural Light may not have won any fans for itself, but its advertising had served its purpose. It confused people about the difference between light beers. Anheuser-Busch wanted that confusion, because it had something else up its sleeve. (More on that in a moment.)

In perhaps the final victory it would enjoy in its sports-spending war with Anheuser Busch, Miller successfully grabbed beer advertising rights to the 1980 Summer Olympic games. It would prove to be a hollow victory, in more ways than one. First, Jimmy Carter would protest the Soviet invasion of Afghanistan by leading more than sixty countries in a boycott of the games. Suddenly it seemed a lot less American to have any sponsorship ties to the event. But the truth was that even if the U.S. had participated—even if the U.S. won every damned medal from gymnastics to cycling—Miller couldn't have fully enjoyed its high profile in the games. They'd bought the package well in advance with the belief that by the time the torch reached Moscow, Miller would have a victory of their own to advertise: their ascension to number one.

They would never make it. By 1978 the sales gap between Anheuser-Busch and Miller had closed to ten million barrels, from twenty-one million just six years earlier. It was the closest they would get. Six years later the gulf between them would be twenty-seven million barrels and climbing.

In 1982, fully nine years after the world first tried Lite, Anheuser-Busch would finally get serious about the light beer segment. Natural Light, which hadn't seriously rivaled Lite in terms of volume, was on its way to being put out to pasture as a discount brand to make way for a new premium-priced Anheuser-Busch-brewed light beer. August was ready to pull out the stops, including his previous reluctance to involve the franchise name in the fledgling category. Bud Light emerged from test markets and rolled across the country.

Now, ordering a light beer at the bar became confusing, which was good for Anheuser-Busch. It is a basic fact of American consumer existence at the end of the twentieth century that no one wants to seem to have generic tastes, as least when it comes to personal pleasure products like beer or cigarettes. One doesn't say, "I'll have a beer," one orders by brand name. The uncertain tone of asking for "a Lite" became pronounced following the introduction of Bud Light, and the decision to call its brand Lite Beer from Miller suddenly came back to bite Miller in the ass.

Bud Light was only too happy to underscore, in a very successful ad campaign, Miller's name problem, while positioning itself as *the* light beer. In each of the campaign's television spots, an unsuspecting fellow would step up to the bar and say, "Gimme a light." The bartender would respond by offering something that was not only completely off the beer subject, but often even life-threatening to the guy, like a lit blowtorch. Realizing his mistake, the guy would say, "*Bud* Light," and be served a frosty mug of beer. The spots would often end with a second guy coming in and saying, "Gimme a light," which would cause the first guy to grab his beer and hightail it out of the way before the torch/bomb/poodle-jumping-through-the-flaming-hoop trick would reappear.

With its clever advertising, and a reported $50 million launch, Bud Light proved to be Anheuser-Busch's best weapon in the fight against the resurgent Miller. Though it would take Bud Light well over a decade to catch up to its progenitor in the sales column, it did manage to stunt Lite's growth almost immediately and in the process bring Miller Brewing's meteoric rise to a halt. Over the next half decade, while Miller's sales numbers stayed dead flat, Anheuser-Busch's sales would grow 28 percent. Miller would end the eighties with exactly the same market share it had at the decade's start, 22.5 percent. (The beer market as a whole grew 8 percent over the decade.) Down in St. Louis,

August and his MBAs watched their fortunes go from 30.4 percent to a whopping 44.8 percent share.

The first major battle of the Beer Wars was over, and the King of Beers had sent the Miller army packing. No question Miller had fought bravely, had managed to alter the rules of battle, and had held on to a respectable amount of turf; but Miller needed to regroup if it was ever going to hope to rise up against the King ever again.

And, oh yes, there were the peasants. The Pabsts, Schlitzs, and Strohs . . . they were present while the fighting raged. And the peasants suffered the same fate that peasants always do in these feudal wars: they had their villages burned and their fields plundered. But the cunning peasants, the Coors and the Heilemans, managed to stay away from the worst of the fighting and against all odds emerged from the first round of the Beer Wars with little fiefdoms of their own.

6

The Wisconsin Hare and the Rocky Mountain Tortoise

"It's like elephants dancing on gnats," said a Pabst brand manager about the effect the Anheuser-Busch/Miller spending race was having on other beer marketers. "There could be tragic consequences for some breweries."

He was mostly right, but not completely. The waltzing of the elephants was a great *boon* to one brewer, actually.

G. Heileman Brewing, of La Crosse, Wisconsin, made its fortunes as a carpetbagger. When the national brands forced regionals to the brink of bankruptcy, Heileman often stepped in, buying the regional for a song and appropriating its labels into Heileman's large brand portfolio. Those purchases were often made for barrelage reasons: by buying regional breweries on the edge of financial collapse, Heileman could land additional brewing capacity (in which it could brew any number of brands) at fire sale prices, provided it wasn't terribly picky about the condition of its purchases. Beer industry magazine *Modern Brewery Age* estimated that in 1973 Heileman was paying $3 to $4 a barrel for increased capacity, where Anheuser-Busch was paying $35 to $38 a barrel to build state-of-the-art facilities. Like the corporate raiders who gained infamy a decade later, Heileman simply sold off the assets it didn't have use for.

It was a marvelous way to grow, for a time. A decade after *Modern Brewery Age* explained the math of Heileman's business strategy, the brewer had shot up from the tenth spot on the sales list to the fourth. From its base in the Midwest, Heileman spent the seventies and early eighties buying up everything it could to the west (like Blitz-Weinhard of Portland and Rainier of Seattle), the south (notably Lone Star of San Antonio), and the east (Carling National of Baltimore, which owned the rights to Tuborg). With the exception of Tuborg, Heileman was content to leave each brand in its own region.

Heileman's initial spurt of growth, a few decades earlier, had come at the expense of a Wisconsin competitor, Pabst. In 1958 Pabst made the bold move of buying out Blatz, which was then the number one-selling beer in Milwaukee. The addition would eventually launch Pabst from number thirteen to number three in size, behind Anheuser-Busch and Schlitz. Things were looking good for the "Blue Ribbon" company.

Until the feds stepped in. A decade after the purchase, Pabst would be forced to divest itself of Blatz as part of an antitrust settlement with the government. Blatz was sold to Heileman. The role of Uncle Sam in Heileman's first big volume boost would prove to be ironic.

A half decade later, in 1972, the government stepped into the beer biz again, this time to restrain the beast they had created. The Department of Justice, stunned by the rapid growth of Heileman, slapped a restriction on the brewer forbidding it from buying anything new in its major twelve-state midwestern marketing region (though it continued to buy up breweries in the rest of the country). The one exception, coming in 1975, was the purchase by Heileman of Grain Belt Brewing in Minneapolis, which Justice allowed as a hardship case.

In 1981 fourth-place Heileman attempted to merge with third-place (and sinking) Schlitz. Even though their combined volumes would still leave them thirteen million barrels shy of number two Miller's forty million, Justice said no. The fact that the four largest brewers accounted for 67 percent of the marketplace, said the assistant attorney general, was just too much concentration. So number seven, the Stroh Brewery Company of Detroit, was able to sneak in and buy Schlitz, using the combined volume to leapfrog Heileman on the following year's sales charts. It was a bitter Russell Cleary, president of Heileman and architect of its ascent, who started an all-out campaign to buy Pabst in 1982. Two years later he worked out a complicated deal, involving the selling off of certain Pabst assets to a third party, that Justice was ready to approve. Stroh, a vindictive loser in the hunt to buy Pabst, managed to block the deal in court. Cleary's goal of a third-place spot on the sales charts for Heileman would never happen, thanks to his Motown nemesis. While the giants of only a decade earlier were marching to the auction block, there for the taking, all Cleary could do was gnash his teeth and rail at what he perceived as the unfairness of the very Justice Department that had boosted him up in the first place.

Though Justice's decisions regarding Heileman might have seemed arbitrary and even contradictory, they were actually quite logical when considering the trajectory of the beer business during the sixties, seventies, and eighties. For the first half of those three decades, regional brewing continued to be a major factor in the industry, and Justice protected midwest breweries, first by insuring Pabst didn't grow too large by gobbling up its competition and then by doing the same with Heileman. Once Miller's quick ascent—combined with the heated competition between Anheuser-Busch and Schlitz—put the industry into a national context, it was only right that Justice consider the total market dominance of the top four brewers in its decisions. Which meant that Cleary's days as a carpetbagger were over.

Once he ran out of things to buy in other regions, Cleary had to take a good hard look at what he'd wrought: a jerry-built company of fair-to-middling brands that had withered from lack of attention. (While Cleary built the national network, Old Style, the brand Heileman is most closely associated with, went from a nearly 50 percent share of the Chicago market to something under 20 percent.) The drill had been simple for over a decade: buy small regional breweries, use them to brew established brand names from the Heileman stable, don't put any real money behind supporting the brands, sell any extra property, and watch your stock go up, up, up. The drill worked as long as there was always something new to buy, something with a cheap price tag.

When potential acquisitions dried up, or were blocked by the government, a new drill emerged at Heileman: the line extension game. Major Heileman brands saw the light; of the seven new light beer introductions by major brewers in 1981, as reported in *Impact Databank,* five were Heileman brands. In 1984 six of the ten low-alcohol beers introduced came from Heileman breweries. Because they were regional, the onslaught of Heileman bandwagon brands rarely competed with each other. And they rarely sold well. For a company saddled with a large brewery network operating farther and farther from capacity (because it had so neglected its established brands, like Old Style), there didn't seem to be any other choice *but* line extensions.

This was the problem that Heileman faced by the end of the 1980s: keeping the liquid up. In the parlance of the big brewer, "liquid" is what comes out of your brewery. Liquid production is the total volume of beer you brew; liquid usage is the total volume of beer you sell. Heileman had to keep liquid production up in order to prop up its network of small regional breweries, because consolidating production and closing some breweries would mean brewing brands meant for one part of the country in some other part and then going to the extra expense of shipping them. That was an option that Heileman didn't find too appealing.

So it found a worse option. To boost liquid usage, Heileman started a third drill, which would ultimately bring the company to its knees: it started playing the discounting game. By cutting prices, the company not only lost revenue for itself and its distributors, it did something even more damaging. It cheapened the brands imagewise, not just costwise.

There is almost no coming back from price discounting in the eyes of the public, as anyone who's ever sold anything will tell you. From time to time some genius will attempt a short-term price drop to boost sales, only to find it impossible ever to return to the original pricing structure. Once someone gets used to paying less, why would they ever pay more? You've convinced them your brand isn't worth it. You've "price classified" yourself. In the beer business, the problem is exacerbated by the levels of distribution: the brewer sells to the wholesaler, who sells to the bar/restaurant/liquor store/grocery store, who sells to John and Jane Q. Public. The two middle levels build their margins in and are loath to cut them. This is especially true in bars and restaurants, where there's often space to carry only a limited number of brands. Why should the bar manager carry your discount brand when he can charge far more for a premium-priced brand? He shouldn't, and he won't.

In 1955 Anheuser-Busch created Busch Bavarian, a so-called popular-priced (read: discount) brand intended chiefly to bridge gaps in capacity for its flagship brand, Budweiser. By the end of the 1980s many of the flagship brands coming from Heileman's regional breweries *were* discount brands, and Heileman no longer had the option of closing breweries and consolidating production in any meaningful way; it could no longer afford to. The cost factor had become a catch-22: if you're brewing Lone Star in Texas and selling it for, say, $4 a case and making almost nothing, how do you close the brewery and move production to Chicago, where it will now *cost* you, say, $7 a case, after shipping?

If you can't figure out a way, you're in good company. Neither could Heileman. In 1987 the company was bought by Bond Holdings Ltd. of Australia, an international brewing conglomerate eager to own a piece of the American beer market. Within two years Cleary was gone, leaving behind a company so deeply in the hole that it was unclear whether Bond could even keep up the debt payments. It became clear in 1990. Bond couldn't. The once great Heileman spent much of 1991 under bankruptcy protection, emerging in November of that year with a new business plan and a lot fewer brands and breweries. As I write this, in the spring of 1996, Heileman, teetering on the edge of bankruptcy once again, has just announced a plan to merge with another ailing major brewer: Stroh. Don't you just wonder if Russell Cleary sees the humor in that?

Heileman collapsed because it reached too far, too fast. No one could accuse the folks in Golden, Colorado, of that particular sin.

The Coors Brewing Company, the fourth largest brewer in the United States in 1973, was a regional outfit doing national numbers. Up from forty-ninth place in 1948, Coors had managed to reach fourth place while serving just eleven states, and all with one brewery. About half the total 1973 Coors volume was sold in California, where its flagship brand, Coors Banquet, held a whopping 40 percent share. In states like Oklahoma, the share was as high as 67 percent. With that kind of concentration, it was clear to the industry that Coors, the brand, was ready to spread its wings.

Coors, the family, wasn't.

William and Joe Coors, grandsons of founder Adolph Coors, were horrified by the very idea of borrowing money. If the brewery was to grow, it would be paid for from within. The same self-reliance that had gotten them to produce their own bottles and packaging would keep them from falling into the same trap that would eventually ensnare Heileman: overwhelming debt. Unfortunately, of course, the extremely conservative fiscal dealings of the brothers Coors would also keep them from enjoying the same good fortune that would visit Miller later in the decade: overwhelming growth.

The demand for Coors in the rest of the country was certainly there. Indeed, Coors had obtained something of a mythical quality east of the Rockies, and it was not uncommon for people to return home from a western jaunt with a case or two of Coors, to impress their friends with the brand that couldn't be purchased nearby. At a time when most beer drinkers would've been hard-pressed to describe the taste differences among most premium domestic lagers, Coors had earned a strong reputation for being the smoothest and the least heavy or bitter. Movie stars like Paul Newman were seen swigging cans of the stuff, and its lack of availability in most of the country made it that much more desirable.

The problem was that lack of availability didn't make Coors any more *available.* It's nice to be wanted, but desirability doesn't add anything to your bottom line if your brand isn't on the local store shelf or in the local bar refrigerator, ready to be purchased. Bill and Joe were flat out unwilling to beg, steal, or borrow the extra capacity needed to make Coors a national brand by the early seventies. It wasn't as if they didn't know *how* to raise funds: when Adolph Coors Jr. died in 1970, the company was forced to publicly sell shares to pay off the huge estate tax on the brewery. Had they been willing to sell off a bit more, or at least borrow against it, they might have changed the course of the Beer Wars dramatically.

Coors Banquet had always been considered a light beer, in the "not heavy-tasting" sense of the word. In fact, the old joke about Coors goes like this: What does Coors beer have in common with making love in a canoe? They're both fucking close to water. But this was not actually a bad way to be thought of, in the days before light came to mean reduced calories. Light meant refreshing; a light beer was the bottled stuff you pulled from the refrigerator and rolled across your forehead on a hot summer day. And there's no question that Coors cornered the market on light lager. Unfortunately for Coors, the market consisted of only a handful of states out west by 1975, when a new kind of light was introduced nationally: Lite Beer from Miller.

Lite, from a flavor standpoint, was not terribly different from Coors. Lite was light, and unfortunately for Coors, it was also *light:* it had just about all of the taste of a Coors Banquet and far fewer calories. And, much more important, it was *available.* Lite was everywhere, and

Coors was not. Though it's arguable that the caloric benefit of Lite would've blasted it ahead of Coors anyway, a more national sales base in 1975 might have softened the blow, or at least served as a solid launching pad for Coors Light. Where Heileman's overeagerness led to unsustainable growth, Coors's reluctance led to missed opportunity.

To underscore the effect of Lite on the growth of Coors, note the following: After thirty-two years of continuous sales advances, Coors ended 1975, the year Lite hit the shelves nationally, down 3 percent in sales—and out of the number four spot on the sales charts, replaced by Miller Brewing. Where Lite Beer would average an astounding 36 percent annual growth over its first five years as a national brand, according to *Impact,* Coors Banquet would mark those same five years with an average loss of 0.5 percent. By 1981 Coors had fallen to sixth place on the sales chart.

The Coors brothers had another major problem, one of the public relations variety. The problem, simply stated, was the Coors brothers.

Bill Coors got personally offended when his workers struck for higher wages in 1977. Forget that inflation was rampant at the time, and the workers did what workers do in companies of every stripe; this was a slap at Bill Coors, and he wasn't going to have it. He wanted the unions to know just how angry he was, and he vowed never to hire their members again in his operation. Strikers were fired and replaced with nonunion labor. Maybe Bill figured if Three-Sticks could stand up to the Teamsters, he could do the same with the AFL-CIO. If he did, he figured wrong. The AFL-CIO branded Coors union busters and launched a national boycott of the brands—as national as Coors was in 1977, anyway—which was joined by other unions. The boycott couldn't have come at a worse time, because now anti-Coors sentiment was reaching union strongholds in the East just before the brand itself. Auto workers in Detroit pointedly ignored the arrival of Coors; so did construction workers in New York.

The animosity served to heighten public awareness of the far-right political leanings of the Coors family. Joe Coors was a member of

Ronald Reagan's "kitchen cabinet," a group of business leaders who advised the new president on domestic policy. While advising Reagan wasn't in itself a problem, especially considering Reagan's wild popularity at the time, the degree of Joe's reported right-wing fervor was. Bob Woodward, in his book *Veil: The Secret Wars of the CIA, 1981–1987,* alleged that Joe had bought a $65,000 plane for Oliver North's beloved Nicaraguan contras.

Charges of racism dogged the family as well. Nine years after the Equal Employment Opportunity Commission (EEOC) brought suit against the brewery for discrimination against minorities and women (a suit Coors settled out of court), the *Rocky Mountain News* would quote Joe Coors's alleged assessment of Zimbabwe's economic woes. The blacks in Zimbabwe, Joe was quoted as saying, lack "the intellectual capacity to succeed." Joe successfully sued for libel (he got the *News* to settle out of court), and the paper issued a halfhearted apology, but the damage was done. In Southern California, the alleged "intellectual capacity" comment prompted a five-day boycott of Coors in nearly five hundred liquor stores.

Though rarely corroborated, stories began emerging from Colorado of large Coors family donations to right-wing groups like the John Birch Society and the Moral Majority. Noting the decidedly antihomosexual leanings of the groups Coors was allegedly bankrolling, gays stayed away from the beer in droves. Robert Burgess, a Coors research analyst and the author of *Silver Bullets,* a book on his experiences there, noted that animosity among gays toward Coors was so serious that he and his co-workers were warned not to reveal their company affiliation when on business in San Francisco, for fear of retribution.

One oft corroborated story was Coors's insistence on polygraph testing as part of their hiring procedure. Beyond the traditional uses for lie detection, the weeding out of drug users and potential thieves, Coors asked two additional questions. The first was understandable. The Coors family, devastated in the 1950s by the kidnap/murder of Adolph Coors III, used the polygraph as a security measure. Applicants were asked point-blank if they intended any harm to anyone bearing the company name. The other nontraditional question also traced its roots back to an event of the 1950s: the McCarthy hearings. Coors wanted to know if any of their prospective employees were Commies.

It was all too much for Paul Newman, who publicly switched to Bud (and gained a sponsor for his race car in the process).

All of the wackiness, real and imagined, going on in Golden, Colorado, added up to one thing: a whopping migraine for anyone unfortunate enough to be in the public relations department. In *Silver Bullets*, Burgess recalls one flack's half-joking rationale for a raise request: "I've been doing some figuring. Gays are 10 percent of the population. Right? Blacks are about 10 percent, union workers are at least 15 percent of the population, and women are 51 percent. So, I figure right there that at least 86 percent of the population hates Coors. And that doesn't even include liberals, environmentalists, MADD [Mothers Against Drunk Driving], or a lot of other groups. So I figure my job is at least eight or nine times harder than it would be at another company. So I think I should get paid eight or nine times more."

Growing public enmity, coupled with the explosion of the very similar Lite Beer from Miller, caused Coors's slump to deepen in the early eighties. A 1982 total volume drop of 10 percent seemed to set off the panic buttons in the management offices, and Coors finally made the one move that could revive their fortunes: the move east. Forced by increased competition on the West Coast—a region Anheuser-Busch had barely spent in before Philip Morris catapulted Miller into the number two spot—Coors dipped into some of the money raised during their public offering of 1970 and expanded their distribution.

By 1985 Coors was available in forty-five states, including all of New England and most of the South. A year earlier, in a nod to their image problems, the brewery had signed agreements with both African American and Hispanic groups, promising to hire more minority executives and to boost minority-owned businesses where possible. Coors pledged, as part of the agreements, $325 million, some of which would go directly to minority causes and organizations in the form of contributions and the rest of which would help increase minority ownership of Coors distributorships.

Thanks to their newfound willingness to expand and to deal with their bad reputation, Coors was on the way back up. In the end, one man was largely responsible for Coors's ascension to the number three spot on the sales chart (the spot they reached in 1990 and still hold today), one man who, more than anyone else, convinced beer drinkers that Coors was not only socially acceptable, it was actually *desirable.* That man was Mark Harmon.

Harmon was one of the stars of television's *St. Elsewhere* and a former UCLA quarterback. He was the perfect spokesman for a beer brewed in Colorado. Standing next to a cool mountain stream in a flannel shirt and hiking boots, Harmon, with his rugged good looks and soft-spoken, believable delivery, made most people forget that Coors had ever had image problems. Here was a clean-cut guy (whom *People* magazine would soon dub "the Sexiest Man Alive") assuring drinkers that Coors was "the one." The Rocky Mountain imagery that had been such a large part of the product myth for years was back big time. Coors seemed to realize that the romance of the product imagery was almost as important as the product itself.

Foote, Cone, and Belding (FCB), Coors's ad agency, had managed to find a spokesman who was somewhat recognizable, but not quite so famous that he could escape being known as "the Coors guy." That meant that each new achievement of his, like the *People* "Sexiest Man" crowning, would hold reflected glory for Coors. FCB had found a way not only to halt the skid of Coors Banquet, but also—because consumers seemed to just automatically carry over the brand imagery—to kick the growth of Coors Light into overdrive. FCB had managed to draw women, not traditionally big beer drinkers, to Coors products. FCB was clearly full of advertising geniuses.

Advertising geniuses who, within a few years, would manage to screw it all up with a single ad. (See the last few pages of chapter 7.)

THE SEARCH FOR THE NEXT BIG THING

While the Mark Harmon ads for Coors Banquet also managed to push Coors Light into the stratosphere, the fact remained that the brand played at a permanent disadvantage. An ad campaign would eventually dub it "the Right Beer Now"; truth was, Coors Light was the right beer a little too late. Though unquestionably a success, it was a muted success because of the brand's late arrival in the marketplace. It didn't matter how good Coors Light tasted, or how perfect the Rocky Mountain cool, clear water imagery was; by the time Coors got around to introducing it in 1978, Lite Beer from Miller had become so established that only a brewer with a bottomless bank account and a great deal of patience could hope to catch up. (Bud Light, anyone?)

Embarrassed by Lite Beer's lengthy free ride, no one in the brewing industry wanted to miss the next bandwagon, whatever it might be.

They didn't have to wait long to find out: in 1983 Hudepohl in Cincinnati claimed to have introduced the very first low-alcohol beer, Pace Pilsner. By year's end Christian Schmidt announced its own entry into the fledgling category, Break Special Lager. It was all the prompting the big boys needed.

Anheuser-Busch, amid much fanfare, gave the world LA in 1984. Following in the footsteps of Miller, which had named the first national light beer Lite, Anheuser-Busch was content to use the category name as the product name. Only no one was going to belly up to the bar and say, "I'll have a Low-Alcohol, please," so they shortened it, winning automatically the enmity of drinkers in N.Y.C., S.F., and other initial-happy markets.

With the introduction of LA, the leader had declared the category viable, and an industry anxious for the Next Big Thing was off to the races. Stroh followed first, with Schaefer LA, which had to be renamed when Anheuser-Busch successfully took them to court for trademark violation. Heileman got into the game (and into the courtroom, where they challenged A-B's right to trademark the LA designation) with typical Heileman understatement: they launched Blatz LA and Black Label LA, followed shortly by Old Style LA, Rainier LA, Lone Star LA, and Schmidt LA. Miller joined Heileman's lawsuit and introduced something called Sharp's LA, a name they'd resurrect a few years later when LAs turned to NAs (nonalcoholics). Pabst, with an eye toward keeping legal costs down, relaunched their failing Pabst Extra Light as Low Alcohol Pabst Extra Light, beating out the moniker Anheuser-Busch Natural Light lengthwise by one word (or two, if you want to get picky about the hyphenation). The winner for oddest name, though, was Latrobe Brewing's Light-N-Lo—no one could decide if it was a beer or a nondairy creamer.

Everyone was in the marketplace, but no one knew quite what the marketplace consisted of. Who wanted low-alcohol beer? Though the theory within the industry seemed to be that there was a market for a beer that offered a reduced buzz, Light beer drinkers already assumed that their brands had less alcohol, so the product benefit for them was unclear. Heart patients and expectant mothers, two groups forbidden by their doctors from having alcohol, were only teased by the new products.

The PR benefits were nonexistent as well. Low-alcohol wasn't exactly no-alcohol, so groups like Mothers Against Drunk Driving certainly weren't going to applaud the brewers or slow down their efforts against them.

Soon enough, it was clear that the new category, in the eyes of the marketplace, was neither fish nor fowl. In its introductory year, amid all the hype that Anheuser-Busch, Heileman, Miller, Pabst, and the others could muster, *Beer Marketer's Insights* pegged combined low-alcohol sales at half a million barrels, compared with 180 million barrels of beer sold overall. The underwhelming sales performance of the category led one brewer's director of brand management to remark to the press, "We've come to the conclusion that people drink to get buzzed."

Shocked by the immediate failure of the category, which never grew beyond its half million barrels in 1984, the big boys were slow to see the tiny bud of potential market share growing from within the wreckage: nonalcoholic brew.

Europeans got there first, and not entirely because they were adept at reading the public: it was because they were adept at reading profit-and-loss statements. In Europe a number of countries tax beverages by alcoholic content, so nonalcoholics, which could be sold at regular beer prices, became the closest thing to pure profit European brewers were likely to find. The added pluses in America were these: Import prices could be charged, and Americans were more likely to believe that a German, Irish, or Dutch brewer could surmount the taste problems associated with removing the alcohol. So in came Germany's Clausthaler, Ireland's Kaliber, and Holland's Buckler.

Along with the imported imagery, the foreigners brought respectability in a way that hadn't occurred to the domestics. None of the imports used the NA designation in their names, for a simple reason: no one *wants* to drink nonalcoholic beer; they do it out of necessity. Whether they're the designated driver, the person with the health problem, or the bartender on the job, nobody wants his nose rubbed in the fact he can't drink or that he's settling for an imitation brew.

In the macho world of beer, Anheuser-Busch, it turned out, had committed the ultimate sin with their low-alcohol entry. In their fevered quest to introduce the Next Big Thing, they'd created a product name and labeling that screamed "This isn't really beer." It was a mistake they would not repeat when, five years after the failure of LA, they would introduce O'Doul's, a nonalcoholic brew. Not only would it carry an imported-sounding name, O'Doul's would come in a green bottle, like two perennial top-selling imports, Heineken and Molson.

Import imagery would also figure heavily in a Coors gambit to capture some of Anheuser-Busch's Michelob drinkers. The idea behind the new Coors product was sound: partner with a foreign brewer to create a domestically produced beer with a heavier flavor and some reflected cachet. The idea was sound . . . if one had never heard of Löwenbräu.

To be fair, the idea for what would become Masters III Beer didn't come from within Coors; it was the brainchild of Molson Brewing, the largest exporter of Canadian beer to the U.S. The similarity with Löwenbräu was that Masters III would be, according to its advertising, an import-quality beer, produced in America under the supervision of the Kaltenberg Brewery in Germany. (After Coors and Molson, Kaltenberg was the third I in Masters III, though the name wasn't originally intended to carry a roman numeral at all. It seems the Masters golf tournament was none too keen on having a beer named after it, import quality or not.) The difference between Löwenbräu and Masters III was that Masters III would actively and openly celebrate its American connection. Anheuser-Busch and Miller both turned Molson down, and nine months after the Masters III introduction, Coors would wish they'd followed suit.

Coors developed the recipe for the brand, in consultation with Molson. Molson shared the cost of overhead. Coors did the actual brewing and packaging. Kaltenberg's role was to smile at the thought of whopping royalty checks. In an amazing show of faith in the idea, Coors and Molson set up a new company to front Masters III, which would operate separately from either brewer in terms of marketing and sales. The product was launched in four cities, Washington, D.C., Boston, Miami, and Columbus, the first three of which were huge imported beer markets. The advertising, themed "Together Is Better," explained to beer drinkers how the three companies had pooled their experience to come up with Masters III.

Imagine, if you will, the following scenario: The owners of the upscale Ruth's Chris chain of steak restaurants decide one day to open a midpriced chain of steak places. They partner with Sizzler and obtain the blessing of a famous Argentine restaurant. The first question you have to ask yourself is, who's going to eat at the new chain? Too low-brow for the folks used to Ruth's Chris, and with too many spices on the meat to suit true blue Sizzler fans (who are going to gag on the check, to boot), the answer is almost no one.

So it was with Masters III. Coors drinkers found it too heavy (a certain "heaviness" being the most common characteristic of imported beer, at least in relation to domestic lager); import drinkers complained that it wasn't heavy enough to live up to the billing it was getting in its advertising. Coors drinkers didn't *want* some full-bodied Germanic treasure, they wanted something smooth, cold, and light. Import drinkers heard the word "Coors" and were reminded of the joke I told in the last chapter, the one with the f-word in it. And as if the taste and imagery problems weren't enough, the separate sales force idea thoroughly pissed off the sales staffs of *both* Coors and Molson, who found it not a little insulting and a bit too directly competitive and who went out of their way to sabotage Masters III distribution.

It wasn't as if Coors didn't know better. In 1981 they'd made their first foray into the superpremium category with a brand called Herman Joseph's. Perpetually in test markets, Herman Joseph's came in brown Coors bottles and attracted little attention and even less repeat business. Feeling they needed to be in the higher-priced end of the marketplace, Coors hung on to the brand for years before finally pulling the plug. (Killian's Irish Red, introduced in 1982, was another brand that Coors hung on to even though it sold next to nothing for years. In Killian's case, though, Coors's stubbornness paid off when specialty beers soared in the early nineties, taking Killian's along with them.)

Masters III, with a life span of nine months, had the distinction of surviving almost twice as long as another 1985 Coors introduction.

In the summer of 1985 my college roommates and I mapped out a postgraduation jaunt. Though we didn't take the clichéd trip through the youth hostels of Europe, we still managed a cultural journey, of sorts: we found a way to quite cheaply see a ball game in each of the five ballparks in California within a two-week time frame. (It works, provided one has enough relatives and friends to cadge accommodations from.) We even remember most of the trip, which says something about the lack of German-style brewhouses along the Pacific Coast Highway. The point of all of this is that on a warm evening in late June, we found ourselves in the very alien Dodger Stadium—alien to us denizens of Yankee Stadium, anyway, for its general cleanliness and quite pleasant fans.

The oddest thing we found that night, though, wasn't the lack of shouted obscenities or even the spotless concession areas; it was what the vendors walking up and down the aisles were calling out along with their offers of cold beer: "Coolers. Get your wine coolers, here." This L.A. really *was* a strange and unnatural place, we decided.

Only cooler-wise, it wasn't so strange.

By the summer of 1985 wine coolers were turning up in lots of places traditionally reserved for beer. Beach coolers, nightclubs, corner saloons, and—most troubling—supermarket shelf space. Supermarket shelf space previously occupied by beer brands.

Wine coolers, essentially carbonated white wine flavored with fruit juice, were the brainchild of Californian Michael Crete. Crete, who started mixing wine coolers in plastic tubs during the early seventies for his volleyball-playing friends, founded California Cooler in 1981. He and a partner, Stuart Bewley, both twenty-eight at the time, started the company on an investment of $10,000 and grossed only $12,000 in their maiden year. Their bottled version of Crete's concoction didn't take long to catch on, though; by 1984 California Cooler grossed $72 *million.* A year later Crete and Bewley sold their company to Kentucky distiller Brown Forman for $63 million in cash, plus payments tied to future sales worth up to another $83 million. Not bad for a couple of beach boys.

Smoother and lighter than sangria, wine coolers were perfect for the sun-and-fun crowd and immediately more acceptable to women than beer. While the beer business was looking to manufacture the next alcohol fad by degrees (of alcohol), the real thing was swelling off the beaches of Santa Monica. Anheuser-Busch, Miller, and Coors would miss the first wave.

For the Big Two, the hesitance to get into the wine cooler market wasn't based on an unwillingness to venture outside of the world of malt; it was based on a healthy dose of denial. They just didn't believe that that particular dog would hunt. Coors was pleased to see the potential in the wine cooler market, especially since, conceptually, wine coolers were awfully similar to a flavored beer idea Coors had been developing for the same female drinkers who were buying California Cooler products by the case. Unfortunately, reacting well to a market development is not the same thing as reacting quickly, and the product that Coors had been developing as early as 1983 wouldn't be ready for the shelves until halfway through 1985. In the meantime, Pabst and Heileman had each gotten involved in the cooler market, Pabst with Margarita Cooler and Heileman with Country Cooler.

There are two reactions, according to one executive who's held posts at both Anheuser-Busch and Miller, that the beer giants will have to any development in the marketplace. The first is, "That's not going to work, because that's not the way you do it," and the second is, "Man, this is going to be great, we better dominate." It's either resolute denial or rose-colored glasses time. Within a few years of adopting the first stance when it came to wine coolers, Anheuser-Busch and Miller would learn a third reaction: "What the hell do we do about this?"

What they'd forgotten was that dismissing something as a fad isn't enough; even a fad can hurt you if it's left unchecked. It's a question of speed, really. If you hop on the next bandwagon quickly, in a controlled way, you can protect your distributors and your shelf space by not allowing the competition to encroach, even for a little while. (And by spending wisely, you can even make yourself a little money, no matter how short the fad's life span.) Wine coolers were the perfect nonbeer category for the big guys to jump into: profit margins were great, as it was inexpensive to make and less fluid product was sold at a higher price than beer. Better still, wine coolers were drunk primarily by women, so cannibalization—luring your customers away from one of your brands to another—was almost nonexistent.

By 1985, when Coors and Anheuser-Busch were ready to get into the wine cooler market, there were already two more major players. Liquor giant Seagram's had Seagram's Golden Wine Cooler and a very hot Bruce Willis as spokesperson. (Though the ads were great, they had the unfortunate effect of convincing Willis that his crooning was vinyl-worthy—"The Return of Bruno" was released soon after, to resounding critical and popular drubbing. The *Die Hard* movies, though, were terrific, Bruce.) Gallo, an honest-to-God winery, got involved in the category as well. Its Bartles & Jaymes Wine Cooler was pitched quite amusingly, and effectively, by the fictional Ed Bartles and Frank Jaymes, two rubes who ended each commercial with the phrase "Thank you for your support." Within a year of its launch, the Gallo brand easily overtook California Cooler for the top sales spot.

The lateness of the day wasn't the largest factor contributing to the swift deaths of the Coors and Anheuser-Busch coolers; it was each company's stubborn refusal to play by rules set by others. Neither would actually introduce a *wine* cooler—at least not at first, in the case of A-B—and both would fail miserably.

Coors was first, with its Colorado Chiller, a malt-based cooler. Greenish in color, and with an overpowering scent of lime-flavored beer, Colorado Chiller was no one's idea of a wine cooler. If anyone *had* mistaken it for a Bartles & Jaymes competitor, the advertising was enough to straighten them out. Featuring mechanized penguins in a bar setting (penguins who spouted slogans like "Less chilling . . . tastes great"), the spots were clearly *beer* advertising, when *beer* drinkers were exactly *not* the people drinking coolers. The product stank (figuratively and literally), the advertising was targeted in the wrong direction, and Coors pulled the plug within a few months.

Anheuser-Busch didn't fare much better with either of its two attempts to break into the wine cooler business. The first product, launched in the fall of 1985, didn't come from the brand development department at August Busch's headquarters; it reputedly came from the brand development department at Busch's estate: his wife, Ginny. One of August's underlings at the time says that Baybry's Champagne Cooler was born when Ginny suggested to her husband that, among her tennis friends, wine coolers were not nearly as popular as champagne mimosas. Why not sell those?

Well, first off, a champagne mimosa in a bottle is going to mean champagne tax rates for the product. (Brewers have historically managed to keep the federal excise tax on beer much lower than those of other alcoholic beverages, arguing successfully that beer is the drink of the common man and its price should be within his means.) Though Busch's own people told him that they couldn't viably charge enough extra to make up the profit erosion, Busch insisted that the product was high value and consumers would pay more. Second, the crowd that drinks mimosas is used to fine champagne blended with fresh fruit juice. They're not going to sit on the terrace at the country club and drink preblended, mass-produced champagne cocktails. (Okay, maybe they will at whatever country club August and Ginny belong to, but probably not anywhere else.)

The second attempt Anheuser-Busch made to grab a piece of the cooler business came within a year, and again, it wasn't content to have a directly competitive product. This time it would introduce a low-calorie cooler. The same man who had declared the name Anheuser-Busch Natural Light "too damn long" would now give the world Dewey Stephens Premium Light Wine Cooler and inadvertently help speed up the demise of the wine cooler category.

Here was the problem that Dewey Stephens created just by its very existence: women already thought that wine coolers were low-calorie. In fact, it was a widely held (and completely unfounded) belief among cooler drinkers that wine coolers were already very low in calories, if not calorie *free.* Anheuser-Busch hipped them to the truth, and, according to one executive there at the time, many wine cooler drinkers simply dropped the whole category, rather than trading down to what they thought they were getting in the first place. Dewey Stephens was gone within a year and a half, along with much of the growth of the segment.

Just as the category was headed downward, Miller limped in with the last major brand introduction, Matilda Bay. Made with domestic wine and imported fruit flavors from Australia, Matilda Bay differed from major cooler brands in that it was noncarbonated, something a Miller exec later admitted was "a horrendous idea." Hamish Maxwell, then chairman of Philip Morris, had asked casually of his Miller people why they weren't in the wine cooler business. Mistaking the query for a command, Miller quickly developed Matilda Bay and rolled it out. According to a joke that made the rounds of Miller headquarters shortly after the brand's failure, Maxwell told the Miller people, "I didn't say roll it out, I said throw it out."

To this day, a number of folks who'd made quite a tidy sum in the wine cooler business insist that Anheuser-Busch and Miller purposefully tanked the segment, by introducing ill-conceived or just plain lousy products and spending heavily behind them. (Coors isn't included in this conspiracy theory because, well, it's Coors; and with the Golden, Colorado, brewer's luck in the product introduction game, any attempt to sabotage the segment probably would have resulted in its tenfold growth.)

Whether by design or the more likely natural course of fad products—the definition of fad being a category or brand that grows very quickly and fades almost as fast—wine coolers were on the wane not long after the midway point of the eighties. (Crete and Bewley showed just as much genius by their timing of the sale of California Cooler as they did in starting the company in the first place.) The shelf space slowly returned to the beer category, though not to the usual suspects. By the time coolers were disappearing from the competitive radar, a new blip was gaining strength. The Next Big Thing had arrived. As it would turn out, the Next Big Thing was an old Big Thing, now in the hands of someone who knew how to market.

With High Life's sales tumbling by double digits annually, the folks in charge of new products at Miller were desperate for another Lite. It was a dilemma largely of their own making: because of the success of light beer, and the interest in new categories and new products, the traditional pull of, well, the *traditional* was disappearing. The big brewers, by putting hundreds of millions of marketing dollars behind introductory products, had conditioned young drinkers especially to look beyond established brands and crave the newest, splashiest market entries. They'd sacrificed the romantic allure of heritage for the eager anticipation of the new.

Not even the timely "Miller, Made the American Way" campaign, unleashed as it was at the height of Reaganism, could help Miller's flagship brand. The stereotypical yuppie (young urban professional) of the eighties seemed less interested in blue-collar imagery than his counterpart of ten years before. So what was Miller to do? The answer came from a Philip Morris guy. In Japan.

Hamish Maxwell, wine cooler query notwithstanding, was renowned for his ability to keep not only a multicorporate perspective, but a multinational one as well. A Philip Morris cigarette executive running the (extremely lucrative) Japanese cigarette market casually mentioned a local beer development to Maxwell one day in 1984. Soon after, Maxwell interrupted the underwhelming presentation of a Miller new products manager with the following comment: "This draft thing is doing so well in Japan, why don't you check it out?" The next day, New Products had someone on a plane. Within a year something called Plank Road Draft was being tested by Miller. While the specific product didn't test well, Miller researchers found a great deal of curiosity about the concept. Though Plank Road Draft never got out of the test markets, there seemed to be something there.

What there was was a great gimmick, though not a new one. It was cold filtration, a process that replaces heat pasteurization as a means to extend the freshness of beer. (Most brewers agree that heat pasteurization, necessary to protect the shelf life of packaged beer against the effects of sunlight and temperature fluctuation, damages the flavor.) The BATF decreed that Miller could label cold-filtered, nonpasteurized packaged beer as "draft" beer.

Coors had been cold filtering for over a quarter of a century, though until Miller Genuine Draft arrived in 1985, Coors hadn't made much of its cold filtration in terms of hype. Miller, as it had done a decade earlier with Lite, was about to trump Coors again, this time with a card stolen from its hand.

"Bottled draft beer" may be an oxymoron, but it's a sellable one, like "jumbo shrimp." When labeled with the Miller name, instead of the unrecognizable Plank Road, Genuine Draft caught fire. Packaged in a clear glass, long-neck bottle bearing a striking black-and-gold label, MGD cast off the blue-collar appeal of its parent brand. It stressed an ice-cold, thirst-quenching quality in all of its advertising and merchandising material. It was an immediate hit among the fastest-growing segment of the marketplace, the very people who were rejecting the flagship brands of the Big Three in favor of whatever the latest trend was: younger drinkers.

It was not a hit at Coors. As part of their successful "Coors Is the

One" campaign featuring Mark Harmon, Coors put a lot of emphasis not only on the cold filtration, but on cold shipping and cold storage, both of which further extend the shelf life of their brands. Coors's commonly understood product benefit—its smooth, clean taste—was a direct result of its insistence on keeping its beer cold until the moment of purchase, the brewer said. Because the company had spent millions on refrigerated trucks and boxcars to move their brands in, and required their distributors to refrigerate their warehouses, it made sense for Coors to beat the "colder is better" drum. Two things dampened their message, though.

The first was an unbelievable screwup on the part of Foote, Cone, and Belding. Just as the Harmon campaign was picking up steam, and it seemed the public was getting the concepts of cold filtration, cold shipping, and cold storage, FCB produced a new Harmon spot, this one set in a retail setting. No problem with the location. Nor were the lines Harmon spoke wrong in any way. The display of Coors was. The beer was sitting out on nonrefrigerated shelves, *at room temperature.*

Never mind the consumers who picked up on the goof and wondered if the cold-storage line they'd come to accept was nothing more than hype. The real problem came when Coors distributors saw the spot and wondered the same thing. If Coors wasn't even going to bother to sell the cold-storage feature, why had distributors shelled out so much damned money—at Coors's insistence—for warehouse refrigeration units? Though Coors would argue that keeping the brands cold made them taste better, some distributors privately questioned whether there was *that* much difference to justify the expense. Why was Coors shipping cold, those distributors wanted to know, when the money could be used to fight the Big Two in the marketing arena? What the hell was going on in Golden, anyway?

What was going on was that Coors was opening the door wider for Miller Genuine Draft. Inexplicably, two years after Harmon had become the Coors spokesman, he was gone—fired to make way for a new, fast-paced ad campaign themed "the American Original." So much for the romance of the brand: the new ads walked completely away from product attributes and therefore could have been ads from any major brewer. The primacy of Coors's cold-filtering claims was abandoned, and along with it any hope for competing with Genuine Draft. Within five years MGD would outsell Coors Banquet, and most consumers would still have no idea that "bottled draft" was what Coors had been selling for decades. (In an odd attempt to rectify that, Coors dropped the "Banquet" from its flagship's name in 1988, changing it to Coors Original Draft. Realizing this served only to make them sound like copycats; they changed back early in 1989.)

Anheuser-Busch reacted to MGD just as they had reacted to Lite: denigrate, regulate, replicate. A propaganda war was launched with a single pamphlet. Titled "Hey Bartender, How Much Do You Know about Draft Beer?", it was clearly positioned as an educational flyer, but the true intent of Anheuser-Busch's draft missive to bars around the country was obvious from the first line of copy inside: "Do you know enough to tell a keg from a crock?" Anheuser-Busch went to bartenders for a simple reason: the BATF would *never* have allowed them to be so competitively nasty in their advertising, an area over which the bureau had jurisdiction. Though the pamphlet carefully avoided naming Miller Genuine Draft, it went to great lengths to characterize cold-filtered, nonpasteurized beer as cheaper to make, harder to keep fresh, and generally less tasty.

That the King of Beers would bad-mouth the competition, however indirectly, wasn't surprising. What *was* surprising was the very public way in which it was bashing Miller Genuine Draft. In the past, Anheuser-Busch had used others to trash new trends or brands, or it had used word of mouth. The pamphlet was educational all right. It taught the industry that August's camp was very, very afraid.

Miller loved it. Genuine Draft, a brand that ended 1987 with less than 7 percent of the company's total volume, was eliciting panicked attacks from a company that held over 40 percent of the *entire* beer market. Miller released a flyer of its own, this one titled "Cold-filtered Miller Genuine Draft. It's Got the 'King' Genuinely Nervous." Calling the Anheuser-Busch flyer a "Busch league tactic," Miller defended cold filtering, described pasteurized beers as "cooked," and raised the counterissue of additives and preservatives, pointing out that while Miller brands didn't use any, Budweiser contained the additive tannic acid.

By pointing out that all their brands carried the "contains no additives or preservatives" claim right on the label, Miller gave Anheuser-Busch its angle for the "regulate" phase of its campaign against Genuine Draft. Miller brands found their way into the Anheuser-Busch laboratory.

In what it called a "routine analysis" of competitors' brands, Anheuser-Busch claimed to have found a longer-lasting head on both Miller Genuine Draft and Miller Lite. Further studies, the brewery said, showed that the "artificial foam" was due to the use of a "man-made" hop extract. The findings were immediately brought to the attention of the BATF, where Anheuser-Busch filed a complaint against Miller for misleading consumers. The BATF disagreed. Pissed off at the loss, Anheuser-Busch threatened to take its case to the Food and Drug Administration, and even directly to consumers, if it had to. Miller sat back and smiled. "The best barometer of competitive success," one Miller flack told *The Wall Street Journal*, "is Augie Busch's temper."

Unfortunately, Augie Busch's temper and Miller's glee in needling him were none too popular with the BATF. The bureau hated being middled in this kind of mudslinging, because it was constantly being called upon to take sides when it in fact needed to remain on friendly terms with both giants of the beer business. What people outside the industry didn't realize was that the BATF's very existence relied on the support of its larger charges. In the early eighties, according to one bureau official, the BATF was in danger of being dismantled as part of a Reagan administration attempt to please the gun lobby. It was Miller's parent, Philip Morris, which provided much of the lobbying effort in Congress that saved the bureau from extinction.

So the BATF decided to step into the pamphlet fray before it could get out of control. A conclave was called, where counsel from both breweries met with bureau officials. More accurately, counsel from both breweries received a lecture from bureau officials, with a very simple theme: "Play nice . . . because if we have to take sides, *all* of us stand to lose." The pamphlet campaign stopped.

Anheuser-Busch had nowhere to go but the replication stage. It seemed that cold filtration was only a bad thing when someone else did it, because by 1990 the King was straight-facedly fielding three draft brands: Bud Dry Draft, Busch Light Draft, and Busch Cold Filtered Draft. The fourth draft introduction, early in 1991, would leave no doubt that Anheuser-Busch was willing to assimilate every detail of Miller Genuine Draft. Michelob Golden Draft came in a clear glass, tall-neck bottle, bearing a black-and-gold label. The advertising tag line, "It's pure cold," sounded suspiciously like Genuine Draft's "Get into the cold." Miller couldn't resist another tweak: "At Miller, we innovate, not imitate."

8

Honey Tree Evil Eye Is a Bitch

Anheuser-Busch and Miller had no idea how lucky they were that the BATF acted informally and stopped them from turning the bottled draft debate into another reason for the beer industry to look bad. By that time it was pretty damned unattractive already, from a public relations standpoint.

Just a few years before the draft flap, the BATF had had a second go at Anheuser-Busch over illegal trade practices, and the record settlement of $750,000 that the King had paid in 1978 would be bested by $1.25 million just six years later. Apparently, August's men had been a bit overzealous in their pursuit of sports domination. According to the BATF, "A-B required or induced retail beer dealers at various ballparks, racetracks, stadiums, expositions, and other entertainment facilities to purchase A-B products to the exclusion, in whole or in part, of its competitors, in violation of the trade practice provision of the FAA Act." As with the first crackdown, this one didn't indicate a seriously corrupt company as much as one in need of a slap for ignoring the maxim that rules are rules . . . no matter how unfair they may seem. (Again, Anheuser-Busch was being punished for trade practices that were perfectly acceptable in the cola business.)

August's $2 million "agreement in compromise" settlement with the BATF ended the investigation without an admission of guilt on Anheuser-Busch's part. Legally he had paid his way back into the clear, but in terms of public opinion—where the minor nature of his infractions wasn't really understood—his brewery was looking more like Goliath than ever.

All anyone had to do was ask Sophia Collier, of Brooklyn, New York.

Sophia entered the burgeoning sparkling water market with something called Soho Natural Soda in 1977. Her product had its share of imitators, including a brand called Zeltzer Seltzer in the mid-eighties, which went so far as to copy Soho's unique checkerboard label design. Normally just the threat of a lawsuit will cause a copycat competitor to back down, but not when that competitor is August Busch III. Zeltzer Seltzer was his latest attempt to diversify beyond the flattening beer market, following the disaster of Chelsea and the failure of a root beer–flavored carbonated drink called Root 66. Anheuser-Busch countered Collier's lawsuit with one of his own, citing Collier for defamation. Somebody should've told August about people from Brooklyn. They don't take no crap. Not from nobody. Ya hear?

Collier played an excellent David. She brought the fight right back to August's turf, talking to his hometown paper, the *St. Louis Post-Dispatch.* "They think by this kind of hardball they can scare me," she told a reporter. "They have millions of dollars to promote their product. We have only my lone voice."

Anheuser-Busch blinked. Just before a 1987 court hearing in the case, the company settled with Collier's American Natural Beverage Corporation. Though no money changed hands, Zeltzer Seltzer would stop using the ersatz Soho Natural Soda label, and Anheuser-Busch would drop its defamation suit. Not long after, Anheuser-Busch sold off the brand.

The Goliath image itself didn't hurt the King with consumers. As with the copycat image Anheuser-Busch weathered over the lifetime of the Natural Light ex-jock ad campaign, it was doubtful that the guy on the barstool was going to change his preference because a brewer was getting too big for his own britches. All the same, the bully image Anheuser-Busch seemed to cultivate through the first half of the decade had an unpleasant effect: it made the King of Beers seem like a bad guy, and no one much wants to protect the bad guy when he gets attacked. The timing couldn't have been worse: as they had done over half a century earlier, opposing forces were massing against the entire beer industry, nearly half of which comprised Anheuser-Busch brands.

It's hard to be sure what most directly contributed to the rise of what August Busch III dubbed "neoprohibitionism" in the early eighties. Perhaps it was the industry deregulation brought on by Reaganism, which launched a number of court battles between states and federal agencies, both sides vying for jurisdiction. (Jurisdictional squabbles usually draw extra attention to the parties being watched over.) Perhaps the Justice Department's assertion—when it denied Heileman the right to buy Schlitz in 1981—that the big boys were getting too big fed into some larger, vague public concern about the industry. Perhaps it was even the realization by many politicians that, with revenue drying up under Reagan tax cuts, alcoholic beverages were an easy target for increased levies.

Whatever caused the growing governmental and public animosity toward the beer business, one of the more interesting contributing factors to it was a wrecked black Corvette, found seventy feet from an

Arizona highway one morning in November of 1983, with a dead girl nearby.

The car belonged to August Busch IV, then nineteen years old. Though he denied being involved in the fatal crash, when August IV was questioned by sheriff's deputies in Tucson the next morning, he was partially covered in dried blood. Empty cans of Bud Light were found at the scene, though blood and urine samples taken from young Busch were either lost or destroyed at the hospital, so it's never been determined if alcohol was the cause of the crash that threw twenty-two-year-old Michelle Frederick from the car, killing her. Blood matching August IV's type was found inside the car, as were a radar detector and a .44 Magnum. So was some identification erroneously listing August IV's age as twenty-three, which would have made him appear legal to drink in all fifty states at the time. (He was already legal in Arizona.)

The result was a prickly, badly timed public relations problem for Anheuser-Busch: whether or not it could be proven in court, it seemed to a number of people that the teenage son of the most powerful man in the beer business had quite possibly smashed up his car while drunk. It didn't look good for a company trying awfully hard to convince folks that it wasn't attempting to appeal to underage drinkers.

Earlier in the same year August IV's car was wrecked, a watchdog group called the Center for Science in the Public Interest (CSPI) petitioned the Federal Trade Commission (FTC) to ban, or at least severely limit, alcoholic beverage advertising. The petition called for a complete ban on any advertising that seemed to speak to young or heavy drinkers, with what remained tied to mandatory counter-messages: ads about the dangers of drinking. All print advertising would have to carry a warning similar to the one mandated on tobacco ads. Youth marketing would be out, as well, including beverage alcohol sponsorships of concerts, sporting events, and taste tests. The restrictions asked for by the CSPI included a widening of the ban on athletes from alcohol product endorsements to include even former athletes.

Suddenly the government was listening. Though the advertising limitations were rejected (largely because the broadcast industry would have been badly hurt), the push for warning labels gained lobbying support from groups like the American Society of Internal Medicine, and efforts toward a federal drinking age bore fruit. In 1984 the federal government found an ingenious way to guarantee a twenty-one-year-old drinking age without trampling on the rights of states: it tied federal highway funds to compliance. Though twenty-seven states started the year with a legal drinking age of something less than twenty-one, by the end of 1984 all were considering raising it. (And very shortly thereafter, all would do it.)

Though the beer industry fought each attempt to limit its ability to advertise what it saw as a legal product used moderately by the majority of drinkers, it found itself demonized in the arena of public opinion again and again. Beer is as bad as narcotics, said some opponents. It's as harmful as cigarettes, insisted others. Beer is just like hard liquor, said another special-interest group.

Oddly, that special-interest group was a liquor company.

As if the beer industry didn't have enough problems, Joseph E. Seagram & Sons chose 1985 as the year to launch an equivalency debate, claiming in a $5 million ad campaign that "a drink is a drink is a drink." A giant liquor distiller headed up by Edgar Bronfman Jr., Seagram wanted to get liquor back on the airwaves and taxed at the same rate as beer. (Liquor had long been outlawed from television advertising and taxed at a much higher rate.) The three largest TV networks, ABC, CBS, and NBC, refused to air Bronfman's spots, which pointed out that twelve ounces of beer and five ounces of wine had as much alcohol as one and a quarter ounces of liquor. (Show me a bartender in Manhattan who makes a screwdriver with just over an ounce of vodka, and I'll show you an empty bar.)

A miffed Bronfman accused the networks of "contributing to the problem of public misinformation, rather than joining in the solution by broadcasting the facts." What did he expect? Did he honestly think the networks would alienate advertisers who spent hundreds of millions of dollars annually for a lousy five mil?

Though the BATF sided in part with Seagram and approved the ads as "technically correct," it was uncomfortable with the debate, again because it would force the bureau to take sides and potentially alienate some of its most powerful charges. While public-interest groups bombarded the agency with demands for tighter reins on alcohol, the largest companies under its jurisdiction were having a public pissing contest over who got folks drunk quicker. The CSPI called the Seagram initiative a "Trojan horse intended to open the airwaves to advertising for distilled products and promote consumption of hard liquor." Their solution? Kick 'em all off the air, and good riddance. Thanks to the publicity generated by the intraindustry sniping, two sets of congressional hearings were held on the subject of alcohol advertising restrictions in 1985.

Neither hearing resulted in either the banning of beer advertising or the equal time for countermessages requested by the CSPI. Nor did the group find support from the FTC, with which they had filed a separate ad ban petition. In ruling against them, the FTC said there was little evidence linking beer ads to alcohol abuse or that the ads were deceptive or unfair. The CSPI retorted that the FTC ruling "underscores the need for a more enlightened and objective congressional response to control the marketing of America's number one drug."

The D-word was all the beer industry needed to hear. In response to both Seagram and the CSPI, the industry put together a booklet aimed squarely at state and federal regulatory agencies, called *Revealing the Facts about Alcohol Equivalence.* The booklet refuted Bronfman's claims about alcohol equivalence, pointing out not only the potency difference between the average mixed drink and the average beer, but also that alcohol content comes built in (and regulated) with beer, where the alcohol content of a drink is up to the bartender or the drinker himself. The booklet also suggested that if Bronfman's main aim—parity in beer and booze taxation—was realized, it would serve to promote irresponsible drinking.

The amazing thing about the booklet was that it was a unified effort. Endorsed by the country's five biggest brewers, and all the major brewer and wholesaler associations, *Revealing the Facts* was the first time in anyone's memory that the industry had put aside its collective differences and agreed on a way to fight an outside threat.

Unfortunately, the industry couldn't agree on a way to stop an inside threat.

On Super Bowl Sunday 1987, the world met the most controversial spokesman ever chosen by a beer company: a female by the name of Honey Tree Evil Eye. Short, not particularly attractive, and unable to speak, Honey Tree was not the type of female you'd expect to find in a typical beer ad. Then again, the campaign built around her was anything but typical.

Honey Tree Evil Eye appeared in a dozen spots for Bud Light over the next few years, though she was known by a different name: Spuds MacKenzie. Honey Tree was a bull terrier, and her commercial alter ego was an instant lightning rod.

Spuds, during (his) career as Bud Light pitchdog, partied on boats, while *Lifestyles of the Rich and Famous* creator Robin Leach enthused loudly about his popularity. Spuds rode on skateboards and piloted his own submarine. Spuds danced on conga lines and was surrounded by incredibly voluptuous babes, known as the "Spudettes." Spuds was dubbed "the Party Animal." Noting that the depiction of actual drinking was legally forbidden in beer commercials, *Adweek* critic Barbara Lippert wrote that "the brilliance of this campaign . . . is that Spuds comes off as the embodiment, the visual equivalent, of a pleasantly inebriated state."

(Spuds had more in common with drunks than anyone knew. Actress Lela Rochon, one of the stars of *Waiting to Exhale,* relates that during an early career, three-year gig as a "Spudette," she had to endure Spuds's bouts of flatulence in the limousine. The offending odor was dealt with in the traditional fraternity method: lighting a match or two.)

Spuds was wildly popular with young drinkers, and with his help, so was Bud Light. In 1987 sales rose 21 percent, giving the brand the largest volume increase of any beer brand. Unfortunately, Spuds was also wildly popular with kids. Antialcohol forces suddenly had a poster boy. Girl. Dog. Whatever.

In fact, "poster boy" was his first designation. Anheuser-Busch marketing director Michael Roarty told *Sports Illustrated* about the genesis of Spuds: "Some guy in our Chicago agency drew a rough sketch of a dog called the Party Animal, for a Bud Light poster. That meant we had to find a real dog that looked like his drawing. That meant Spuds. Orders for the poster of this strange-looking dog were monumental. We still can't explain it. It's like everything else in advertising. You just hope you get it right, but you never know for sure."

Roarty didn't need to be coy. Everyone knew that Anheuser-Busch had gotten it right with Spuds; all they had to do was look at Bud Light's sales figures. Or the avalanche of Spuds merchandising. Especially the unauthorized stuff. All they had to do was notice the children's products bearing the pilfered likeness of Honey Tree Evil Eye. God knows Washington noticed.

Standing before the Senate one day in 1987, Strom Thurmond, Republican from South Carolina, delivered a blistering attack on Anheuser-Busch while holding a stuffed Spuds toy, charging them with "targeting youthful drinkers. The stuffed animals, children's toys, and T-shirts small enough to fit twelve-year-olds indicate the real purpose of the campaign." Anheuser-Busch, lamely, argued that Spuds was intended to sell beer to those above the legal drinking age and that the products mentioned were not authorized by the brewery. Clearly, though, whether or not Spuds was intended for grown-ups, he was big with the kids. Though no one ever credibly suggested that Spuds's underage allure was intentional, Anheuser-Busch didn't help its company image by seeming to say, "Hey, don't blame us if our spokesanimal makes a cuddly plush toy."

Things got worse in December of the same year, when Bud Light packaging and promotional material featuring Spuds as Santa Claus was banned in Ohio. ("Nah, we're not pitching to kids. Have we shown you the terrific Spuds-as-Easter-Bunny campaign?") To counter the growing animosity, Anheuser-Busch decided to use Spuds in their "Know When to Say When" holiday television commercials. For industry critics, and a lot of other folks, the public service ads had the opposite effect. Was the campaign a wink? Was Anheuser-Busch making *fun* of moderation by putting a dog dressed as a human being in the spots?

Spuds was the lightning rod, but there were plenty of other targets for the ire of public-interest groups, thanks to the beer industry's lousy record of self-policing. Next up were celebrity endorsers with their own (often well-documented) drinking problems. Anheuser-Busch had to pull an ad in its wildly popular "Night" campaign for Michelob, when wildly popular singer/guitarist Eric Clapton followed the celebrity trend of checking himself into rehab. Clapton told *Rolling Stone* that he was "actually in treatment in Minnesota when that came on the TV. I was in a room full of alcoholics, myself being one of them, and everybody went, 'Is that you?' "

The most oft criticized advertising gimmick, though, was the promotion of beer brands at the annual rite of spring break, celebrated by college students at beaches throughout the southern and southwestern states. Because the drinking age was a very steady twenty-one by the late eighties, over half of all college students lining the beaches of Florida, Texas, and California were underage. Didn't stop the big boys. Giant inflatable beer cans stood vigil over beachside bars. Wet T-shirt contests, brought to you by Bud, were all the rage. Miller nights provided sunburned coeds with new baseball caps to wear back to school.

From Spuds to rockers to spring break, it was clear that the beer business was more interested in what worked than what was responsible. As it was doing more and more with its new brand introductions, it was letting its marketing strategies be guided far more by fierce competitiveness than by common sense. It was looking at the short-term volume gains it could achieve when it should have been looking at the long-term problems it was creating for itself.

The bill for the beer industry's foolishness started to come due in 1988. Senator Thurmond put down his Spuds doll long enough to champion, with Democratic representative John Convers of Michigan, warning label legislation that would require all beverage alcohol containers to carry a rotating set of messages about the dangers of the product. In October Congress passed a modified version of the legislation, requiring a single warning label with two permanent messages:

> **Government Warning:** 1) *According to the Surgeon General, women should not drink alcoholic beverages during pregnancy because of the risk of birth defects.* 2) *Consumption of alcoholic beverages impairs your ability to drive a car or operate machinery, and may cause health problems.*

Though the National Beer Wholesalers Association (NBWA) opposed the legislation, its protests were muted, for two reasons. First, it knew when to fold 'em. The drumbeat was so loud in the halls of Congress to punish the reckless beer folks that the NBWA was faced with two options: stand by and watch warning labels pass, or prepare for renewed talk of advertising bans. The second reason it kept relatively quiet was self-interest: as with the cigarette industry, it became clear that warning labels would provide some cover against consumer lawsuits. The irony, of course, is that there was no evidence to suggest that warning labels would deter problem drinkers from getting smashed and doing themselves (or others) harm, so the net effect of labeling was to protect . . . the industry.

Even with the passage of mandatory labeling, the beer business was not completely out of the woods with the antiadvertising crowd. Right after labeling became law, Surgeon General C. Everett Koop held a three-day drunken driving workshop, which he had initially intended to include only his own handpicked panel. No invitation was given to the beer, liquor, or broadcast industries. Koop's heart was in the right place: at the time, alcohol-related car crashes were the leading cause of death for Americans aged fifteen to twenty-four.

Unfortunately, it was clear from previous public statements that Koop and groups he invited to the workshop already felt that the answer to drunk driving fell largely in the realm of advertising regulation, something that could be handled strictly on a federal level. What they missed was the clear indication that the recent federally mandated rise in the drinking age was already having a positive effect on traffic fatality rates, which might have pushed them in the direction of advocating tougher DWI (driving while intoxicated) laws on the state level. It would have been a much more winnable battle, because the financial interests of a) the beer industry, b) the sports industry, and c) the broadcast industry wouldn't have been tied so closely to the outcome.

The National Association of Broadcasters, fearing ad bans, joined the NBWA in legally challenging the closed-panel nature of the surgeon general's workshop. Koop gave in and agreed to let them participate. He might well have been calling their bluff: shortly after winning the right to attend, both groups publicly refused to do so, citing what they called the antialcohol bias of the groups the surgeon general had originally invited. In the end, the broadcasters and the sellers of alcohol had fought for the right to make a show of *not* attending.

The outcome of the workshop was as predicted: proposals including restrictions on ads, the elimination of advertising tax deductibility, the banning of both celebrity endorsement and sporting event advertising.

Koop lost on all counts, as none of his panel's advertising proposals were enacted by government agencies. The NBWA did a smart thing, which was accusing the surgeon general of not going far *enough,* at least not in his study of the drunken driving issue. In an open letter to him, the NBWA offered to back a plan to curb drunken driving, provided a more in-depth look at the problem could be taken. Considering Koop had half a year left as surgeon general, it wasn't much of an offer.

On his way out the door in June of 1989, the surgeon general fired his last shot at the alcoholic beverage industry, and it was a doozy. Addressing the drunk driving issue one final time, Koop suggested another method to discourage drinking. Apparently he hadn't read George Bush's lips: he joined the call for increased taxes.

Oh, that's right; Bush said "no *new* taxes." That must have made it okay, then, for the federal government, one year later, to double the *existing* federal excise tax on beer. The tax on a six-pack went from $.16 to $.32 and on a barrel from $9 to $18. Though it was far from the fivefold increase proposed by some legislators, the tax increase, coupled with the now mandatory warning label, showed just how tough Washington was willing to get and how defenseless the beer business was. With public opinion squarely against the big brewers, thanks largely to Spuds and spring break, politicians were finding a new way to make names for themselves: beer bashing.

In 1990 a young representative from Massachusetts by the name of Kennedy pushed, along with pre-VP Senator Al Gore, legislation banning beer advertising outright. "Like it or not," Joe Kennedy warned, "beer ads educate Americans that taking a drink is needed to win that race or score with that new girl or guy." (A wonderfully ironic stand to take, considering it was his grandfather's dealings in the alcoholic beverage business that would largely bankroll the family's political dynasty.) Antibeer fervor reached an absurdist crescendo that year, with the release of an American Automobile Association (AAA) report called "Beer and Fast Cars." Calling fans of car racing "lower on the educational ladder," the report finds them more susceptible to beer advertising done in conjunction with racing events. At one point, "Beer and Fast Cars" breathlessly asserts that 30 percent of all beer drinkers are unemployed. That would have meant that of the eighty million beer drinkers at the time, twenty-four million were looking for work: four times the number given by the Bureau of Labor Statistics.

Of course, quibbling with the findings of the AAA was akin to August Busch III's conundrum over the antigun rumors; how can you possibly win, whatever you say? The people involved in the antibeer-advertising crusade weren't in it but for the best of reasons—they genuinely cared about the health and safety of their kids. The beer industry, though, seemed at times to go too far in its efforts to portray them as wild-eyed fanatics. (In one particularly angry interview with *The New York Times,* August tried the full-tilt demonization boogie: "When I go home tonight at dinner, I'll have a beer. My children will look at me drinking a beer. These critics would say that my children should look at that the same as me snorting cocaine. Beer is legal, legal, legal!")

What the industry needed to do was stop picking on the messengers and start dealing with their message. What it needed to do was build a calm, rational—and consistent—message of its own. First, of course, Spuds would have to be put down. *(Author's Note: The preceding sentence is a joke and in no way indicates a suggestion that animals should ever be harmed, for any reason. No animals were harmed during the writing of this book.)*

In April 1990 an exasperated Pete Coors stood before the California Beer & Wine Wholesalers and decried the disunity in his own industry. "If we continue on the same track in the nineties as in the eighties, we should start looking for other work," he told them. "Let's not lose the war." The latest and most crucial of the great Beer Wars, he told his audience, wasn't being fought in the supermarkets, bars, and liquor stores, it was being fought in the halls of Congress and in fifty state legislatures.

And it wasn't just about kids and advertising, though Coors took a verbal jab at one of his competitors for playing both ends at spring break. (They'd put up huge, inflatable six-packs not far from their own moderation-themed billboards.) It was about recycling, interstate trade, and a host of other subjects, all currently legislated differently from state to state. One of the most complicated aspects of the beer business, he knew, was figuring out how to comply with all the different laws in all the different states. The hardest thing for Pete to swallow was that it was the industry's own fault. By not making effective use of the lobbying groups they had, the Beer Institute and the NBWA, brewers had allowed much of their legislative fate to be decided with no united input of their own. On top of that, they'd allowed the stupid decisions of a few (there's that darned Spuds again) to tar the whole lot of them.

It was time, Pete told the wholesalers, for the industry to "unite under a banner of proactive programs . . . we need to learn how to hang up our competitive six-shooters, get into a room together, work on problems together as a united industry. Not defensively—we do that very well—but offensively."

A year after he gave his speech, it felt as if Pete had been heard. The Beer Institute awarded a $300,000 grant to a substance abuse and education program. The NBWA and the Beer Institute began a very public push against underaged drinking. Most impressively, an alliance of brewers, vintners, and distillers known as the Century Council was formed, headed up by John Gavin, former U.S. ambassador to Mexico. Its sole purpose was to fight alcohol abuse.

Oddly, three names were missing from its membership roster: Anheuser-Busch, Miller, and Coors.

It's hard to say whose rejection of the Century Council was the most befuddling: the company that had contributed so much to the problems that had necessitated the council's creation, Anheuser-Busch; the tobacco (read: public relations–sensitive) guys at Miller; or the man who had basically begged for the council's creation just a year earlier, Pete Coors. Each of the three publicly gave some lip service to the effectiveness of the Beer Institute, hollowly suggesting—in the face of major legislative pushes against them—that they didn't need to band together with vintners and distillers by joining the Century Council. Theories abounded about the boycott. Maybe, it was suggested, the animosity between the beer business and Seagram (a founding member of the council) was just too great. Maybe the Big Three had something else up their sleeves.

And maybe there was a deeper reason they weren't putting aside their animosities for the common good. Maybe the Beer Wars hadn't been fought by men who could recognize their own failings, shift strategy to reflect hard-learned lessons, or recognize allies. Maybe the leadership of the Big Three comprised men who'd been made soft by success; men too arrogant to realize when it was time to hang together, rather than be hung separately.

Maybe that explains why, over the mid- and late eighties, the fastest-growing and most written about segments in the beer industry had nothing to do with Anheuser-Busch, Miller, or Coors.

Part Three

Border Skirmishes

9

Show Us Your Badge

There's only one word needed to explain the phenomenal growth of imported beer during the 1980s: badges. People need their stinking badges.

Okay, maybe there's a second word as well: Yuppies.

Not for a moment do I mean to suggest that yuppies bought imported beer in quantities sufficient to fuel the category's average annual growth of 11.4 percent over the first half of the eighties (an amazing figure considering the domestic beer industry's flat performance over the same period.) Instead yuppies repopularized the notion of badges (stuff you buy to impress people) in their pursuit of status. The kid making $80,000 a year right out of college on Wall

Street was the trendsetter of the decade—his tastes often became yours, mine, and ours. We coveted his BMW, but we couldn't afford it. We envied his time-share on the beach in the Hamptons every summer and his other one in Vail every winter, but they were both out of our league. We wanted his Armani wardrobe, but we hadn't the guts to rob a bank so we could buy it. As baby boomers, more financially strapped than our parents, we had to look to yuppie badges we could afford, like shirts with little alligators on them and designer ice cream.

And expensive beer.

The math is simple. Very few of us can walk into a Porsche dealership and say, "Hi. You sell the best sports car in the world. I'll take two. In red." Similarly, most of the Rolex watches sported by the average working stiff are of the lower-end variety, if not the "Who'll give me twenty dollars?" street-corner variety. *Anybody,* though, anyone from a corporate president to the guy in the mailroom can belly up to the bar and for an extra fifty cents or a buck buy what they have been told is the best beer in the world. And they can be *seen* having the best beer in the world. Imported beer is a badge, a status symbol. And it is an affordable one.

Want to know why most beer importers would rather have their bar accounts sell bottles instead of draft beer, even though the latter is generally thought to be better tasting? Because they know that unless you, Joe Consumer, can have that bottle in front of you on the bartop, where everyone can see what great taste you have, you're not going to spring for the extra dinero.

While we're at it, let's add four more words to the list of reasons imported beer took off like a shot when it did: Leo Van Munching Jr. His father's gift was one-on-one salesmanship. His gift was a unique understanding of the discussion above. His father, through sheer will and personality, gave Heineken beer a solid toehold in America. It was Leo Jr. who positioned the brand—and by extension, the category—for tremendous growth. Here's how.

With Löwenbräu no longer an import competitor of Heineken, Van Munching & Company, Inc., faced the mid-seventies as the importer of the clear front-runner in the tiny imported beer category (so tiny that in 1975 total import sales accounted for just 1.1 percent of the U.S. beer market). Leo Sr.'s loyalty to the Heineken company and to the Dutch government through World War II had been rewarded with exclusive multiyear contracts to import Heineken, which were eventually replaced, in 1960, with a single agreement granting the company exclusive rights to Heineken through the lifetime of Leo Jr.

Father and son were a terrific pairing, in some ways. Father, to mix a few languages, was the chutzpah of the company: the self-promoting bon vivant who provided the flash needed to establish an image-based product. A Donald Trump without the bad hair or the sneer, if you will. Son was the level head: the workhorse with the business degree and a detailed vision of how the company could expand. Leo Sr. seemed satisfied to be the big fish in a very small pond. Leo Jr. wanted to get the hose out and make the pond big enough to allow a little growing room. Unfortunately, the balance of power was the same at Van Munching headquarters in New York City as it was at Anheuser-Busch headquarters in St. Louis. The father had all the power, the son had all the good ideas.

As would happen at roughly the same time in St. Louis (from the mid-sixties through the mid-seventies), the fortunes of Van Munching & Company rose as the son grew more bold in his attempts to circumvent the father. The first noticeable change in the structure of Van Munching & Company was the makeup of its distribution network. Because he knew them from his days of selling wine and liquor along with beer, Leo Sr. was comfortable using liquor wholesalers for Heineken in key markets like Southern California. It was just bad business, because when liquor wholesalers made calls on accounts, they were peddling dozens of brands at a time. They sold scotch-gin-rum-vermouth-vodka-cordials-whiskey-you name it, all in the same sales pitch. What kind of time would they give to pushing one brand of beer, especially when the profit margin on booze was so much bigger?

Not much. Leo Jr. realized in the mid-sixties that distribution would skyrocket if only Heineken could be sold by beer people, where its profit margin suddenly looked tremendous compared with those of Budweiser, Schlitz, or Pabst. (Most beer wholesalers represent at least one major domestic brand.) More than that, though, having Heineken represented by beer wholesaler salesmen meant that it got sold when bar managers and store managers were in beer buying mode and were thinking of their overall beer needs. The immediate competitiveness actually made Heineken an *easier* sell, because it could be pushed as a segment unto itself from a pricing standpoint, and (until the explosion of imported brands in the eighties) it was often the only import in a wholesaler's stable. You need a domestic? We've got a lot of choices for you there, Mr. Buyer. You need an import, with its extra profit? We've got Heineken.

In New York City, always Heineken's biggest market, Leo Jr. convinced his father to end decades of self-distribution and take advantage of the clout that came with being sold by a large wholesaler. The key was manpower. Whereas Van Munching & Company could afford only a few salesmen to canvas the thousands of accounts in the city, and a few trucks in which to deliver beer, a large wholesale operation meant dozens of salesmen and trucks and the legitimacy of being sold along with at least one large, well-established domestic brand.

Van Munching started doing business with independent beer wholesalers for exactly the same reasons domestic brands embraced them in the fifties and sixties: wholesalers made distribution easier and much, much cheaper. (Even Anheuser-Busch, with its network of breweries situated near major markets, sells its brands through independent wholesalers in a vast majority of the country.) As a supplier, Van Munching could sell Heineken directly to a local wholesaler in each of its markets and let the wholesaler worry about storage, transportation, and complying with local ordinances.

The secret to Heineken's success was not just the transition to a beer wholesaler network during the late sixties and early seventies, though. It was also the retention of the internal sales force even *after* the transition. Unlike any other importer at the time, and unlike most domestic brewers even today, Van Munching & Company built a national sales force independent of wholesaler personnel. Not just regional managers, but street guys who pounded the pavement every day, taking orders to be filled by local wholesalers and solving problems. Sure, it often amounted to checking up on the wholesalers, but it also provided them with extra manpower (which they didn't have to pay for) and, more important, extra order pads. The complaints were minimal.

And the rewards were maximal. As the Van Munching & Company network of beer wholesalers grew over the seventies, the brand exploded. In 1972 Heineken sold 3.5 million cases in the U.S.; by 1975 that number doubled. (Cases are 2.25 gallons of beer, or twenty-four 12-oz. bottles. A barrel holds 31 gallons, so in 1975 Van Munching's total barrelage was still just over 500,000, to Anheuser-Busch's 35.2 *million.*) Some of the initial burst in sales, of course, came from the disappearance of Löwenbräu as an import, but as Heineken reached nearly 25 million in case sales by the end of the decade, it was clear that something else was happening.

A few something elses were happening. First, Van Munching & Company was showing some marketing sophistication . . . whether Leo Sr. liked it or not. Like Gussie Busch, Leo Sr. had long frowned on advertising expenditures; he found them unseemly for the brand and generally wasteful. Advertising was so . . . *common,* and so expensive. For Leo Sr., the purchase of quarter- and half page black-and-white ads in magazines like *The New Yorker* was enough. His son was not satisfied.

Leo Jr. returned to Van Munching & Company's New York headquarters in 1972 after a six-year stint setting up and running a West Coast office in Los Angeles. He immediately brought color to the ads. Heineken's distinctive bottle began showing up in print advertising in all its green glory, immediately separating it from domestics, which tended toward the rather drab brown bottle standard. Heineken also made the leap to television advertising, much to the dismay of Leo Sr. (Leo Sr. got over his television phobia a year later, when he himself was asked to appear in TV ads for his beloved *New Yorker* magazine.)

The Heineken television advertising carried none of the warmth or humor of domestic beer ads. No jocks, no beaches, no animals . . . no people. Just the bottle, and a little bit of voice-over copy touting Heineken as "America's number one–selling imported beer." Dull, dull, dull. And *effective,* as the sales growth showed. Though the copy changed a bit over time, the backgrounds were different every year, and a jingle or two found its way in; the same basic commercial ran for fifteen years and saw the brand through tenfold growth in that time.

It was apparent to Leo Jr. that some things would have to be done behind his father's back, if the company was going to continue to grow. His father was far enough removed from the nuts and bolts of the operation that Leo Jr. was able to introduce canned Heineken outside of the New York market without his father's knowledge. Cans had been a sore spot for years; Leo Sr. would have no part of them, feeling they cheapened the brand, though Leo Jr. knew that they were a necessary evil. With glass bottles banned in many beach communities and at events like golf tournaments, what was the choice? Miss the perfect opportunity for people to sample the brand while on vacation or enjoying a spectator sport? He quietly had a United States version of the can designed, got BATF approval on it, and had canned product shipped in.

Some time after Heineken cans had established themselves as potent sellers, Leo Sr. walked into the office of his traffic manager, the guy responsible for the movement of product from the brewery order stage until pickup by wholesalers, and spied a Heineken can on his file cabinet. Mistaking it for a foreign version, he said, "We'll *never* have these here." The traffic manager let slip that cans *were* available. In fact, he told his boss, we're moving quite a lot of them. Exasperated, Leo Sr. threw the can across the room and stormed out.

Storming, unfortunately, had long been a part of Leo Sr.'s modus operandi. Perhaps the can-throwing episode, coming as it did in the mid-seventies, was attributable to what doctors would later diagnose as the onset of Alzheimer's disease. Leo Sr. was legendary for his temper. From time to time over the years, his tirades had ended in the scrapping of good plans and the departure of good people. A decade earlier a bout of foul humor would inadvertently contribute to the health of one of Heineken's largest competitors—Molson.

One of those run out by the mercurial Leo Sr. was Gerald Regan, who'd led the New York sales force for Van Munching in the early sixties. Leo Sr. fired him in 1964, largely because Regan was earning a reputation as a bit of a show-off in the trade, and Leo couldn't abide any loud personalities within his company but his own. After his departure Regan initially put his import experience toward another Dutch beer, Amstel, which irked his former boss beyond measure. (More on Amstel shortly.) In 1968 Regan landed a job as a consultant for the Molson Brewery's U.S. effort. That led to his foundling of Martlet Importing in 1971, which was created to handle three of Molson's brands: Molson Export, Molson Canadian Beer, and Molson Golden.

Canadian beers had an advantage in the import category: no costly ocean voyage, just a little extra rail or truck time from the Great White North. As a result, their pricing was just above domestic superpremiums, but still below Europeans. While domestics were segmented according to price (discount brands, premiums, and superpremiums), imports were, because of their low overall volume, one big happy category. So why weren't Canadian beers leading the way? Lack of self-image.

Though Labatt was a perennial fixture on the import sales charts, it found its own growth stymied by a self-delusional marketing approach. Figuring that its true competition must be the domestic superpremium segment, because its pricing was closer to Michelob than to Heineken, Labatt puts its efforts behind off-premise (supermarket and liquor store) sales rather than on-premise (restaurant and bar) business. The off-premise push was a bit of wishful thinking for Labatt, which let the allure of potential volume (as in, "Hey, the domestics sell a lot more off the shelf than over the bar") blind it to the reality of its situation (as in, "Hey, the domestics still cost a lot less than I do"). Rather than taking its price advantage over Europeans as a way to grab real share of the import market, Labatt went the other way and positioned itself as a slightly higher-priced alternative to good domestic brands. It didn't work. Americans didn't understand why they should pay more for something that seemed like a domestic.

Molson Golden gave them a reason, although it did so accidentally at first.

True mystique is rarely manufactured or designed; it is often bestowed on products when they're looking elsewhere. Though Regan insisted from the moment he signed on with Molson that its Golden brand was the way to go in the States, the brewery stubbornly pushed the much heavier-tasting Export on him. He was allowed to take on Molson Golden, with the proviso that he put his efforts behind Export and Canadian and not spend anything on Golden support. Export and Canadian languished, the victims of America's distaste for overly heavy beers.

Meanwhile Molson's Canadian efforts for the Golden brand inadvertently sowed the seeds of the brand's success in the U.S. Television advertising for Golden in major Canadian cities like Toronto was spilling across the border, thanks to the strength of some stations' signals. Before long, a small market for the beer bloomed in states like Michigan, Vermont, and New Hampshire—not much in the way of volume, but a far sight past what Export and Canadian were doing. Molson Golden's initial U.S. sales were a happy little accident.

From that modest start, Molson developed a case of "the Coors Phenomenon," thanks to a few hundred thousand college kids. There are some good schools in the border states, schools that attract kids from all over the country. Thirsty kids, who drink an amazing amount of beer—just ask any Dartmouth grad. As vacationers had done by bringing cases of Coors back east with them, college students created a mystique around Molson by bringing it home with them. Home where you often couldn't get it.

Unlike Coors, Molson was ready to capitalize on its good fortune and even expand upon it. Learning from Labatt's positioning mistakes, Martlet grabbed on to a little imported imagery. Regan convinced

Molson to switch from its drab brown to the brighter green of the Heineken bottle. He also oversaw the creation of advertising that would position the brand as a sophisticated, classy proposition. In one of the best remembered and most effective campaigns the imported beer segment ever had, a pair of actors named Garrett Brown and Ann Winn became the Molson Couple, who spent years and countless radio ads bantering about the allure of Canadian beer. In one particularly memorable spot from the mid-seventies, Brown played a truck driver attempting to cross the border into the States while border guard Winn questioned him about that one extra case of Molson Golden he kept in the truck's cab for his own use. The flirting throughout the campaign was sensational, made more so by the mysterious quality of radio: you never see their faces, so they look however you want them to. The spots were intelligent and sexy, and by extension, so was the beer.

But Regan brought more to the table than the ability to improve a brand's image. He knew a thing or two about distribution as well. To sustain growth, he knew, Molson's spread across the country had to be managed carefully. Overextend beyond demand, and you risk having product in the trade that gets old, which leaves you with unhappy distributors and disgusted customers. It's awfully hard to recover from bad beer. Just ask Schlitz. Move too slowly, and someone else will jump into the breach with a product that will make the public forget you. Just ask Coors. Regan stage-managed Molson's growth a few markets at a time; it became his standard late-in-the-year joke with the younger Leo Van Munching that he was holding back a couple of states for next year's overall volume increase.

In the years following Löwenbräu's early-seventies defection from the ranks of imports, Molson Golden grew into the number two spot, somewhat by default. The only other German beer of any size at the time, Wurtzburger, was just too heavy in taste to appeal to mainstream drinkers, and Beck's was not yet widely available. (And, truth to tell, the average beer drinker wasn't sophisticated enough to recognize the difference between Holland and Germany, so Heineken picked up a lot of Löwenbräu's slack.)

By 1979 Molson Golden was outselling Labatt's Blue in the U.S. by a three-to-two margin; by 1982 the margin was larger than three to one. Of course, Leo Van Munching Jr. could afford to joke with his former employee: Heineken was outselling number two Molson Golden by a margin that was better than two to one and gaining on three to one.

On the eve of the Regan era and the rise of the yuppie, the import segment's top five shaped up this way (1979 year-end tally, as compiled by *Impact Databank*):

Rank	**Brand**	**Sales (million cases)**
1.	HEINEKEN	24.8
2.	MOLSON GOLDEN	9.7
3.	LABATT'S BLUE	6.2
4.	DOS EQUIS	3.1
5.	BECK'S	2.6

In all, imports accounted for 2.65 percent of U.S. beer sales, up from only 1.1 percent in 1975. The huge increase was fueled mostly by the explosion of Heineken from a seven-million-case brand in 1975 to a nearly twenty-five-million-case brand. Of the 150 imported beers *Impact* counted in 1979, 90 percent sold less than five thousand barrels, or sixty-nine thousand cases. The top three sellers accounted for two-thirds of the category's sales.

It was a lofty time for Heineken, which itself accounted for 41 percent of import sales. Looking back on a decade that had seen nearly tenfold growth for his brand, Van Munching Jr. wanted to branch out, for a simple reason: it was the only way to substantially boost profit for such a labor-intensive company. The problem, of course, was that his father, who'd strenuously resisted the shift to beer wholesalers and who allowed canned beer only after it'd been established behind his back, drew a line in the sand about adding products to the lineup.

Much in the way August Busch III's people had taken to meeting at his farm rather than under the nose of his old man, Leo Jr. had established a more private working relationship with the brewery's export director, Paul Snoep. Discussions about the future of the company were held by early morning transatlantic phone calls from home or during Leo Jr.'s infrequent visits overseas. It was during one of the latter that Leo Jr. first broached the subject of portfolio building with Snoep.

As most prosecutors and married people know, there is a basic trick involved in getting what you want out of someone. When you want them to do something they might be hesitant to do normally, it usually helps to scare them with an unpleasant alternative first. So it was that Leo Jr. asked Snoep in late 1978 if the brewery would have any objection to Van Munching & Company going after the rights to import Guinness Stout. Leo's fear was that Heineken, now that it had an idea of the profit potential in the United States, might not want to put all of its eggs in the Van Munching basket. Now that the import segment had been established, it might want to keep all the profits from other brands for itself.

Snoep was floored; until that moment, Van Munching & Company hadn't even hinted that it saw a world outside of Heineken. Why now? Leo Jr. told him that because his company maintained its own sales force to work with distributor salesmen, it didn't make financial sense to carry just one product. After letting his question sink in, Leo proposed an alternative: Would Heineken be willing to supply an additional brand for export? More specifically, a light brand? Light beer, Leo Jr. pointed out, had shown significant growth and staying power; perhaps the timing was right for an imported brand. Snoep was enthusiastic and said he'd bring it up with the Heineken board.

Oh, and one other thing, Leo Jr. told him that day. I won't import Heineken Light. Not now, now ever. Snoep asked him why and what else he had in mind. The problems, Leo Jr., told him, were twofold. The first was cannibalization. Why make the extra effort to establish a second brand when so much of its consumer base would probably come from the first brand? Even A-B had shown an awareness of the cannibalization potential when it named its first entry into the category

Anheuser-Busch Natural Light. By the time it introduced Bud Light, it almost *had* to use its flagship's name in order to be competitive with the well-established Lite. Heineken had no directly competitive reason for taking a similar risk.

(Leo's belief that Heineken Light posed a major cannibalization threat was boosted over a decade later, when marketing professors David Aaker and Kevin Lane Keller conducted a study of consumer attitudes toward line extensions for the *Journal of Marketing*. Aaker and Keller created twenty fictitious line extensions, including Heineken Light and a Häagen-Dazs candy bar, and had subjects rate each concept on a number of levels. Of all twenty, Heineken Light rated the highest—5.56 out of a possible 7—in the category dealing with the substitutability of the extension for the original product.)

The second problem Leo had with the idea of Heineken Light was potential damage to the Heineken brand. If an imported light turned out to be a disaster, he didn't want it tarnishing the franchise by being so closely tied in. Moreover, light beer may have been accepted, but it wasn't exactly seen as high-class by consumers. Remember, in the late seventies, Joe Ortleib was on television pouring water into beer and suggesting that's how light beer was made. Leo Jr. was convinced that a beer like Heineken, a beer pitched to drinkers as uncompromising in its quality, would invite a mountain of cynicism upon itself by being the next "me too" light beer producer. Rather than Heineken Light, he told Snoep, he wanted the brewery to take another brand in its portfolio that wasn't available in the States and create a stand-alone brand. In fact, Leo Jr. already had the brand in mind: Amstel. The question was, would the brewery make him an Amstel Light?

Snoep became an immediate advocate, even though he realized quickly he'd been snookered by the Guinness proposal. The Heineken board of directors took to the idea of Amstel Light as well. A formula was created, as was a new label. Brown was chosen for the bottle color, to keep the brand as removed from Heineken as possible. Alfred "Freddy" Heineken signed off on both the brand and the packaging. By the fall of 1979 Amstel Light was ready to go. Now Leo Jr. had to play a heartbreaking waiting game with his father's health. He told the brewery he'd need a little time before he could launch.

In January of 1980, after a string of medical problems and bouts of disorientation, doctors told Leo Jr. that his father's mental and physical conditions had deteriorated to the point where he could no longer return to the office. The son quietly assumed the role of company president and signaled the brewery to begin production on Amstel Light. Within three years it would crack the list of the top-ten-selling imported beers, a feat unmatched by any of the imported light beers that followed, even to this day.

Amstel's success lay in its deliberate appeal to women, on a few fronts. From a heaviness standpoint, Amstel Light was the first European import light enough in taste to appeal to many women. From an imagery standpoint, it was the first light beer—imported *or* domestic—to be both highbrow and non-gender-specific in its marketing approach. As with Heineken, the advertising was all bottle-and-glass stuff, with a straightforward tag line ("95 calories never tasted so imported") that hit the same points as "tastes great/less filling" in a slightly more sophisticated (if less entertaining) way. Macho imagery, whether it had to do with the perception of how strong a brand was or whether it came out of a brand's advertising, had long been used to sell beer to men. Leo Jr. was banking on sophisticated imagery to sell beer to women, as well. Women quickly accounted for slightly over 50 percent of Amstel Light sales. Rather than simply cannibalizing his efforts by drawing men away from Heineken, Leo's tactics, it became apparent, were drawing women away from domestic lights.

It helped greatly, with both genders, that Amstel Light was a stand-alone brand. Regular Amstel Beer hadn't been available in the United States since 1968, when the Amstel Brewery in Holland was taken over by Heineken. The Van Munchings Sr. and Jr. convinced the Heineken board that continuing (or strengthening) export of Amstel to the U.S. only undercut existing Heineken sales, and exports were stopped. Because it therefore had no "parent" brand, Amstel Light didn't carry the stigma of being, in the consumer's mind, a watered-down version of something else. Not to put too fine a point on it, it meant that women had a beer that wasn't considered a watered-down version of something their date might be drinking.

There is no question that packaging played a large role in Amstel Light's success. I started the chapter by talking about badges: Amstel Light may have been the first import created largely for show, inasmuch as the name was conceived before anyone gave the first thought to what the stuff would taste like. It was created to cater to people who wanted to feel sophisticated about drinking a light beer. It was created to be a badge.

Other imports, like Molson, were repackaged to be badges. Moosehead, another Canadian beer, had done middling U.S. business until its importer, All Brand, convinced the brewery in the late seventies to drop its short brown bottle and redesign its label, which *Inc.* magazine described as having "a metallic red background with a white triangular insert that featured what appeared to be a tiny molting moose." Suddenly the green-bottled brand with the bright green, tan, and red label featuring a moosehead five times as large as before was a hot seller. The brand made the top ten list in 1979 and was number four three years later.

All Brand pulled off a similar remake with another of its brands, Australia's Foster's Lager, in 1980. Foster's had also been coming into the country in a squat brown bottle, this one with a short neck that proved unattractive to Americans, though it was a hit in Australia. All Brand got the brewer to switch to another package popular Down Under, the twenty-five-ounce can. (Texas, in an effort to stress moderation, had passed a law prohibiting the sale of twenty-five-ounce beer cans. All Brand showed a little Aussie ingenuity: they had the brewer supply the same full twenty-five-ounce can, but with graphics altered to read "24-oz.") It was immediately noticeable on store shelves and on bartops, and it fit in with the macho image America had of Australia.

The irony was that as imports worked harder on coming up with distinctive packaging, they moved further away from filling that packaging with distinctive beer. This was not through neglect; it was a conscious act. Yuppies, as the import beer trendsetters of the early eighties, were proving to be a bit contrarian: whereas drinkers in the past had accepted the extra cost of imports in order to get heavier-tasting beer, young urban professionals often seemed to gravitate toward brands that would allow them to spend more money without forcing them to move away from middle-of-the-road tastes. This is not meant as a value judgment; the fact of the matter is that most Americans don't like heavier beer. Our tastes as a nation haven't changed much since the lighter pilsener style of lager beer became popular here a century and a half ago.

Heineken, not all that heavy a brand to begin with, defined the outer limit of heaviness for the typical yuppie taste bud. Though thick, dark Guinness Stout—easily the heaviest beer on the import top ten sales chart—took the number six spot in 1979, it dropped steadily before disappearing from the chart completely in 1985. (Thanks largely to the rise of the fuller-bodied micro- and craft brews, Guinness returned to the chart in 1991.) In fact, in Guinness's last eighties appearance as a best-seller, in 1984, it was beaten out of eighth place by a newcomer to the list—one from the opposite end of the taste spectrum. The brewing personification of yuppiedom, Corona Extra.

Mexican Soda Pop

Though he was a fierce competitor, Leo Van Munching Jr., my father, rarely begrudged any of his competition their success and rarely said anything bad about them unless provoked. In fact, I only twice caught him belittling another beer brand publicly.

The first instance came at a press launch for a new Heineken campaign. One of the reporters asked him what he thought of the strategy of France's Kronenbourg beer, which ran ads in 1980 saying "Europeans like Heineken, but they love Kronenbourg." He paused for a moment, then he smiled, as he does before saying something he intends to be both unkind and funny at once. "Kronenbourg is the reason the French drink wine," he said.

The second instance came in 1986, after Corona Extra had leapfrogged past Molson and Beck's to take the number two spot on the import list. With sevenfold growth in two years, Corona's West Coast importer, Barton Beers, was crowing that it was only a matter of time before Corona overtook Heineken as the country's top-selling imported beer. The *Chicago Tribune* called Leo for a quote. What did he think of Corona? "Mexican soda pop," he sniffed.

Having just been handed the role of public relations director, I was aghast. Hadn't I been told never to bad-mouth a competitor? Hadn't I been instructed, under threat of parental lecture, corporate expulsion, and possible disinheritance, that I should always take the high road in my dealings with the press? I asked him about the quote. I wondered aloud if he was worried about Corona stealing drinkers from Heineken. He sat me down and asked me a simple question. "Ever had a Corona?" I had, so he asked a second question. "Do you think for one minute that there are people out there in bars saying, 'What should I have, a Heineken or a Corona?' " I understood: it was like wondering if people had a hard time choosing between Coke and 7Up. The flavor difference was too great. Sure, a Beck's drinker might switch to Heineken, or vice versa, but rarely will Heineken and Corona drinkers trade off.

He never did tell me why he chose to jump off the wagon in terms of polite discourse, but I knew it was fear of Corona, though a more indirect fear than that of poached consumers. It was the fear that Corona would trivialize the import category beyond any hope of being taken seriously.

Corona started its ride as the fad brand of the eighties as a quirky little alternative beer in Texas and California. In Texas, where Lite Beer from Miller had found one of its first strongholds, Corona played into the popularity of another Mexican drink, tequila. Like tequila, Corona was often served with lime. (Its chief quirk came from a problem with the bottle fillers in the Mexican brewery where Corona was made for export; they didn't work well, and the clear glass bottles in the six-pack were often filled at different heights.)

As beer expert Bob Klein pointed out in his book *The Beer Lover's Rating Guide,* Corona was a very light lager, à la Coors. (His description read, in part, ". . . very light, airy, and essentially tasteless . . . it is refreshing—but then, so is plain water.") As such, it became the ultimate beer drinking experience for people not particularly fond of beer: stuffing a wedge of lime into the bottleneck of a Corona, as was the popular custom, created a taste not particularly different from citrus-flavored seltzer. Again, that's not meant as a value judgment; Corona's light drinkability made it perfect for the younger drinker of the time, who was looking for more of what marketers call an "external product benefit" than the traditional import drinker. (That's fancy lingo for packaging bells and whistles.) And Corona was no slouch in the external product benefit area. The package was fabulous—a clear glass long-neck with a painted-on blue-and-white label—and, at the time, one of a kind. Most important, like Coors and Molson before it, Corona was a brand that was awfully hard to come by outside of a few markets at first.

As scarcity was one of Corona's strengths, the brand's U.S. importer wisely avoided advertising it for the first four years of its surge in popularity, for fear of making it look commonplace. Barton Beers rolled the brand across the West and Midwest and watched the sales go from 1.8 million cases in 1984 to 5 million in 1985 to 13.5 million in 1986, which put Corona in the number two spot on the sales chart. Some might call that kind of growth "out of control," and they'd be literally right: Corona's first major problem, though it hardly seemed like one at the time thanks to the sales figures, was that it literally had no control over its own distribution in the East.

While Barton did a tremendous job for Corona in the western two-thirds of the nation, the brewery looked at the potential of the brand east of the Mississippi and decided to cut out the middle man. There are two likely reasons why the brewery didn't make any attempt to reclaim western distribution rights from Barton: first, they'd have risked a lawsuit right at a time when funds were needed to sustain the growth of the brand, and second, they'd have risked a serious disruption in the brand's distribution while they attempted to build their own wholesaler network.

Gambrinus Importing was created by brewery executives to take the brand into the last third of the United States. "These guys absolutely were not geniuses or students of the industry," recalled one wholesaler who worked with Gambrinus. "They just had something that clicked and was hot." While Gambrinus dithered over wholesaler agreements in the East, the brand was already being distributed there in the worst possible way: transshipping.

A wholesaler network brings order to the marketplace. You, the supplier, deal with your wholesalers on issues of quality control, marketing, etc., all with an eye toward sustained, long-term growth. You work together out of mutual interest, and usually you have a legally binding agreement that dictates your obligation to stay with a wholesaler in a given market based on certain aspects of his performance. In most states wholesalers can be granted exclusive rights to a brand by the brand's supplier, within a specific territory.

Transshipping, though, is chaos. What it means is that a wholesaler (or any third party with a truck) in one territory sells product to a wholesaler in another territory, without the consent of the supplier. The wholesaler on the receiving end is usually a small-time operation, thrilled to get his hands on a major label. Obviously transshipping undercuts the designated wholesaler, because it costs him sales, but it's also a nightmare for the supplier, because it removes any chance at quality control. A fly-by-night operation selling transshipped beer is not going to perform basic services for accounts, like picking up beer that's gotten old; worse still, there's every likelihood that he's selling old or bad beer to begin with, because there's no way for him to know how old the beer he bought through the back door was when it came in. Truth is, he mostly doesn't care. Last week he had Beck's, this week it's Heineken, next week he'll have something else.

In some cases transshipping is done into markets that don't officially have a product yet or a wholesaler. That was Corona's fate in the Northeast, where demand for the beer was so strong that a wholesaler in Denver, Colorado, had established a sort of gray market for it. (Gray market because the brewery hadn't yet obtained the state permits required to sell its brand in the Northeast; this was a hard thing for states to do much about since the brewery wasn't shipping beer there directly.) Though it's not clear whom he was buying from—some believe it had to be one of Barton's wholesalers, but others insist he was sourcing directly from the brewery in Mexico—the Denver connection reached the huge New York City market before Gambrinus. This created two problems for Gambrinus. The first was that the bottles, long Corona's biggest selling point, looked like hell by the time they hit the bartops of Manhattan. Whether the transshipper had bought inferior product or was subjecting the packaging to incredible wear and tear on the trip eastward, the result was a belief among some drinkers that the brewery was not the most sanitary place. That general feeling, though it was completely unfounded, turned into a full-fledged rumor in 1987 that Corona had urine in it.

The Corona rumor, absurd as it sounded, was taken quite seriously by Barton, which told the *Los Angeles Times* in July of 1987 that one Corona distributor in Southern California had thirty-five separate retailers ask about it *in one day.* The story was circulating (at least, this is how we heard it from some of our salesmen) that the television newsmagazine *60 Minutes* had done a piece on Corona, showing a sewage ditch feeding into the brewery. There was no such piece, as the *Times* pointed out, but that didn't stop the rumor from spreading across the country. Corona was able to trace it back to at least one competing distributor: Luce & Son, Inc., of Reno. (Among other beers, Luce carried Heineken). Luce, as part of a settlement with Barton Beers, agreed to state publicly that Corona was "free of any contamination."

The problem for Barton and Gambrinus was that the rumor was funny, in a Howard Stern/schoolyard/bathroom humor kind of way. Though Corona's importers dealt effectively with it, by going public with both the rumor and the Luce settlement, it hung on for a number of months. Late in 1987 the bar two doors down from an apartment I lived in had a Corona night. I assume that one of my friends decided this was somehow disloyal of the bar owner (who got a lot of my business), and he played a practical joke: he put a sticker in the urinal with an arrow pointing down and the legend "Free Corona Refills." One of the bartenders told me about it the next night. Worried that I'd be suspected, I went downstairs; it was still there, as he'd put it far enough into the urinal that no one wanted to touch it, for fear it had been used for target practice. I found the owner and offered to scrape off the offending sticker. "Leave it," he said. "Hell, everyone thinks it's hysterical. They keep bringing their buddies down to see it."

The second problem Gambrinus faced because of the early arrival of Corona in the East was animosity based on the pricing. Consumers don't distinguish between legitimately distributed product and the transshipped version, and they were not happy when their first experience with Corona came at a hefty premium. But that's the problem with the gray market: scarcity drives up prices all the way around. Had Gambrinus brought Corona into a market like New York City in a controlled way, bars and restaurants would've been able to buy it at its intended pricing, which was roughly equivalent to that of Canadian imports or slightly higher than that of domestic superpremiums. They, in turn, would've had to price it competitively, as the bar or restaurant next door was likely to have it, so overcharging would've driven customers elsewhere. As it was, Corona was often literally sold off the back of a truck, and savvy bar owners knew that with such spotty distribution, Corona pricing could be jacked up beyond even that of European imports.

The pricing problems were ironed out as Gambrinus set up a legitimate distribution system in the Northeast and the urine rumor faded off, as such rumors do. But the brewery executives who dreamed up Gambrinus as a way of maximizing profits must surely have asked themselves this: Did our greedy insistence on doing it ourselves, unprepared as we were, get in the way of a more organized—and more fruitful—move into the most lucrative import markets?

We had our own problems to worry about at Van Munching & Company in 1987, but they had nothing to do with distributing or even beer. They had to do with dollars and cents—or, more accurately, guilders.

A healthy economy had pushed imports to their 11.4 percent growth average over the first half of the 1980s, while the domestics remained largely flat. It wasn't just the creation of the yuppie class that fueled that growth; it was also a currency situation favorable enough to allow importers to keep their prices reasonable. It was largely the strong U.S. dollar that made imports—especially European imports—so attractive to American beer drinkers. It allowed imports not only to keep the spread in price between themselves and the superpremiums to a manageable level (for instance, Heineken cost about 33 percent more than Michelob), but also to invest a little money on advertising.

Here's why the exchange rates matter: One way or another, all imported goods are paid for in U.S. currency. Whether a supplier has to do the conversion to his own currency after receiving dollars, or an importer must pay the supplier in foreign currency (as was the case with Van Munching & Company), an exchange is taking place. When the exchange is favorable to an importer, and profits are strong, pricing can stay down. If he's willing to forgo some additional profit and invest in marketing support, whether it's increased advertising, public relations, price promoting, or point-of-sale material, the importer can also use a favorable exchange rate to go after more market share.

Which is exactly what Leo Van Munching did. For SSC&B/Lintas, Van Munching & Company's advertising agency at the time, Christmas came often during 1983, 1984, and early 1985. During the course of those years in particular, Leo would regularly send his advertising director to Lintas to instruct the agency to revise their media plans upward. Though planning was normally done at the beginning of each year, and based on the previous year's sales (with growth projections factored in), the currency exchange was done throughout the year, to take advantage of shifting rates. Because of that, Leo would kick in extra funds for marketing sporadically and without warning, and Lintas, making a 15 percent commission on all media spending, eagerly anticipated the ad director's next visit.

By 1987, though, the money train had come to a halt as the dollar withered and died. Over the span of three years, from the close of 1984 to the close of 1987, the price of the Dutch guilder *doubled*, from $.28 to $.56, according to Bloomberg Financial Markets. Now Leo didn't have to worry about how much extra money he had to spend; he had to worry about making any profit at all on the beer he was buying. Suddenly ad spending went back to being pegged on case sales (which meant a decrease in exposure), and the pricing of the beer had to be raised. Other importers of European brands, almost equally battered by the weakened dollar, raised their prices as well. But not all other importers had currency problems. In fact, one type of currency spent 1987 in even worse shape than the dollar: the peso.

Aside from the contamination rumor, Corona spent 1987 in the catbird seat. With Gambrinus getting ready to open new markets throughout the East, and the dollar still strong against the peso, the brand bested its 1986 sales figure of 13.5 million cases by nearly 10 million. Heineken lost 2 million cases off its 1986 all-time record of 35.2 million cases. The press had a field day, declaring the imminent death of the import king. *Adweek's Marketing Week* wrote in late 1987 that Heineken "has its finger in the dike, but the hole is getting wider." The magazine pointed out that along with the amazing popularity of the lighter-tasting Corona and the unfavorable exchange rate, Heineken was faced with another problem: "Heineken has simply gotten too big and has been around too long to communicate exclusive cachet to many drinkers."

As public relations director of Van Munching & Company, I was faced with one major obstacle in my attempts to deal with the business press. My father. Leo almost never spoke with reporters, for two reasons: first, he was terrified of appearing like a glory hound, perhaps because his own father was so clearly an animal of that particular stripe; and second, he believed that the mystique of Heineken was better maintained by being mysterious. He was the Greta Garbo of the industry, if you will. Let the other guys do the common thing and run around seeking press adulation: the less Joe Consumer sees about

Heineken in the paper, the more above it all the brand seems. And the fact was, as the president of a privately held company, he didn't *have to* speak with the business press, and he didn't particularly worry about what they wrote about his operation.

The fact that he didn't worry saved my hide in February 1988. I had used the evenhandedness of the *Marketing Week* piece quoted two paragraphs back to convince Leo to grant a rare interview. I argued that with so much being written about Corona's rise, and with so little being reported about the currency problems facing the European brands, the time was right to go on the offensive. My father didn't buy it, but he was feeling indulgent when he asked whom I wanted him to talk to. Unfortunately, I chose *Forbes.* The same folks who ten years earlier had labeled August Busch III "complacent" in the face of the Miller threat were about to do the same with Leo, and I was going to help them. The story *Forbes* pitched to me as "an overview of the segment" turned into a carbon copy of the Anheuser-Busch/Miller piece: complacent leadership falls asleep at the wheel while hungry newcomer gets ready to win the race.

The problem with a magazine like *Forbes* is that a reporter covering computers one week might be dealing with candy bars the next and home insurance the week after. Many of those reporters have a tendency to sweep into an industry, look up a few numbers, make dramatic pronouncements about what's happening, and walk away to cover something different. I ran to a newsstand on a frigid Saturday morning when a friend called to say her copy of *Forbes* had arrived in the mail and that I wasn't going to be happy. I leaned against a mailbox to read the piece and watched my short career flash before my eyes.

BEER BLUNDER was the headline, and the large-type synopsis at the top of the page was as far as I got before swearing loudly: "For years Heineken has been the top-selling import in the U.S. Now it looks like it's losing the top spot to a Mexican brew that did a lot of things right while Heineken sneered." The smile on my father's face in the photograph that accompanied the story (the photograph I had to talk him into letting them take) now seemed enigmatic. Was it the pinched smile of someone who hates to be photographed? Or was it a sneer? Would he smile when he told me to clean out my desk?

The reporter quoted "market analysts" as declaring that "later this year . . . nothing will keep the Mexican brew from pushing the Dutch beer off its perch." The reportage was breathless, if not always sensible: in one paragraph, for instance, she blasted us for not updating Heineken's Lintas-created ad campaign; three paragraphs later she noted that we were in the process of leaving Lintas for a new ad agency, quoting Spencer Plavoukos, Lintas's chief executive, thus: "When the market changes and there is increased competition, some clients panic." In all, it was the kind of article that public relations directors lose their jobs over. While I didn't really expect that fate, I did not sleep much that Saturday night. Rather than get my dressing-down in public, I sought the coward's way out on Sunday. I called my father and read it to him on the phone.

He did the strangest thing. He laughed. He actually laughed when he heard that *Forbes* was predicting our fall to number two. He listened silently through most of the rest, but he wasn't silent when I followed my reading of the article with an apology. "Why are *you* sorry?" he said. "*You* didn't write it."

Though I should've been relieved at my quick exoneration, I pressed on, because I truly did feel guilty about the photo and the interview. "But I talked you into it," I said.

He laughed again, which was condescending, but condescension beat the hell out of the anger I was expecting. "You didn't talk me into anything," he said, "but now you know why we don't talk to the press." The use of "we" was disconcerting, because I wasn't sure if it was the papal "we" or if I was being told that I was no longer to talk to the press, either. But that was a clarification best left for another day.

Besides, my father was much more interested in discussing a matter tangential to the *Forbes* article: the love life of the woman who'd come to our offices to photograph him. "Are you ready for this?" he asked me. "Remember Shonna?" Shonna Valeska was the photographer's name. "Someone told me that she dates Bruce Cutler." Cutler was a famous attorney who'd counted among his clients one John Gotti, reputed Mob boss. I was amazed by the revelation—not that Ms. Valeska had a famous beau, but rather that with all the nonsense I'd just read him, my father was more interested in a little gossip. I slept like a baby on Sunday night.

The reports of Heineken's death, it turned out, were greatly exaggerated, as developments in the category during 1988 would show. *Forbes* had gotten at least one thing right in its discussion of Corona: it had called the brand "a trendy brew." Though *Forbes* had meant it as a positive, trendiness was exactly the thing that would prove to be Corona's eventual undoing. Trendiness, like beer, has a limited shelf life.

As *Marketing Week* correctly pointed out late in 1987, Heineken had a problem communicating with the younger beer drinkers fueling the growth of Corona and other fad brands. Because of its size and relative age in the marketplace, Heineken seemed old and stodgy; the bottle-and-glass advertising that had been aimed at people interested in straightforward quality imagery was just wallpaper to those interested in the sizzle as well as the steak. Heineken needed sizzle, if it was going to remain relevant to the people spending money on imports.

But sizzle worried Leo instinctively. He'd seen too many brands come in as "the hot new thing," only to be discarded as the notoriously short attention span of the consumer turned to the next "hot new thing." Foster's Lager, for example, having fallen off the top ten list in 1984, returned in 1987 on the coattails of a very popular man named Paul Hogan. Better known to America as the star of the popular *Crocodile Dundee* movies, Hogan had first appeared on our shores as the spokesman for Australian tourism. He was the guy who popularized the phrase "I'll throw a shrimp on the barbie for ya" and taught Americans the hearty Australian greeting "G'day, mate." Hogan's rugged, humorous appeal translated well to the brand—for as long as Hogan was popular. In 1987, one year after the first *Crocodile Dundee* was released, Foster's pushed passed Mexico's Dos Equis for the number nine spot at 3.2 million cases. A year later the sequel appeared, and Foster's pulled ahead of St. Pauli Girl for the number eight position, with 3.8 million cases. By the time *Almost an Angel*, Hogan's first non-*Dundee* movie, failed miserably at the box office in 1990, Foster's was clinging to the last position on the top ten list, with 2.7 million case sales.

(Foster's eventual resurgence—1994 sales figures put the brand in eighth place with sales of 4.3 million cases—came after Foster's import rights went to Molson in 1989. Molson found an interesting way of keeping down the cost of importing Foster's from Australia—it stopped importing Foster's from Australia. The beer that continues to be pitched as "Australian for beer" is still an import, though. It's now brewed in Canada.)

When Leo asked Lintas in 1987 to replace the latest incarnation of Heineken's bottle-and-glass advertising (the current version was tagged "Satisfy your thirst for the best"), he asked them to look beyond the traditional approach and try to find a way to communicate to younger drinkers without walking away from a message of product quality. Whether they didn't believe that he was willing to try something new, or they were fresh out of ideas, three rounds of creative proposals went by without anything Leo found appropriate. The fourth round—which we referred to later as the "everything but the kitchen sink" round, saw better than a dozen different approaches; from jocks drinking Heineken after the big game to testimonial ads, Lintas decided to present everything it had and let Leo decide which way to go. Nothing impressed him.

Leo decided to let other agencies pitch for the Heineken account. The brief remained simple: find a way to reach the trend conscious without alienating the existing Heineken consumer. It was a tall order.

One agency pitched a very domestic-feeling beach commercial, with rowdy friends enjoying Heineken to the strains of a jingle the agency promised would become a catch phrase: "Let's get some Heineken goin' on!" Though the wrongheadedness of the approach was breathtaking—we would have been positioning Heineken against

Bud and Coors, at a hefty premium—the agency clearly believed in its own idea of hip lingo. That Christmas, while the review was still "goin' " on, my father received a card from one of the agency's execs, on which he'd written, "Dear Leo: Let's get some advertisin' goin' on!"

Another agency wanted us to use high-tech special effects to transform the Heineken bottle into a huge dirigible that would be shown flying across the Atlantic toward America. We wondered if that agency had been asleep during the brief, when we explained that part of our problem was the perception that we were too big to appeal to trend seekers.

A third agency—N. W. Ayer, one of the largest agencies in the land—told us that the best approach for Heineken was a historical one: a series of advertisements romanticizing the history of the brand. They were doing fine until they showed us a proposed execution. In the thirty-second television spot Ayer pitched to us, the Heineken brewery would be shown being overrun by Nazis during the 1940 invasion of Holland. The (historically inaccurate) ministoryline was this: Jack-booted thugs put the brewmasters up against a wall at gunpoint, demanding a sample of Heineken's special "A" yeast (the brewing equivalent of McDonald's secret sauce) but getting nowhere with the stoic Dutch. At the end of the spot we would learn that the sample was cleverly hidden in a fake mole on the face of one of the female brewery workers. The tag line: "Heineken. The taste they couldn't capture." Beaches, blimps, and Nazis. We were no closer to solving our image problem.

Until a small agency named Warwick Advertising presented their idea for a campaign.

Warwick's pitch was based on a very simple premise: all fads face a backlash eventually. Rock bands that are all the rage one year are ridiculed the next; the clothes that were praised for their individualistic sense of style one season are dismissed as too mainstream four issues of *Vogue* later. Though Corona was hotter than ever in 1987, with sales of twenty-three million cases (just ten million behind Heineken). Warwick found in preparing their pitch that people were already seeing the first signs of a backlash or, more precisely, hearing them.

Our guys were also aware of the backlash against the faddishness of Corona, fueled largely by the brand's import pricing, which didn't jibe with its domestic flavor. Here and there in reports came word that the still strong cry for Corona was peppered once in a while with derision, as in friends were teasing each other about being faddish by choosing Corona or by ordering one with a lime in it. Warwick found a way for us to fuel that derision and to enlarge it to include the faddish packaging and promotion of some other competitors as well. Warwick won the account.

The campaign Heineken debuted in the spring of 1988 was designed as a single-year effort, to knock faddishness and in the process reinforce the general perception consumers had of Heineken as the real deal, beerwise. In a way, we had to make product quality—real or perceived—the hottest trend of all. The trick was to do it in a way that didn't attack fad chasers too directly; we had to make consumers see that fads were silly without making them think we were calling *them* silly. Warwick copywriter Andy Mendelsohn and art director Alden Ludlow managed it by creating a series of characters who were maxed out on faddishness and who would talk to the viewer in a manner so extreme that no one would see themselves being lampooned.

In one of the spots, a man sits at a table in what looks like a seaside restaurant, wearing a pastel T-shirt and a white linen sport coat, à la *Miami Vice.* On the table sits a cordless phone and a clear-glass, tall-necked bottle of beer with a lime wedged into the top. You never see the label, but you know what it is. Talking to the camera, he starts listing all the things that make him feel cool: "Foreign films, okay? Answering machine for my car phone. My beer? So hip, with a twist." As he reaches the final word, he is literally pushed out of the frame by another piece of film: a straight-on bottle shot of Heineken, with the campaign tag line "When you're done kidding around, Heineken."

In another, a man stands in a very New York bar, all wood

paneling and brass railing. He's dressed head to toe in Banana Republic clothes, circa 1988: khakis, bushman's jacket, etc. Among his personal observations: "All my plastic? Gold. I live in the city, but my clothes say safari. My beer?" He picks up a twenty-five-ounce can—not labeled, but clearly a Foster's—and puts on an Australian accent. "The biggah the bettah, *mate.*"

Though Leo was not comfortable at first in going after the competition so directly, as he felt it might make Heineken look like a bully, Mendelsohn and Ludlow convinced him that what we were ridiculing was packaging and other external factors. We never said the other guys made bad beer; we made fun of the reasons why the characters in the commercials chose their brands, whether it was for the size of the package or some trendy way of serving it. To explain the strategy behind the commercials to the press, I developed something of a mantra: "It's not what's 'in' that counts; it's what's in the bottle."

(The ads were something of a personal triumph, but perhaps a professional misstep for me. While we were shooting them on the soundstages of the Silvercup Studios, the daughter of Warwick's chief creative officer, Bob Fiore, brought her boyfriend by, as he was curious about commercial production. Much to her father's initial trepidation, Christina and I struck up a friendship. As proof that I am lucky beyond any measure, she married me seventeen months later. This was a professional misstep because now I was not only working *for* my father, I was working *with* her father. To my father, I was an employee responsible in part for giving direction to the agency. To her father, I was the client. From then on, whenever the two disagreed on creative matters, I could always count on alienating one of them.)

Though our wholesalers loved our combativeness (except maybe for the ones that also carried Corona), there is no way to quantify the effect the Heineken ads had on consumers. I suspect that we couldn't have taken a great deal of credit for Corona's 1988 flattening out (the brand dropped a million cases to twenty-two million), because our ad budget was not at the size where many drinkers were seeing the ads with any regularity. The point of the ads, though, seemed to be creeping into the collective conscious during 1989, when salesmen's reports noted an increase in derisive comments made by consumers *and* retailers about fad brands and fad packaging. Though price increases brought on by the comatose dollar kept pushing Heineken down in terms of volume, the pain of our 9 percent sales drop in 1989 was softened by the 27 percent dip suffered by Corona and the 36 percent drubbing of Foster's.

Heineken started the nineties in much the same way it had started the eighties: outselling its nearest competitor by a margin greater than two to one. (In 1980 it sold 2.23 times more than Molson, and in 1990 the margin over the still sliding Corona was 2.35 to one.) Thanks to a new phenomenon in the domestic beer market, though, we never got a chance to enjoy the restoration of the import status quo.

11

SAM ADAMS: BREWER, PATRIOT, PAIN IN THE ASS

Mired in the faddishness of Aussie movie stars and clear glass bottles, tinfoil-wrapped necks and wedges of lime, as the import segment was in the latter half of the eighties, it was easy for us at Van Munching & Company to become dismissive of anything that smelled like a trend. It was also stupid. For while we were busy defending our turf against other foreigners, a new threat to import sales was emerging from dozens of tiny domestic breweries: the microbrew.

For fifty years VM & Co. had stressed the view that the beer business was made up essentially of two categories: domestic and imported. That's not to say that we were unsophisticated when it came to recognizing the pricing differences within those categories, only that it served our interests to simplify. To the press, adopting our outlook meant covering Heineken as a very big fish in a well-defined pond, as opposed to noting that the brand sold less than one-twentieth of Budweiser's volume. To our wholesalers, that view meant an easy way for us to delineate profitability: Sure, you sell a lot less of the imported stuff, but your margins on it can't be beat. To the public, the word "import" meant class and sophistication, traits not associated with American brewing since the Big Three had swallowed the domestic beer industry whole. But by the mid-eighties our view of the industry had grown myopic from a product imagery standpoint, and dangerously so.

Because of the tremendous growth of imports, a number of entrepreneurs began asking themselves if the traits that made foreign beers sell couldn't be replicated here in the States. In asking the question, they—overnight, it seemed—redefined the beer business. No longer was the equation domestic/imported; now it would be mainstream/sophisticated. However they defined it, it would mean direct competition for the imports.

Though the microbrewing industry had its roots in San Francisco, where Fritz Maytag had rescued the failing Anchor Steam in the sixties, the fellow who would do the most to turn it into a revolt against the foreigners, appropriately enough, was a rabble-rousing Bostonian.

With his Ivy League love for pin-striped suits, his slight build, and his insinuating voice, Jim Koch (pronounced "Cook") didn't look or sound much like a brewer. But he sold beer like one. Within just a few years Koch's Boston Beer Company, founded on $400,000 in 1985, would completely dominate the micro boom. Koch knew the reason microbrewing hadn't yet really gone beyond the brew pubs that spotted the West Coast (especially the cities of Portland and Seattle) was basic economics: very few aspiring microbrewers had the access to capital to build enough capacity to launch anything more than a small local brand. Koch's common sense told him that the capacity to launch his own brand didn't *need* to be built; it could be leased from any number of existing regional breweries. If Julia Child brings her ingredients and cooks in someone else's kitchen, he would later argue, isn't the result still a Julia Child dish?

His Samuel Adams Boston Lager was equal parts brewing and bluster. His bold blue-and-silver label, which featured a portrait of Samuel Adams in roughly the same size and shape as the portrait of George Washington on the dollar bill, oozed patriotic nobility. (It didn't hurt, of course, that the style of lettering used on the label was strikingly similar to that found on currency.) Underneath the portrait were the words "Brewer" and "Patriot." It was a label only a Communist could hate.

To those in the industry, who weren't quite sure what all the patriotism had to do with *beer,* Koch's product imagery seemed so contrived that spending time with his packaging for Sam Adams was not unlike a visit to Disney World: though the details were uncannily recreated and the production values unmistakable, you couldn't shake the feeling of hollowness just under the surface. Of course, like Disney, he was an instant smash. (It didn't hurt that he made a terrific beer.)

And a marketing genius. A tireless promoter, Koch spent his days on barstools, convincing Boston's pubs and restaurants to take in his product. Like a certain Dutch immigrant a half century earlier, he built his business on personal contact, one bar at a time. He didn't hide in an office, rearranging numbers on a page and poring over focus group findings; he talked to people. He made loyal followers out of bartenders, drinkers, and—maybe most important—the press. He convinced them all that he was the classic little scrapper; never mind his Harvard education or the six-figure salary he'd until recently been receiving from the Boston Consulting Group. In a self-created analogy that would come up again and again, he was David. The Goliath he would direct his marketing efforts against was imported beer.

More than anything else, Koch went bar to bar selling a little nostalgia. He knew the most important ingredient in beer is *romance*—that affinity beer drinkers feel for their brand based not just on its taste, but on imagery and heritage as well. Beer, whether it's used as a reward, a relaxant, or a refresher, is a gift people give to themselves, and as such, it should come nicely wrapped . . . and not only in pretty packaging, but also in good mental associations, like craft brewing and patriotism. To take the romance analogy a bit further, Koch knew that the selling of beer should be a sort of seduction, not just of the consumer, but of the bar manager, the store clerk; anyone who had a say in ordering beer. The big boys had gotten so large and so sophisticated that a smart fellow like Koch could win distribution largely by flattering his customers with an old-fashioned, personal approach to selling.

Despite our inability to take him seriously based on a huge volume difference (Heineken sold some 33.2 million cases in 1987 to Sam Adams's less than 500,000), Samuel Adams posed a much bigger long-term threat to us than anything south of the border. The signs were all there; Koch meant to take us on, and he'd done his homework. With our notes.

For starters, Samuel Adams's premium pricing, often even 15 percent above Heineken, was meant as proof of quality: you have to pay more, it must be better. (Just ask the folks at Chivas Regal, whose sales soared once they raised their price to the point where it was significantly higher than their competitors'.) Some mistakenly thought that Koch advertised his expensive ingredients because he felt some need to justify his higher price. Just the opposite was true; he wanted to bring attention to it. Pop quiz: You're going to visit friends, and you stop in the liquor store for a bottle of Chardonnay. Do you grab the $4.99 bottle (thus risking the "cheap bastard" tag), or do you double it and buy a little self-image insurance? If you answered "depends on the friends," good for you, but you don't get off that easily. Koch knew full well that the "bring a coupla cases over and we'll belch in front of the football game" crowd was locked up by the domestics, and he didn't waste a breath going after it. He set his sights solely on people who were aware of what things cost and were not immune to the need to impress.

Instinctively, Koch knew the reason Heineken has always sold better in bottles than on draft, no matter how much better draft beer may taste: as I said at the start of chapter 9, beer is a badge, just like clothes and cars. No one can tell how much you paid for your beer when it's in a glass—you're counting on that bottle on the bar in front of you to show you've got taste . . . and maybe to show that you've got bucks as well.

And there was no getting around the fact that Koch and his fellow upstarts—like Pete Slosberg, the creator of Pete's Wicked Ale—just plain made great beer. Unlike the big brewers' answer to imports, the "superpremium" category of brands like Michelob, the micros were making beer with honest-to-God character: full-bodied, rich, and every other adjective they could reclaim from the tired advertising of the comparatively bland domestics. Call it snob appeal, part two: Not only do we cost more, because of the quality of our ingredients, but we are the real deal—beer as it was meant to be brewed. If you drink our brand, the logic goes, it is because you have taste . . . unlike Billy Bob over there, sucking back his long-neck Bud.

Along with the pricing, this set the micros apart from many of the imports, effectively narrowing down the competitive set to the European brands: Heineken, Beck's, and to a lesser extent, St. Pauli Girl. These were the quality benchmarks—quality as defined by pedigree and strength of taste. These were the beers with the most snob appeal.

To combat the Europeans, the micros were able to trade on a home-grown appeal. Think about the mood of the country in the mid- and late eighties: Reagan, Bush, flag-protecting constitutional amendments, amen. Was it any surprise that some folks would rally around Koch's admonitions to throw out the foreigners? Of course, the lure of domestic micros wasn't just a rah-rah America thing. It was also about the aesthetic pleasures of equipment. Cool-looking brewing equipment. The big domestics had long been unable to show their kettles and tanks with a straight face; at their volumes, their breweries resemble petrochemical plants more than anything else. But up at the Commonwealth Brewery in Boston, you could actually see where the beer you were sipping was made—an on-premise product if ever there was one. Brewers like Koch and Richard Wrigley, the founder of the

Commonwealth Brewery (a Boston Brewing rival), fell all over themselves to have newspapers photograph them peering out from the inside of shiny copper brewing kettles. You could just about smell the hops in their public relations, and if you had an hour for the tour, you could smell the hops for real.

Finally, Sam Adams and the other micros had size, or the lack thereof. They were nothing compared with Heineken or Beck's. This is where the David and Goliath analogy came in. Everyone loves to root for the little guy.

The irony, of course, was that with scarcely 1.3 percent of the American beer market, Heineken somehow found itself in the Goliath role.

Understanding that mass-produced is often considered a synonym for lousy, I made it a point as Van Munching's public relations director to inject the following into any conversation possible . . . call it a beer-biz sound bite: "Budweiser spills in a week what we sell in a year." Imagine my horror, then, when this eventually showed up in a Sam Adams ad: "I brew in a year what the largest selling import makes in just three hours, because I take the time to brew Samuel Adams right."

Whereas my claim had always been taken by the press as one of those folksy overstatements meant to make a general point, Koch's claim was by its exactness deliberately misleading. What consumer was going to spend the effort to reason that statement through and realize that he was talking about volume, not brewing time? As he would do with so many subjects, Koch played the brilliant obfuscator and used a little pretzel logic to make an important point: Heineken came from a very big brewery.

In fact, even our Europeanness couldn't protect us from the taint of size. Koch once told an interviewer that Heineken was "the Schlitz of Europe; a beer you buy at a gas station." The guy ought to run for president; *that's* a sound bite. It neatly punctured the notion that Heineken must be good because it was so popular in Europe (where they know their beer), and it equated us with, well, *Schlitz.*

But for all of his disdain for us, it quickly became clear that Koch wanted what we had cornered the market on for half a century: mainstream prestige. With his three-pronged appeal—ingredients, cost, and taste—he was staking out our turf, playing in our yard, dancing with our girl. And oh, what he was whispering in her ear.

Relentlessly, Koch went after Heineken's quality on two fronts: the recipe and the freshness. From his initial advertising, Koch claimed that Heineken was legally forbidden in Germany because it contained "adjuncts and preservatives" and couldn't pass the country's strict "beer purity law." When the ads broke this was, in its way, true. In addition to the classic ingredients (water, yeast, malt, and hops, as defined by Germany's purity law), Heineken used corn in its brewing. Corn (or maize, as the brewery prefers to call it) acts as a stabilizer and is often used by larger breweries to add crispness to a beer that may take a while to reach its destination. Rice works in much the same way.

The German beer purity law Koch referred to, the *Reinheitsgebot,* was established in the sixteenth century to protect that country's thousands of small breweries. By eliminating the use of stabilizers, natural as they were, Germany cut the chances that any foreign brewer would enter the country or any domestic brewer would expand to a size that threatened large numbers of other, smaller outfits. The law was successfully challenged and struck down by the European court overseeing the formation of the European Economic Council (EEC) on the grounds that it was protectionist. Though that happened in early 1987, Koch continued to run the "purity law" advertising for years afterward.

And why not? It was misleading enough to be effective and just close enough to the truth to be unassailable for all practical purposes. A lawsuit on our part, or on Beck's or St. Pauli's, would've been difficult to win at best (try proving damages against a guy selling a tiny fraction of your volume) and would've given Koch even more of the David and Goliath publicity he wanted. In fact, he damn near *begged* us all to sue him. He told *Adweek,* "If what I said was untrue, they could bankrupt me [with a lawsuit]." He assured a Boston paper, "I spent six months making sure my claims were factual because if I'm wrong, the litigation costs would wipe me out." The Associated Press quoted a more colorful variation: "If I were wrong, do you think they would let me get away [with] saying there's something fishy in their beer? They'd squash me like a bug."

The danger Samuel Adams posed to us, at the time, had nothing to do with his potential as a sales rival. His threat was to our image, our authenticity—in the realm of imported beers, that meant our stock in trade. Whether or not Koch sold one case of his own stuff, his constant knocking of Heineken began to eat away at our stature and put us on the defensive. Letters from Heineken drinkers, once little more than admonitions to keep up the good work or questions about why the case that had been down in the basement for three years tasted funny, now were filled with questions about adjuncts, preservatives, and German law. As public relations director, I was, to be Ross Perot–ian about it, busier than a one-legged man in a butt-kicking contest.

Koch's lawsuit bravado had its intended effect. When the national press picked up on the story, the veracity of his claims went unexplored in favor of the far more sexy squashing-the-bug question. After a half hour phone interview with *Newsweek* in June 1986, I was chagrined to discover that the only quote I had landed in their Koch story was this: "I don't think any of us are going to sue and give him the fight he's looking for."

The *Newsweek* story, more than any advertising Koch had done, forced Leo to take the Sam Adams threat seriously. More than that, it just plain pissed him off. Heineken had spent a bundle over the years advertising in *Newsweek,* and while he didn't expect favored treatment, Leo expected fair treatment. *Newsweek* had printed Koch's allegations without comment, even though I had meticulously detailed our response to the writer. Leo felt slighted. So he pulled his ad dollars.

At the time, I objected to the move, concerned that we'd cut off our nose to spite our face. *Newsweek* was a respected magazine with a readership well suited to our ad message. Why reach fewer consumers over something that was already done?

Because word gets around, that's why. Two friends in the magazine business called me within a month of our pullout from *Newsweek* to tell me, off-the-record, that similar stories had been altered out of fear that importers—and possibly even domestics—would boycott their publications as well. *Newsweek*'s editor in chief sent Leo a two-page letter copping a plea that had the piece been longer, the issues might have been clarified. "I do wish we had been able to explain the [brewing] process in more detail," he wrote, adding, "We did not intend to suggest that Koch and his beer are a threat to the 'majors,' nor to portray Koch in a particularly positive light." It was too little, too late. Van Munching products remained out of *Newsweek* for three years.

But aside from my father's fit of pique, the management at Van Munching adopted a haughty stance and seemed unwilling to answer Koch's attacks. Though there was the requisite name-calling (privately, anyhow)—including a pointed phonetic mispronunciation of his name—and a bit of hand-wringing, I couldn't get company executives to agree on a plan of action. And then it occurred to me: the company just wasn't prepared to deal with unsportsmanlike behavior. Accustomed as we'd become to being "above it all," by virtue of our product imagery, even our category's imagery, we had no idea how to respond to a scoundrel. We sat around, wondering about the proper etiquette for the knife fight Koch had picked with us. Swatting *Newsweek* was our first tentative jab back at the guy—okay, it didn't exactly hurt him, but at least we were doing *something*—and it felt good. Though I wasn't getting any help in the "how" department, I wanted more. I'd get my chance soon enough.

Shortly after the *Newsweek* story ran, I was approached by public television's *MacNeil/Lehrer NewsHour* in regard to a similarly themed piece they were doing. I passed along the recommendation to Leo's vice president/national sales manager (and my boss) that I agree to an on-camera interview, provided Koch wasn't going to be on hand to grandstand. The VP laughed. "These guys [microbrewers] are a dime a dozen," he told me, though it didn't exactly answer my recommendation. Can I do the interview? I asked. "Do you know what Koch sells?" was the answer. (The temptation to answer, "Beer, actually," was almost overwhelming, but I held my tongue.) I tried a different tack, reminding the VP that we were minuscule compared with Budweiser, but that didn't mean Bud should ignore us. That got me an answer and a glare. "No," he said. But suddenly the issue was age. I was too young, the VP told me; end of discussion.

A more seasoned PR director might have found a way to convince the VP, but the company didn't have one, it had me. In some fairness to myself, that was by design: my father loathed dealing with the press and had a public relations function mostly to issue polite "No comment's." When he hired me right out of journalism school in 1985, I suspect he felt that my ability to write simple press releases more than qualified me for the job. (Within a year of joining the company, I was spending the majority of my time learning the advertising end of the business.)

I learned a valuable lesson about going over your superior's head on the day the VP and I argued about *MacNeil/Lehrer,* and it was this: When you're the boss's son, it can't really hurt. Frustrated that the national sales manager was refusing to deal with Koch, I wrote Leo a memo outlining my reasons for wanting to tell our side of the story in front of the camera. He said yes to his son, not his PR director. I know that because I'd never heard of another company president who felt the need to remind his PR director to speak slowly, be polite, and wear an appropriate suit. The VP was equally respectful of my position in the company: since I didn't copy him on the memo to Leo, he stopped talking to me for a couple of weeks.

As we didn't have a brewery to use as a backdrop for the interview, it was conducted in a distributor's warehouse across the river in Long Island City. This was great for scenery but lousy for acoustics. I learned my second valuable lesson in a week: Don't give interviews in warehouses. Ten minutes in, it became apparent that all my answers had to be completed in ten seconds or less, because anything longer risked being drowned out by the sound of a forklift moving pallets of beer around. (I didn't dare ask them to stop working for five minutes, as my father would have gone apoplectic at the thought of me pushing my weight around at a distributorship.) The noise didn't faze my interviewer in the least; he'd calmly ask me to repeat answers over and over, until they got a clean take on each. I, on the other hand, was doing my best to keep lunch down. I had visions that I was becoming the "corporate spokesman" character Martin Short played on *Saturday Night Live*—the sweaty, tremulous weasel puffing away on a cigarette with an impossibly long ash between evasive answers: "I know *that.* Why do you think I don't know that? It's interesting you think I don't know that."

Somehow I managed to get through it without cursing or weeping openly. I was relieved when they finally turned the camera around to film the interviewer. We continued to chitchat with him on camera; having seen the movie *Broadcast News,* I knew that this footage would be inserted into my answers to give the impression the interviewer was actually paying attention. (I'd also seen it done at a college press junket for the movie *Starman.* While an auditorium full of us aspiring Woodwards and Bernsteins asked director John Carpenter what Jeff Bridges was *really* like, one enterprising student videotaped his replies, later filming himself asking all of our questions and patching it together into a faux one-on-one interview. I saw it on a local cable show and wondered if anyone else found it disconcerting that while the interviewer looked off camera to the same spot, Carpenter was addressing his answers in eighteen different directions.)

The final piece aired a few weeks later, and I, blissfully, didn't come off all that badly. Awkward, sure; but I managed to speak in complete sentences. And it helped that for all of his obvious charm with print reporters, Koch wasn't any more comfortable on camera than I was. It really helped that his worst moment—eyes bulging almost homicidally while he pronounced imports "frauds"—came sandwiched in between my only two appearances in the piece. It did *not* help that the voice-over before I first appeared identified me as "Philip Van Munching, importer of Heineken." The day after the piece aired, Leo's VP ended his silent treatment of me thus: "So you're runnin' things now?"

As *MacNeil/Lehrer* gave us our first chance to combat the "illegal adjuncts" shots, we were mostly happy with the results. The reporter was quick to point out that a beer taste-test the show had videotaped to frame the segment on Sam Adams was pretty clearly set up by Koch so that the tasters would prefer his brand and that Koch was as much huckster as he was brewer. At the end of the piece, though, there was a reference to a bigger taste test that Koch had won: Denver's Great American Beer Festival, where Sam Adams had been named "Best Beer." Though we were annoyed that the piece ended on an up note for Koch, the mention of the prize would have an unforeseen effect. Instant karma—the cosmic payback reserved for those who are less than kind to their fellow man—was about to bite Jim Koch in the ass.

Koch had told *Newsweek* that he was successful at pounding away at the imports because "people like to know some dirty secret." Though he won "Best Beer" in 1986 (and a number of times thereafter), the Great American Beer Festival brought to the fore Koch's little secret: he had brewed his "Boston" lager in Pittsburgh, Pa., right from the start, under contract with the Pittsburgh Brewing Company, home of Iron City beer. We had been aware of this (and not above telling every reporter within earshot), but we had no idea how hated Koch was among those microbrewers who actually ran their own breweries. After the piece aired on *MacNeil/Lehrer*, we found out.

The first to contact us was the Boulder Brewing Company, makers of Boulder beer. The company's executive vice president, Skip Miller, sent us a letter in late August 1986. Like a number of letter writers who would follow, Miller was put out that Koch was trading on the cachet of a brewer without having gone to the start-up expense. And that he was not above misleading people to protect that cachet. "I read an interview with him in the *Boston Globe* where he gave evading answers to questions like 'Do you worry about using Boston's water as an ingredient in your beer?' " he wrote, "with his response being 'The fact is, it's probably the least important.' Well, yes it is [important], especially when it's Pittsburgh water."

Of course, the anti-Koch mailbag was not without its dose of opportunism. Miller himself was looking for an alliance with Heineken that would help him distribute his brand in Koch's backyard. He wanted to, in his words, "capitalize on our negative feelings, transforming them into positive actions which will result in profits for both of us." So did Bill Owens, proprietor of Buffalo Bill's Brewpub in California, which would become known for an eclectic portfolio of brands, including Alimony ale—"the bitterest beer in America." Though I turned both down—can you imagine the press we would have gotten?—I spent a good deal of time on the phone with Owens, learning some interesting theories about the ways in which the Great American Beer Festival victory was being won.

Owens, now also the publisher of *Beer: The Magazine,* was an eccentric, in the very best sense of the word. You have to love a guy whose magazine's masthead once listed Jack Kervorkian as the staff doctor. He was also a realist: he wasn't mad at Koch for coming in as a contract brewer with a lot of promotional cash and—if the rumors were to be believed—"buying" the 1986 prize; he was furious with the festival for letting him. He was furious with the prize, period.

Instead of a panel of beer experts, the grand prize at the festival was chosen by consumer preference poll; if you had a ticket to the event, you could vote. Koch, small brewers (including Owens) had charged, sent his minions out to Denver bars and gave away tickets to the festival, which cost something like $20, asking only that the recipients vote for Samuel Adams in the polling. For those already armed with tickets, the stories went, he had T-shirts and hats, items almost none of the real microbrewers had a budget for. Koch credibly denied the charges, pointing out the tight policing of the event and the fact that with five thousand festival-goers, he couldn't possibly have afforded to give away enough tickets. He attributed the stories to jealousy, and he was most certainly correct that his fellow contestants were jealous: Koch, a man who didn't actually brew his own beer, was getting all the attention. And whether he was buying the prize or not, his bluster was not making him any friends within the Association of Brewers, the organizer of the festival.

Despite the protests of its members, the association didn't eliminate the consumer poll until after Koch won the 1989 prize, his fourth in five years. (He didn't enter in 1988.) Starting with the 1990 festival, prizes were given in thirty-two specific categories, with the winners chosen by a panel of trained judges. Of course, Koch being Koch, he found a way to continue to annoy his fellow brewers. He trademarked the designation "Best Beer in America" and advertised that he'd been named that "four years running" at the festival. When the association tried to force a little disclosure into the advertising of its members—insisting that they include the actual category and year of any medal if they wanted to continue to participate in the festival—Koch showed that he could be Goliath, too: he threatened to sue. The association backed down.

Owens also noted that the "fraud" tag was something members of the association were laying on Koch with as much regularity as he was laying it on us. They loved to point out that Koch wasn't a microbrewer at all; having his beer brewed for hire by an existing outfit ("in *Pittsburgh*," Owens sniffed) meant Koch was merely a contract brewer playing dress-up.

They also loved to point out that for all his talk of product integrity and especially "freshness" (and how the imports didn't have it), Koch was heat pasteurizing his beer, something considered a no-no by hard-core brewing snobs. Pasteurization extends shelf life and allows beer to travel well . . . from, say, Pittsburgh to Denver. (In fact, an early neck label for Samuel Adams carried a swipe that imports weren't fresh because of the ocean voyage—in reality usually ten days long. This was wonderfully ironic when you considered that Koch bragged about Samuel Adams being the only American beer imported *into* Germany.)

Obviously, the name of Koch's product was the target of much derision among microbrewers, but not only because of the "Boston" designation. The declaration "Brewer" under the drawing of Sam Adams on the label turned out to be a stretch as well. As Harold J. Bauld wrote in 1986 in *Boston* magazine:

> [The] beer is currently made and bottled in Pittsburgh, a perhaps forgivable eccentricity for a beer named after a man who never drank a lager and who was not a brewer at all. (Sam Adams was a maltster, a soaker and drier of barley, and not a very eager or adept one at that, according to every colonial record. Sam inherited the malting house from his father and rode it straight into collapse, four times staving off receivership only by bullying creditors with fast talk—the kind of ferment he is better known for.)

The fact that *Boston* would take shots at him must have irked Koch, but it couldn't have surprised him, considering the antagonism he'd already stirred up among other local brewers. Two years after Bauld's slight, *Boston* would run a lengthy piece (Kevin Convey's "Beer Wars") detailing the local PR struggles being waged among Samuel Adams, Richard Wrigley's Commonwealth Brewery, and Rich Doyle's Harpoon ale. Except for Wrigley, no one in the piece came off as especially likable, and the charges were thrown around like handfuls of Bavarian hops: the author said Doyle screwed Wrigley out of his plans for a commercial brewery by asking the state too many questions about Wrigley's brewing license; Wrigley said Doyle rushed the opening of his brewery, causing "serious problems" with Harpoon; Koch—always and ever the bully—threatened them both with having their beers analyzed in front of the press, on the (erroneous) assumption they had yeast and bacteria problems.

The most interesting thing about the article was that it put Koch somewhat on the defensive, a position he was clearly unused to. *Pro*actively, the guy was brilliant: make a charge, laugh off any rebuttal with a wink and a protestation that if he was wrong, wouldn't they be suing?

*Re*actively, he was a bit truculent: "Oh yeah? Well, if you say anything bad about *my* beer, I'm gonna have yours analyzed." In fact, Convey reports, when Wrigley called just such a bluff on Koch's part, Koch switched gears completely and tried to enlist Wrigley in his anti-imports crusade. God bless his soul, Wrigley responded with this: "I am very offended by your attitude about my fellow brewers. . . . If Heineken didn't come in here, and Beck's, and open the market, you would not be able to go to Pittsburgh and buy some beer and sell it and say you're a brewer."

In a way, the article helped us finally settle on a strategy for dealing with Koch's misleading ads. There would definitely be no suit—why give Koch back his little-guy edge?—though we didn't dissuade the Heineken brewery's small U.S. office from continuing to play legal footsies with Koch's lawyer. (In truth, it was nice to see them occupied with *something;* Lord knows we didn't need them here to look over our shoulder.) Instead we would stop praying for an act of God to shut him up and start heaping back some of his vitriol. And, lesson learned from *Newsweek,* we'd appeal to the pocketbooks of those taking Jim Koch's advertising dollars.

(There was talk in our corridors of a third method of combating Koch, one that would have been immoral, illegal, and just incredibly, incredibly satisfying: messing with his ability to build a distributor network. The theory went that our salesmen could apply a little behind-the-scenes pressure on our distributors to avoid taking in his brands. Though our stated objection would be that his pricing made him direct competition, word would be strong on the street that this was payback time. Vengeance would be ours.

Leo scotched the idea quickly, not solely on the grounds that it was illegal. I think he just plain hated the weasellyness of the whole thing; stabbing someone in the back was neither brave nor gentlemanly, and he would not cede the moral high ground. And, truth to tell, there were a few problems with the idea apart from the obvious legal ones. One was that we were already a bit too late; Koch had managed to sneak in to a number of our wholesalers in the first few years of his campaign against us. Another was that while he had a lousy reputation with the competition, he had a terrific reputation among wholesalers. What wasn't to love? His brands were profitable, growing exponentially, and—irony of ironies—he had a Van Munching–esque sales team, which meant that he was going to the expense of supporting the efforts of his wholesalers with his own manpower, as we had for decades.)

My strategy with the press became this: Point out Sam Adams's Pittsburgh roots whenever possible (explaining in loving detail the difference between a contract brewer and an authentic microbrewer), and answer any attacks from Koch about our freshness by pointing out the fact that like Sam Adams, Heineken takes the extra step of heat pasteurization to extend its fresh taste and insure an adequate shelf life. But why, I never forgot to add, would someone who boasts of shipping beer to Germany attack us for traveling the same distance? The some-say-he-bought-the-festival-award story and the Adams-wasn't-really-a-brewer story were reserved for journalists I knew and trusted not to let me come off as petty and vindictive as I was feeling on the subject. A freelance writer I'd spoken to for a number of trade magazine articles, surprised by the newfound bile in my tone when asked about Koch, asked if this meant "an end to the kinder, gentler Van Munching & Company."

"If this is on the record," I told him, "we would never stoop to the classless tactics of some of our competitors."

"Okay, Philip, off the record: Are you going after Koch?" he asked.

"Fuckin'-A, bubba," I replied.

"About time," he said.

Fortunately, he respected the off-the-record bit. Had he printed that, my father would have kicked my tail all the way down Sixth Avenue and out the Holland Tunnel.

Whether he got tired of us as a target, or didn't like being punched back, Koch started to lay off his more direct attacks on Heineken's ingredients, resorting to the "it takes me all year to make what the largest selling imported beer makes in just three hours" advertising. Interestingly, he wasn't even mentioning us by name anymore.

And once he stepped up his advertising spending and started a heavy radio campaign, we had leverage over him we hadn't had with newspapers, where we spent little money. Being Goliath sometimes had its advantages.

Our spending strategy came in two parts. We would contact any station carrying both Sam Adams and Heineken advertising and request that they not run any spot that disparaged Heineken unfairly. If they refused, we told them it wouldn't be possible for us to buy their station during any Sam Adams flights. (A flight means an uninterrupted period of time during which your ad is in rotation. You might be on two weeks, off one, etc.) As we also wouldn't shift our planned flights to accommodate a station, this became somewhat of an ultimatum, though we didn't couch it that way. Our stated rationale was simple and unassailable: We felt that it would be confusing to our consumers if they were to hear Heineken ads in proximity with advertising that disparaged Heineken.

Like national health care and the personal financial dealings of many career politicians, our radio gambit was just too complex and confusing to make for good copy. Koch couldn't sound-bite it, he couldn't make a convincing case that we were strong-arming stations (as we were still buying time on some of the same stations he was buying time on), and he couldn't even talk about us anymore without eliciting a response that included the word "Pittsburgh." He lost heart. By 1990 we got word from Heineken that Koch's lawyer had offered a phraseology change to his advertising, replacing the word "adjuncts" with "corn," provided—what a difference a few years makes—we would promise not to sue him over any of his previous ads.

In the end we won no major victory over Koch; at best we muted the damage he did with his initial attacks on us. If we did anything right, it was what we didn't do: use our advertising to refute him. Though it had been discussed a number of times over the years—at one point Molson even approached us about a joint attack ad—the idea was rejected for a simple reason: people just don't read advertising that carefully, and we'd end up doing little else than making more people aware of Koch and Koch's charges than already were.

To this day my father remains convinced that Jim Koch is the Antichrist, which I find ironic because Koch reminds me so much of *his* father. Both Koch and Leo Sr. owed a debt of gratitude to P. T. Barnum, and both harbored egos the size of a small town. Both proved tireless promoters, and both understood old-fashioned, barstool-to-barstool salesmanship. The major difference between the two is that my grandfather managed to accomplish what he did without pissing off everyone else in his industry.

Part Four

A Soldier's Story

12

Heineken Light, Heineken Chunky Style

(Author's Note: In a general sense, Beer Blast *is about the effects of applied modern marketing technique. It is the story of what happened to a relatively straightforward and unsophisticated industry when outsiders got hold of it—Philip Morris and August Busch's cadre of MBAs, to be more specific—for better and for worse. What follows over the next three chapters is a microcosm of that; a case study, if you will, of the effects big business had on one player in the beer industry.*

Or, put another way:

Every once in a while we read something in the newspaper or see something on public television about the discovery of a tribe of people who've never been exposed to what we think of as modern civilization. They live in the remotest corner of the rain forest, or in the jungle, or far out in a desert no one had ever paid much attention to. We marvel at this, and we wonder how they could have possibly survived all this time without us . . . without our MTV, our fax modems, our fast-food restaurants. Deep down, we feel relief for them: they have been rescued.

This is about the "rescue" of Van Munching & Company, Inc.)

In late 1990 I got two pieces of news. The first was that I was going to be a father. While Christina and I were overjoyed, we handled our discovery in very different ways: she, being irrepressible, told as many people as she could as quickly as she could, and I, being superstitious, tried to keep it to myself until the pregnancy got past the most likely time for miscarriage. Only the news wouldn't keep; I had to tell *someone.* I chose my father, because I saw him every day in the office and because he was exceptionally good at respecting confidences.

My telling him elicited the typical Van Munching family response: a deadpan, "Does she know who the father is?" followed by warm congratulations. After we finished discussing my good fortune, he added three words that I think he'd only spoken to me once before at the office: "Close the door."

I'd have swallowed hard, but my stomach was already in my throat as I did what he asked. In the parlance of my father, "Close the door" was akin to "You'd better sit down."

"You told me your news, I'll tell you mine," he said. "But it stays in this office." There was a long pause. "I've sold the company."

He explained that he'd finally entertained one of corporate Heineken's offers to buy back the rights to their own brand, rights contractually given to my father until his death. We were to become what's known as an operating company of Heineken, NV. Before I could mentally pack my desk, he explained that as part of the arrangement he had agreed to stay on for at least three years, to run the company and help prepare for the transition. I made a joke about using that time to find other employment, and he told me that my younger brother, Christopher, and I were part of the deal; under a side agreement we were to have "every opportunity for advancement" in the Heineken-run company.

His reasons for selling were not terrifically complex. His father had passed away earlier in the year, and the government would have to be paid a mammoth inheritance tax on the value of the company. Though the company's past profitability guaranteed he could easily afford the tax, it was a matter of ease: actually selling it put an immediate value on the company, while the other alternative was to let government auditors crawl into the books and set their own value for tax purposes, which would have been essentially nonnegotiable. But that was only the practical reason. The emotional one—and, I suspect, the weightier issue on my father's mind—was his desire to spare his family even the remote possibility of one day going through the same contortions his father's health had forced him through just over a decade earlier, when keeping the company on track meant reading his father's daily mood swings and eventually convincing him to sign a power of attorney. Pragmatist that he'd always been, it didn't much surprise me that my father was eager to leave while at the top of his game.

As I had done with my news, he asked me to keep his confidential for a while, so that the rumor mill wouldn't cause worry among the ranks. It also meant that I couldn't tell Christina, whose father's agency would likely panic at the thought of a management change at one of their largest clients. This left me about a month to stew all alone over the changes corporate Heineken might bring.

For a few years there were no major changes: 1991 and 1992 passed with only one Heineken-dictated personnel change—the August 1991 addition of Eric Morham to our ranks, initially in the role of assistant national sales manager. Morham came via the company's Amsterdam headquarters, where he'd been a regional export manager. Before that he'd been a marketing guy at the Heineken-owned Amstel Brewery in Canada, his home country.

No one in New York saw much of Eric for the first six months of his stay. As Leo had done with just about anyone who'd come to the company in an executive capacity, he sent Eric out on the road to learn the beer business Jim Koch style: out in the trade, talking to bartenders and stocking supermarket shelves. As far as Leo was concerned, the only way to understand the industry was to spend time working with and asking questions of the guys who were doing the actual selling. Though I started in public relations and my brother, Christopher, had started in what could best be described as marketing services, we'd each done our half year in the trenches.

The New York office of Van Munching & Company might even have forgotten about Eric's presence in the States had it not been for some odd questions coming in from salesmen around the country.

"What's this about seven-ounce packaging?" was a common query in the last half of 1991, as was an even stranger one: "When is Heineken Light coming in?" According to some of the salesmen Eric was assigned to work with, he was confident that once Leo left, and perhaps sooner, the company portfolio would include at least one of the two. At the Christmas luncheon that year, I asked Eric if it was true that he was a proponent of bringing in Heineken Light. Because both the national sales manager and another assistant had already queried him on the very topic, he was a bit defensive. "Why not?" he asked me.

"I'll give you two reasons," I said. "Heineken and Amstel Light. Where else are Heineken Light drinkers going to come from?" I let his explanation that there was plenty of room for the brand to stand as the final word; even bringing up the subject at a festive occasion was not exactly the height of diplomacy on my part. And truth was, I liked Eric; he had a good sense of humor and was about twenty years closer to my age than any of the top three men in the company. So what if I thought he blustered a bit? I'd watched the management of the sales department ride him a bit harder than others, probably out of resentment that he had entered the company at a level as high as assistant national sales manager. I figured he was entitled to a few lofty pronouncements about what he would do if it were his company.

Besides, he was not my department.

As it had been from the days of Leo Sr. pounding the pavement and selling beer a case at a time, Van Munching & Company was first and foremost a selling organization. The company was built around a central sales department; each of the three other departments served the needs of the salesman on the street. The accounting department, aside from payroll, handled monies coming in from wholesalers and going out to suppliers. The traffic department was responsible for fulfilling orders; it communicated our product needs to the brewery and took responsibility for the beer's transportation to the wholesaler. The third department, the one I spent nine years in, was called the advertising department. Not "marketing," because that might have implied some decision-making powers, and the truth was, all decisions were made by Leo, in consultation with the top sales guys.

Still, advertising was responsible for all creative and media, all point-of-sale material, and all sponsorships larger than local charity events. Price promoting, often done at other companies by a marketing or brand manager, was at the sole discretion of the sales structure. At the time, I thought often of how old-fashioned this setup must have been: all of my business-trained friends seemed baffled at our lack of a brand management system, and it irked me that the strategic, nationally focused thinking of an experienced advertising agency could be seriously undermined by an unkind word from a sales guy who'd never lived off of Long Island.

Instead of a textbook corporate structure, we had Leo, and in that sense the company hadn't changed in the two decades since he'd returned to the New York office from establishing the company's West Coast outpost. Though his father had been in the president's chair until the beginning of 1980, Leo Jr. had overseen the functions of each department, right down to giving the final go-ahead for every T-shirt design, every supplier change, every major line-of-credit extended to a wholesaler.

This was not as constricting as it sounds; if he ran the company as a monarchy, Leo was at least a consistent monarch. It was not difficult to anticipate what he would or wouldn't give approval to. He operated according to one clear principle: Everything we do must reflect the quality and stature of the brands we sell. The "everything" was quite literally meant, too. As the industry leader, his edict went, we will maintain our office in a certain way, we will pay our bills as soon as they come in, we will behave in meetings with outsiders or when we're out in the trade with a certain level of class. This had its annoying moments: early in my stay at the company, I blew better than a paycheck on an Italian suit—pleated pants with a European cuff, ventless double-breasted jacket—only to be asked by my father why I hadn't gotten "a real business suit." But it had rewards as well. As employees we were trained to "trade with those who trade with us" and eat business lunches in restaurants that carried our brands. We learned to ask to see managers, so that we could thank them for their business, and ask them how things were going and if there was anything we could do for them. Because of that, we were treated like royalty; we didn't wait for tables, desserts would come on the house.

The psychological effect of Leo's business philosophy upon his employees was simple; forced to behave as if the company they worked for were somehow above it all, most Van Munching employees seemed to come to believe it. The perception became the reality.

Within the advertising department, the notion of "class" had a singular importance because our charge was to oversee ad campaigns, support materials and sponsorships that would motivate consumers to *spend more money for their beer than they had to.* Our messages had to convey *"class,"* because *"class"* was our unique selling proposition.

Class largely dictated the avoidance of certain things. From a media standpoint that meant we didn't advertise on *Married with Children,* for instance, and we didn't buy ad space in *Penthouse* or *Hustler.*

(Because *Playboy* served our brands in their clubs, we ran ads in their magazine. The moment the clubs closed up, we were out.) Van Munching's young media director, Dave Spalthoff, and I met Howard Stern at a cocktail party thrown by his New York station toward the end of the eighties and received a good-natured tongue-lashing by the shock jock because we didn't advertise on his radio show. "C'mon, you guys listen to my show—you know you do—and *you're* in the target, right? You should be advertising on my show." Though he might have been right, and maybe we should have been on his show, neither Dave nor I was keen on making that argument to Leo, who had once become apoplectic after Stern's previous station ran a Heineken ad right after one of Howard's dicier lesbian-themed segments.

From a creative standpoint, class meant aspiration; we had to portray Heineken and Amstel Light as the brands of choice for the people our consumers aspired to be. Again, this was not a difficult proposition to apply, because just about everyone aspires to be recognized for their good taste. We had to, in all things, sell Heineken and Amstel Light as the highest-quality brands in their respective categories. As the point of origin and the packaging bespoke quality, so must all the marketing imagery.

This made media choices and sponsorships (which I'll get to in a moment) relatively easy to agree on, internally. It didn't make creative strategy any easier, though, because there are infinite ways to project a specific image.

In the client/agency relationship, it is often the case that the client believes the best work shows nothing but the product and talks about nothing but the product, while the agency would like to remove the product entirely from the visuals and create an entertainment. Part of this comes from the fact that a client's worldview often extends no further than his own category, and he doesn't think in terms of all the advertising clutter his message must compete with for attention. At the same time, the ad industry is more of a launching pad for writers and directors than it has ever been, agencies are increasingly judged by how "hot" they are as measured by creative awards won, and the client's need to sell is sometimes buried by the agency's desire to have a terrific reel.

The trick is to balance the two impulses; a strong client can anchor a strong agency in the reality of the selling task, and a strong agency can prevent a strong client from boring his consumers to tears. There were two instances during the seven years I worked with the renamed Warwick Baker & Fiore when the balance felt perfect. The first was the "When you're done kidding around, Heineken" campaign in 1988, and the second was a campaign we launched for the same brand in fall 1991. Themed "Just being the best is enough," the campaign again attacked faddishness, but this time in advertising, and this time in a more gentle, sophisticated manner.

Quite literally, Warwick had worked Leo's command that Heineken be positioned as the best beer on the market into the advertising. The new spots—created by Andy Mendelsohn and Alden Ludlow, the same team responsible for "When you're done kidding around"—knocked the competition obliquely, pointed out Heineken's best-seller status, and showed people enjoying the brand—and wonder of wonders, they managed to be interesting. In an ad typical of the campaign, a casually though nicely dressed young man sits at a nearly empty bar, leisurely reading a paper while drinking a Heineken. He and the bartender chat about the incredible nature of professional athletes' salaries.

"I don't get it," the guy says, looking up from the paper, "some guy bats .228 and makes three million bucks."

"Can you imagine what Willie Mays would be worth today?" the bartender says.

As their conversation continues, a voice-over announcer comes on, and says, "No holiday sweepstakes. No blimp with our name on it. No racing team. None of that is what made Heineken the number-one-selling imported beer in America." The screen fades to black, and the tag line is seen but not spoken: "Heineken. Just being the best is enough."

The voices of the actors come back up enough so that we can hear the bartender ask where the guy supposes all the money for such high salaries comes from. The ad ends with the guy's response: "Ticket prices, I guess . . . and all those beer commercials."

As it had with the "When you're done kidding around, Heineken," ads, the brand was once again sharing a laugh with the sophisticated consumer. This time the subject was the inherent silliness of the advertising gimmickry used by most other brands. And again there was an underlying snobbishness to the campaign, but one that worked to boost the ego of the viewer; in effect, the ads said, "Hey, we know you see right through all this gimmickry in beer advertising, and we know you're only *really* interested in quality."

As the first commercials in the campaign were being readied to air at about the same time as Eric Morham was arriving, late summer of 1991, we were sweating out the effects of a major increase in the federal excise tax on beer. According to *Modern Brewery Age,* the tax increase enacted in 1990 to take effect on January 1, 1991, doubled the tax on beer, from an average of $.16 to $.32 on a six-pack and from $9 to $18 on a barrel. As *Impact* correctly pointed out, European brands were the hardest hit by the increase, as their margins had already been eroded by the weakened dollar. Heineken ended the year down a frightening 13 percent, Beck's lost 15 percent. Corona had a schizophrenic response to the tax increase: out west, where Barton used their healthy margin to eat the increase, the brand was fine; back east, where Gambrinus chose to raise prices, the brand's slide continued. Overall, Corona lost 6 percent.

With Heineken about to end the year with its fifth straight volume decline, a lot rode on Warwick's latest campaign. Not only was the industry looking to see if Heineken could turn it around, but those who would remain at Van Munching after Leo's departure felt the eyes of Holland on us as well. We saw 1992, the first year the new campaign would be seen before and during the peak summer selling season, as a test.

In fact, Heineken tested our advertising department quite literally in 1992: they commissioned a research company to do qualitative testing on the "Just being the best is enough" campaign.

Where quantitative research involves compiling a great number of simple responses to questions, and is often done over the telephone, qualitative research concentrates on the in-depth probing of a smaller number of subjects. Where advertising is concerned, quantitative research might tell you who's seen your ads, how often, and in what context. Qualitative advertising research is what you'd use when you want to know how they *feel* about your ads. Rarely, in my experience, does qualitative research elicit an overpoweringly negative response to commercials that have already been produced; the common sense of the people involved usually precludes a full-blown disaster.

In the few instances when it does happen, a wildly, universally negative response during qualitative research is a strong indication that the advertising may harm the product. But a wildly, universally enthusiastic response proves nothing beyond the fact that consumers were entertained. It does not indicate with any certainty that your creative will motivate people to go out and buy your brand. The storerooms of ad agencies are filled with commercials that everyone loved yet never sold unit one for the advertiser. Just ask the folks at Isuzu, whose wildly popular Joe Isuzu character didn't seem to get people into the showrooms.

Cynically, then—and I will grow increasingly cynical over the next few chapters—I look at qualitative research as basically good for two things. The first is as a way to CYA, or cover your you-know-what, because responses in qualitative research can vary so widely that it's possible to pull almost anything out of them. The second is as a way to check up on someone else's work. Which, as the subsidiary of a large corporate entity, we felt was being done to us. Much to our relief, the roughly sixty people the researchers spoke with seemed to really identify with the campaign. This was not particularly surprising to us, as Heineken was on its way back up in terms of volume; it would close out

1992 with about a 6 percent bump. Corporate passed along the final research report to us, without comment.

Our resentment of the research's origins was largely paranoia on our part, because it turned out that Heineken Corporate researched everything, everywhere. No package was created or changed without a research project, no decision made until reams of paper had been amassed. We learned that because we started regularly receiving copies of research projects they'd been conducting on our shores with little or no input from us. One of the qualitative projects they had done, also in 1992, was titled "A Market Structure Study of the U.S. Beer Category," which contained little more than what we could have told our new corporate parent, had they chosen to ask. For instance: "Americans tend to segment beers by origin, domestics vs. imports. . . . There is, however, a sizable segment that consumes and understands the nature of light beer. . . ." Further, "Budweiser is still the 'standard' for American beers, [though] many report preferring the taste of Heineken." For this wisdom, Heineken paid tens of thousands of dollars.

(Actually, we should have been grateful for the "Market Structure" study, in that in its final paragraphs it looked at the notion of Heineken line extensions and declared something else we had considered obvious, whatever Eric Morham thought: "It is inconceivable to most respondents that Heineken could be a 'light' beer.")

Though we chuckled privately that Heineken, in its unwillingness to consider experience over research, was being taken for a ride by overpriced information gathering, one study would force a minor conflict of wills between Leo and Amsterdam. The subject was sponsorship.

Our internal approach to evaluating sponsorship proposals was centered in pragmatism. Would the local distributor's sales boost from a sponsorship be sufficient to earn back a sizable amount of the cost? We were not of the size (or at least substantial enough of budget) to be offered many presenting sponsorships—as in the Blockbuster Bowl or the Volvo Masters Golf Tournament—so for us sponsorship wasn't a matter of buying meaningful name exposure as much as it was buying the opportunity to sell one or more of our brands to a captive audience. We looked at sponsorship as a way of pushing the brand involved with a specific area for a specific time, and we took whatever small media exposure we might gain as gravy.

Not all sponsorships are sports related. For instance: In 1993 someone representing the rock opera *Tommy* approached us about presenting the musical as its sole sponsor on Broadway. While we sorted out with them what that would mean in terms of beer sales in the lobby and any rights we might have to use the music in a joint promotional ad, one of the folks involved invited me to see a preview of the show. He told me before the curtain went up that he had a wonderful idea about actual product placement in the show. He sat behind me and pointed out that during one scene, large beer images would be projected onto screens behind one of the actors. Had he been paying attention, he might have realized that that particular actor played Uncle Ernie, who—while these images were being projected—was singing drunkenly about what he was going to do to the title character while his parents were out. I turned to the man during the intermission and gently offered that we weren't too keen on being the official beer of child molesters. *Tommy* was a smash, but without a presenting beer sponsor.

Our first question in evaluating any sponsorship, even before considering the pragmatic question of local beer sales potential, was "Is it right for the brand?"

Which is why we sat in stunned disbelief when our Dutch masters handed us a global research project that had named yacht racing as an attractive vehicle for sponsorship. Further, we were informed, they had already committed large sums of money to an international yacht race: the Whitbread 'Round the World Race. Further still, they wanted our support—financial as well as in terms of manpower—on the U.S. leg of the race.

Though there might have been a larger waste of promotional

money for Van Munching & Company, we were damned if we knew what it was. The Whitbread was wrong for us on two major counts: one, yacht racing put us right back in danger of becoming the stodgy old brand that Corona drinkers of a half decade earlier suspected we were, and two, no one had ever heard of the thing. No matter how much money Heineken or Van Munching spent on the Whitbread in the U.S., almost no one would be aware of it. No offense, you yacht racers reading this, but the fact that even the biggest yachting event, the America's Cup, is so spottily covered in the press is proof that the sport registers as the most minor blip on the average American's consciousness.

In effect, Heineken was asking us to carve a sizable chunk out of our advertising budget, which was roughly $15 million for our flagship brand in 1993, and spend it creating promotions and possibly advertising to support an event that was at best unknown and at worst harmful to our image. The actual request came in the form of a meeting attended by my father, the advertising department, a brewery executive in charge of the sponsorship, and the promotional firm from Britain that Heineken had retained to run their end of the sponsorship.

J. B., as the brewery executive liked to be known, told us early in the meeting that the name of the race was now officially "the Whitbread 'Round the World Race for the Heineken Trophy." All well and good, until my father pointed out that Whitbread is the name of a brewery in England, so the new name was akin to "the Miller 'Round the World Race for the Budweiser Trophy." Though he said it kiddingly, J. B. didn't laugh. And the meeting didn't get much better. Leo kept brushing aside each new entreaty for money—for public relations support, for a radio campaign—with the promise that we would man the "race village" planned for the Ft. Lauderdale–area stopover of the race in early 1994.

J. B. was frustrated; as we were an operating company, wholly owned by Heineken, he should have been able to dictate a higher level of commitment. Leo wouldn't budge. J. B. shifted the entreaties to include a global perspective. He argued that Heineken was a truly international brand, and Heineken was using its sponsorships to stress that. We were not being team players, he suggested. Finally, in exasperation, my father gave J. B. a lecture. "Look," he said, "you have to understand something. I have to do the best job for our brands that I can with limited funds. Maybe you think we're Budweiser or Miller; we're not. I cannot, in good conscience, throw our resources out the window over a boat race that no on in my country has ever heard of or cares about, just because you think that people in other countries care about it. I'm not selling Heineken there; I'm selling it here." The folks from the promotional firm all looked down at their notepads as though they'd just discovered something fascinating on them. The meeting ended.

I was proud of my old man; he'd stood up to the nonsensical nature of the proposal in a gentlemanly fashion. I took no little glee in hearing that one of the top men at the promotion company complained bitterly about J. B.'s failure to a man he didn't realize was a friend of my father's. "Jesus Christ, I mean, I thought Heineken *owned* the company," he reportedly said. But along with the pride, I felt a certain uneasiness; Leo was not exactly endearing himself to Heineken's emissaries, and Leo himself would soon be gone. As someone with the same last name, I wasn't thrilled about the idea that a lot of bitter execs would soon be my bosses.

One bitter exec I *wouldn't* have to worry about—or at least it appeared that way in the spring of 1993—was Eric Morham. My father's patience with Morham's lofty boasting about what *he* would do when it was *his* company to run had reached an end. Letters and calls from both VMCO salesmen and wholesalers were arriving at an alarming rate, concerned not only about Morham's ideas for new brands, but about his attitude about his current employer. "Leo and his top guys have no idea what they're doing," was apparently the common theme of his field pronouncements. Leo went out into the trade to talk with Morham's accusers firsthand. All confirmed what they'd been complaining about: that Morham was positioning himself as the inevitable leader of the company by openly denigrating the current leadership.

More to the point, all were growing concerned about the rapidly approaching post-Leo era. Would they have to report to, or do business with, a braggart and a hip shooter?

Tired of being slagged to his own men, Leo called in Morham for a chat. Rather than face up to his own words and explain what in his estimation top management was doing wrong, Morham played politician: he denied everything. He was fired.

Actually, he wasn't so much *fired* as he was kicked out of the office; he was, after all, an employee of Heineken. Leo called Amsterdam to let them know Eric was no longer part of the U.S. organization.

Had he had the problem two years earlier, Leo probably would've gotten a little respect from corporate Heineken. Until 1991 the company had been run by longtime Heineken men (like Freddy Heineken himself), who had some historical sense of what Leo brought to the table. Unfortunately, most of the old school of Heineken management had retired, and the decision was made to staff the highest post in the company in the custom of many large companies these days—they hired a marketing guy from a completely different industry.

So when Leo picked up the phone to appeal to Holland to help him with the growing morale problem caused by Morham's mouth, he ended up making his case to a man with absolutely no institutional memory. Karel Vuursteen, named chairman of Heineken's executive board in 1993, hailed from the Philips lighting organization, having spent twenty-three years there before joining the brewer in 1991. Vuursteen might have received Leo's request for help with sympathy, and he might have received it with surprise. He might have received it in a lot of ways; the one he chose was disdain. For Leo.

"You both work for me, and Eric is staying put," was the essence of Vuursteen's initial response. Leo, who hadn't expected an easy conversation, also hadn't expected the annoyed dismissal he was getting, especially from someone who knew nothing about the U.S. operation. He went straight to the only threat he could make: he threatened to walk out on the last half year of his agreement to run the company. Vuursteen, probably fearful of having to explain to brewery owner

Freddy Heineken why his friend of over forty years was departing in anger, blinked. Eric was out officially. At least for the moment.

My greatest fear at the time was that Vuursteen's revenge would be to name Morham as my father's successor when he stepped down as scheduled at the end of 1993. So when a different successor was named, in the middle of that year, I was greatly relieved. And confused. As the new president of Van Munching & Company (they'd bought the name along with the business), Heineken had indeed chosen a foreigner . . . but not a Dutchman. Michael Foley, a chartered accountant hired by Heineken to work at their Murphy Brewery in Cork, Ireland, ten years earlier, would be in charge of the United States, the largest volume (and profit-generating) Heineken market outside of Holland. Without a day of previous U.S. experience, he was going to take over the whole ball of wax.

To assist him Heineken named a marketing director, a man who would oversee the transition from our advertising function to a full-fledged marketing department. This actually cheered me, for two reasons. First, with Leo gone we would need a trained marketing leader; no one in the company struck me as capable of overseeing all of the promotional functions, including the existing advertising director, the man I reported to at the time of the transition. Though I felt perfectly capable of leading the advertising efforts, the structure I'd labored under had kept me far enough removed from pricing discussions that I had no feeling for retail promotion. The second cause for celebration was that the man they'd named as marketing director, Chris Vuyk (pronounced "Vowk"), had already visited and—unlike most of the other Dutchmen who flew in for a few days—was full of questions rather than pronouncements. Vuyk seemed genuinely interested in why we did things the way we did.

The trepidation that I did feel over the impending transition was not an uncommon one; I worried that I'd done nothing to distinguish myself (successful advertising being born of a thousand fathers), nothing to earn the notice of my new masters. And, as I was the son of the man who'd owned the company, nothing to prove that I wasn't just the boss's son. On the eve of the new fellows' arrival on our shores, my problem was solved. By David Letterman.

In late August 1993 David Letterman's *Late Show* premiered on CBS, after a summer-long barrage of promotional announcements. His first week ratings were huge; his numbers in the overnight Nielsen ratings doubled those of the average after-hours variety show.

So a lot of people were watching when Letterman made a joke that first week, during the monologue on his Tuesday night show, about a quality-control problem Heineken was reportedly having overseas. Letterman noted that Heineken had found a problem in a new bottling line, whereby chips of glass could potentially end up in Heineken bottles, so the company had recalled millions of cases of beer. But the recall wasn't to destroy the beer, Letterman quipped, it was to repackage it as "Heineken Chunky Style."

America laughed, and my phone rang off the hook. Was it safe to drink Heineken? people were asking. Wholesalers were calling it a panic. Should we stop deliveries? What Letterman hadn't mentioned was that Heineken's problem was with a new bottle design not used in the U.S., so the recall didn't affect us in any way. Between fear-allaying phone calls, I spent Wednesday morning trying to get the folks who sold us advertising on Letterman's show on the phone. I wanted to know what they could do to help us solve the problem Letterman had unintentionally created. I would learn quickly why Letterman often calls network people "weasels"; the response from the ad sales department amounted to "Tough luck." Not only would CBS's New York sales office not ask Letterman's people to run some kind of clarification, they wouldn't even call Letterman's people on the phone to discuss our situation with them.

So I picked up the phone, dialed information, and got the main number for CBS. I asked to be transferred to Letterman's show, and I ended up explaining my problem to a receptionist. Though she said someone would get back to me, I rather doubted it, and I said, "Look,

I'm not sure there is anything you folks can even do, and I'm certainly not going to threaten to pull our advertising, because we'd only hurt ourselves. I just want to appeal to the show's sense of fairness. By accident, Mr. Letterman caused a problem for us. I'd just like to talk to someone about it." The receptionist paused a moment and said that no matter what, someone would get back to me that afternoon.

They did. An assistant producer called back within ten minutes, and I repeated my story. She promised she'd look into it, and I repeated my line about the show's sense of fairness. I received three more phone calls that afternoon on behalf of the show. The first was to say they were looking into their obligation from a legal standpoint. The second was to say they were sorry, but if they did retract, they might set themselves up for legal problems later. I responded to each of the first two in the same way—basically, "We love the show . . . we're not going to sue . . . we're not even going to pull future advertising . . . anything you could do would help."

The third call came from Rod Perth, CBS's head of late night programming, one of the men central to bringing Letterman to CBS from NBC. Perth said, "I just wanted to let you know that David is going to say something about it tonight, but I'm not sure what. He *will* explain the situation, though." Perth, as any executive working with Letterman justifiably felt, was nervous about what might come out of his star's mouth. I was so thrilled we were getting our retraction that I told him, "I don't care if he calls me a jackass on national television; as long as people understand that it's safe to drink Heineken." I went home and nervously awaited Wednesday's broadcast.

Wednesday's broadcast was the single greatest hour in my professional career. Letterman not only made fun of himself, making reference to his move to an earlier time slot ("Mr. Big Shot wanted to be on at eleven-thirty. . . . At twelve-thirty we could say *all kinds* of stuff that wasn't true"), he spent the rest of his show working in Heineken mentions. It became his running joke, but in a positive way for us. He brought the audience in on the notion that he had a lot of making up to do. When Demi Moore came on and told him she had a present for him in the bag she was carrying, he leaned over and said, "I hope it's a nice cold Heineken," to gales of laughter. When the Spin Doctors performed, he held up their latest CD and said, "This thing sold like a . . . this thing sold like Heineken." By the end of the show, when band leader Paul Shaefer was seen actually drinking a Heineken, Letterman joked that for all the free publicity, we ought to send him a truckload of beer.

On Thursday we did. I met up with our delivery van to drop off some beer at Letterman's offices—it was the least we could do, considering the millions of dollars in free publicity Wednesday's show had given us—and a camera crew came down and taped me unloading beer and bringing it into the building for broadcast on *that* night's show. Letterman got another great gag out of it—he explained that the free beer was as a result of his apology to us, and he went on to kiddingly apologize to Anheuser-Busch for giving us so much airtime—and we got another night of priceless exposure.

Our ad agency put together a "highlight" reel of all of the *Late Show* Heineken mentions that we sent to our division managers, and which Leo looked at for the first time on the day Michael Foley arrived in our New York office. He gave Foley the background and stressed my role in getting the show to correct itself. If he wanted to turn my couple of simple phone calls into an act of public relations genius, it was okay by me. Foley seemed to be impressed.

But more important, Foley seemed to be impressive. A large man with a ruddy face and a boyish head of hair, the forty-five-year-old Foley gave off a strong sense of purpose in the few meetings we attended jointly before my father's retirement. He asked sharp questions; he weighed answers thoughtfully. With an Irishman's quick wit, he charmed many of those Van Munching executives made nervous by the impending transition. The way in which he deferred to Leo over the last few months of Leo's stewardship left little doubt with most of us that Foley appreciated where Heineken's success had come from.

We were *not* sure that our masters in Holland shared Foley's appreciation, though. At Leo's retirement dinner we got a dose of corporate grandstanding when Heineken's export director, Frans Van der Minne, got up to speak. He followed Foley, who'd graciously called Leo "an incredibly tough act to follow." Van der Minne, after generally boasting about the role he'd played in Heineken's U.S. success (he'd been instrumental in making the Heineken king-size bottle a reality, he assured us), pointed out that this was the second time Foley had had a tough act to follow. (Foley had followed Van der Minne as the head of Heineken's Murphy Brewery.) He didn't appear to be joking.

As the emcee of the dinner, it was my job to lighten the proceedings between testimonials, lest things get sappy, which would have ruined the evening for Leo. After Pete Fearon (an old friend and one-time rival from the Molson organization) got overly effusive with the "I love you's" directed at Leo, I joked that we were all proud he'd found the courage to come out of the closet, though I wished he hadn't done so with my mother sitting there. Later on, I joked about the incredible physical resemblance between the current director of the Murphy operation and one of our division managers.

While Van der Minne was at the podium, I jotted some notes with which to tease him; noting that he'd just taken credit not only for Leo's success, but also for Foley's, I wrote the following as he spoke: "For those that would like to stick around after dessert, Mr. Van der Minne has promised to solve the Kennedy assassination *and* find a cure for cancer." I'd have gotten the biggest laugh of the evening . . . and I'd have ended my career at Van Munching & Company. I crumpled the notes in my hand, thanked him kindly for speaking, and moved along.

Truth is, I was too relieved and happy to worry that Van der Minne was using my father's night to beat his own chest. Foley had been great; he'd said exactly the right things that night and in doing so gave a strong sign to those of us who remained that he would try to follow in Leo's example. We were convinced Foley had wholeheartedly embraced Leo's credo that everything the company did must reflect the quality of the brands. We were confident that class would remain as the defining element of the company.

Boy, were we wrong.

13

BEERBARIANS AT THE GATE

Less than two months later, my brother, Christopher, looked at the beautiful, nearly naked blond lap dancer writhing on the seated figure of Michael Foley and came to the realization that Van Munching & Company was changing. His thought was confirmed when Foley looked over at him, smiled, and shouted above the music, "This is fuckin' great!" Christopher, Foley, and a full contingent of Van Munching executives were at the Trophy Room, one of the Houston area's classier strip joints, unwinding from the second full day of Foley's first major initiative as the new company president, the 1994 SWOT meeting.

SWOT stands for strengths, weaknesses, opportunities, and threats and is catchy management-speak for a business self-evaluation exercise. Thirty-three people attended the three-day meeting at a conference center in Houston: all of the New York–based company executives and every Van Munching division manager and assistant division manager in the country. For three days in early February 1994 we discussed what was right with the company, what was wrong with it, where we could get more business, and where we were in danger of losing business we had.

It was a good meeting, if a bit predictable. People got to vent, which seemed to have a therapeutic value. Complaints outweighed positive comments by about two to one, with the sales staff feeling overworked and underappreciated. As some of the complaints about the previous management became more pronounced, Christopher and I noticed some uneasy glances in our direction. No one would come out and say "Leo should've . . ." or "Leo didn't . . ." because his sons were present. One of those clearly growing uncomfortable was Foley; Christopher and I both got the impression he resented our presence at the meeting. I wondered if he actively wanted those assembled to paint a bleak picture of the past so his efforts could seem that much more heroic in the future. As I sat there, though, I didn't much care *why* he was uncomfortable with us, I only registered *that* he was. And if I wanted my contractually promised "every opportunity for advancement," I needed to make him comfortable, pronto.

I'd made one tactical mistake by not joining him for lap dancing; my staying behind at the country-western bar the evening had started in brought a number of good-natured gibes from the sales guys that I was a prude. Foley may have sensed the truth, which was that I didn't find a boys' night out at a strip joint particularly appropriate behavior for a company that prided itself on classy demeanor. Maybe he thought I was judging him, which of course I was.

Whatever bad feelings he harbored toward me, though, were forgiven the next morning when I took a turn at a little public speaking. In front of the assembled group, I said roughly the following: "I hope that no one feels inhibited about complaining about Leo because Chris and I are here. That's what this meeting is for, and truth to tell, there are things about his management that I would have changed." Foley, who'd looked down or at someone else whenever I'd spoken earlier in the meeting, looked at me. I continued, "Here's sort of my take on things: I look at Leo not only as *my* father, but very much as a father figure within the company. So in a way, it's like we've moved out of the house, and while we appreciated all the guidance we got from Dad, now we get a chance to make our own way. It's kind of exciting." Foley smiled and said, "Great, great." After the meeting, he commended me on all my input.

At the end of the third day we all headed back to New York to reshape the company. My great contribution, aside from possible career salvation, was the institution of dress-down Fridays at the company, an idea I floated to Foley after he'd decided I was okay.

Within two months of the Houston meeting, I had a small raise, a new title, and a very guilty conscience. The raise was fine—especially since salary reviews weren't scheduled for months—but the title was awkward, because the man I'd reported to under my father still held the title I was now being told by Vuyk to use: advertising director. Vuyk had decided that the current ad director wasn't up to his job, so Vuyk did something I had heard about from friends in other companies. He froze the man out. When the newly forming marketing department was moved to another floor early in 1994, the ad director was left where he was, even though the secretary he shared with the media director, Dave Spalthoff, and me came with us. His responsibilities were taken away one by one and reassigned to Spalthoff and me. Though neither of us was particularly fond of our former boss, we didn't feel good about the way in which he was being squeezed out. Vuyk told me one day that it was his hope that the ad director, who'd been with the company since the days of my grandfather, would ask for an exit package and leave of his own accord. Vuyk wasn't disappointed, and before spring had much of a chance to catch hold of the trees, Van Munching was back down to one advertising director.

Chris Vuyk was fond of drawing diagrams to explain to his department the marketing concepts he wanted us to adhere to. A straight line with hash marks at certain intervals was used to demonstrate project trajectories; for instance, one member of the marketing team would be involved in a certain project up until the first hash mark, or the strategic planning phase, while another would overlap into the second phase, or executional phase, while a third might climb aboard a hash mark later, at the implementation phase. Other drawings often included circles within circles, to indicate sets and subsets of consumers, or bisecting axis, to map out quadrants of brand imagery. Lacking MBAs, the three Van Munching holdovers under Vuyk—Spalthoff, myself, and our merchandising director, Len Schlachter—almost never understood the drawings until Vuyk explained them to us.

The oddest of all was a departmental structure map Vuyk made for us in the spring of 1994. Oh, we got the idea of pyramidal corporate structures; what we had a hard time with was the way Vuyk's structure lacked any shape, aside from its general horizontal nature. What Vuyk was trying to do was explain to us how our new marketing department would look once he got finished staffing it. At the top, of course, was Vuyk, and the box containing his job title sat at the top of the chart. The odd thing was that the hierarchy ended there; underneath his title was one long row of six boxes. In addition to our existing posts of advertising, media, and merchandising director, Vuyk was going to add two brand managers and one research director. Each position would be equal in authority, Vuyk told us, and each would report directly to him.

Looked swell to me; I had been afraid that I'd report to the brand managers. Dave and Len were more skeptical. Len said he'd had enough corporate experience before coming to Van Munching to recognize a "too many chiefs" scenario when he saw one. Still flushed with my promotion to ad director, I accused Len of undue cynicism and told him to at least wait until the brand managers were hired and worked with us before deciding that chaos was inevitable. I was confident that Vuyk's search process was turning up terrific candidates, and I told Len to have a little more faith. This turned out to be wildly ironic.

As my post-Houston favored-employee status lasted through the entire first quarter of 1994, Foley suggested to Vuyk that I be allowed to interview the finalists for the two brand management positions. Though flattered, I was nervous that my level of marketing sophistication would pale compared with that of the seasoned professionals I would doubtless be speaking with. I was right and wrong in that assumption.

Not one of the three finalists Foley and I interviewed had a day of meaningful beer experience. Or even liquor experience. Though one had spent a few months as an assistant account executive (ad-speak for grunt) at an ad agency that handled Genesee Beer, an upstate New York regional brand, nothing on any of their résumés indicated a knowledge of the intricacies of the alcoholic beverage business. The one candidate who impressed me suggested her first order of business if she got the job would be a self-education on the various legal restrictions placed upon beer marketing. The other two lacked not only the first's MBA, but also failed to give any indication to me that they recognized any differences between different packaged goods. This worried me because one was currently working for a cigarette manufacturer and the other was working on dish soap.

Foley found all three acceptable, as did Vuyk. I recommended we hire the MBA and the cigarette woman, as she'd at least had more varied experience than the dish soap guy. Vuyk agreed, and offers went out. The MBA declined. Cigarettes and dish soap it would be.

I knew I was in trouble on the first day Jessica Arato and Phil Dolan were both in the office. I took them to lunch, as a kind of a getting-to-know-you gesture, and spent the hour listening to the two of them complain that they weren't getting P&L responsibilities. Marketing neophyte that I was, I had to ask what that meant. You'd have thought I was picking my nose at the table. "Profit and loss responsibility," one of them sniffed. I dug my finger in deeper: "What does that mean?" In essence, Arato and Dolan were annoyed that they weren't responsible for setting the budgets on their respective brands, Amstel Light and Heineken. Not having worked a day in the company, much less in the beer business, they felt they deserved full financial responsibility for Heineken's top two brands in its number one export market. This marketing thing was harder to understand than I'd first thought.

Arato, though she had seniority and a more varied résumé, was assigned to the smaller volume brand, Amstel Light, and Dolan was given Heineken, which had roughly six times the volume. Both set about to rethink the way we sold our brands, largely consulting books rather than the three warm bodies who'd spent a combined three decades in the trenches. I quickly apologized to Len for not having respected his experience when he fretted over the coming brand managers, now that I knew how it felt not to have one's experience respected.

The sales department was being restructured at the same time, starting with a dramatic change at the top. Doug Brodman, the man my father had groomed for the national sales manager's job for years before putting him in it about a year before his own retirement, was unceremoniously dumped not long after the Houston meeting. His replacement—I won five dollars betting a co-worker on this—was Heineken Light champion (and recent company rehire) Eric Morham. Turned out that following Morham's ouster from Van Munching & Company by Leo, the masters in Holland had parked him in a management course in California and bided their time until Leo's departure to return him to the fold. Morham, now christened VP/sales, set about remaking the field structure.

The company had long utilized a basic divisional structure, nine geographical divisions overseen by managers who reported directly to assistant national sales managers in New York. The assistants reported directly to the manager, who reported directly to Leo. This kept the levels between actual salesmen and the top management of the company to three on paper and two in reality, as the New York sales management team rarely operated as formally as the titles might suggest. The report of a salesman in Reno eventually found its way onto senior-level management desks in New York. The net of this, of course, was that all meaningful decisions were made out of the head office, though the men in the field answered directly to someone stationed a bit closer.

Many companies, Miller Brewing included, have developed structures known as "regional profit centers," or simply "regional management." This is to decentralize power; it puts decisions about pricing and advertising in the hands of regional managers, which theoretically shortens decision-making time and strengthens accountability. When a product is as straightforward as a paper clip, or even a brand of soda, this structure certainly has its merits.

But in an image-based category, where you are selling a little sizzle along with your steak, regional management increases your risk of trouble by increasing the number of caretakers of your image. It's hard enough for one centralized team to agree on something as subjective as imagery; it is impossible to imagine any consistency of message when four teams are made responsible. It's as though you've put the direction of the company in the hands of four different presidents. Further, the more layering you add, the harder it is to implement policy. For those reasons, my father had kept company decision making centralized and the layers of management manageable. It was a structure that appeared to be working.

Morham went the regional route and, in effect, added a layer of management to the sales department. To drive home the point that power was being decentralized, a northeast regional office was established in New Jersey, so that none of the four regional managers hung his coat at headquarters. The net effect of this was threefold: payroll went up, because regional managers aren't cheap, the predictable infighting went on over which divisional managers to promote into the new slots, and four more experts were created. Experts in everything from creative to sponsorship, from pricing to point-of-sale material; it's amazing how new authority creates self-confidence. To be fair, one of the four Morham installed in the new management position seemed up to the task, in that he weighed the guidance of others before making decisions. Another seemed a bit overwhelmed. The last two started punctuating calls to those of us in marketing with "Let *me* tell *you* how it is out here," which we took as a bad sign in terms of headquarter/field cooperation. Maybe my comment in Houston about moving out from under a father's thumb was more applicable than I'd first thought; having moved out of the house, we were finding out that some of our roommates were jerks.

Some of our other roommates, at least according to the new management, were too old. In a presentation to Heineken's executive board in mid-1993, Foley listed, among other organizational problems, an "aging" workforce, which he complained resulted in "no labor turnover." This is accountant-speak for "Hey, we could boost profit if only we could pay starting salaries, instead of having to pay all these people who've made a career here." Suddenly the experience of the salesmen in the trade—something that had long set the company apart from its competition—was deemed an extravagance by the new guy.

Foley hired a human resources manager, Richard Kapp, who was familiar with the legal intricacies of letting longtime employees go. The new manager, quickly dubbed "Kapp the Knife" and "the De-Kapp-itator" by black-humored co-workers, was sent around the country to offer exit packages to some of the more senior sales staff. According to at least one package recipient, the offer was simple: Accept and sign our settlement offer (and the attached promise to take no future legal action against the company) *right now,* or you will eventually be given nothing except two-week notice and a final paycheck. In every case I could track down, they signed; though some noted bitterly that cost cutting didn't seem to affect the personal perks of Foley's job.

"It was so disheartening," said one regional manager. "Here we were, agonizing over having to let go some of our most experienced and loyal guys, so we could save money off our payroll, and Foley was jetting around following the Irish team in the World Cup soccer tournament."

The question that was asked in the halls of Van Munching & Company often during 1994 was simple: Weren't we doing okay? According to our own figures, Heineken had seen an impressive 10 percent bump up in 1993, and Amstel Light had grown 6 percent. No one outside of the new management team was precisely sure why we needed all these new managers, these inexperienced salesmen, or these new setups. As someone still bearing the same name as the company, a lot of perplexed longtimers came to me for some kind of perspective on what was happening. I tried to be reassuring as I told them that we were dealing with largely cosmetic changes: the structure really doesn't matter if the underlying principles are kept. No way, I said, are these people going to mess with the goose that laid the golden egg. Problem was, I didn't really believe my own words.

As 1994 hit the midway mark, I kept getting mixed signals on the Heineken ad campaign. Word from our own men in the field had been consistently good; their chats with their distributors and accounts were eliciting quite a bit of praise for the work. The research that corporate continued to fund was actually growing more positive by the year. In 1992 the research had found that year's ads successful in delivering the strategic positioning—"Just being the best is enough"—"on both emotional and rational levels." In 1994 the research said that the work had "a clear, on-target message: Superiority—Heineken is the best beer." It concluded that the latest advertising had an "excellent fit with [the] brand image; exactly the approach the leading brand should take. . . ." Best of all, the research indicated that people just plain liked the advertising and, by extension, felt good about the brand.

So why was Foley complaining to me about the advertising's tone? Part of my job as ad director was to screen and evaluate competitive advertising. As part of educating Foley about the U.S. market, I'd show him reels of what the other fellows were doing and comment on what the strategy seemed to be. Disturbingly, he'd often respond to the faster-paced commercials with, "We need something like that." At one point he showed me a tape of some commercials from Ireland. One of the flashier, rock-themed ads prompted him to stand up, point at the screen in our conference room, and say, "*That's* what our drinkers would respond to."

It's hard to know, sometimes, where to begin to pick apart an argument. Looking at the certainty in Foley's eyes, I wasn't sure if I should start by saying that what he'd shown me looked like any one of a dozen candy bar commercials currently airing on MTV. Perhaps I could explain that every other importer who'd adopted hip, flashy advertising (like Beck's and Foster's) was in serious decline. Maybe, I thought, I should point out that with sales growing at between 6 and 10 percent annually, maybe consumers were responding pretty well to the approach we were taking. Not for the first time, I chose self-preservation. "We'll certainly look at this when we plan for next year," I said, hoping he'd forget.

If Foley showed a great love for flash, Vuyk started indicating an affection for all things foreign. He called meetings with Warwick, our ad agency, to show them tapes of ads running in Britain or Heineken ads from around the world. (One such spot, themed "C'mon, taste the world!" featured a jingle and visuals that could've been lifted from any one of a dozen soft-drink ads from twenty years ago.) Vuyk used these tapes as examples of "good advertising," and while we all appreciated that we should be aware of what made an ad interesting to watch, we weren't sure what these things had to do with the future positioning of Heineken.

I asked Vuyk that very question, and he gave me two answers. The first was that his screenings served as a conversation starter; we should all be questioning what makes advertising effective. I bought that. The second answer came in the form of a research study he slapped down on my desk without comment: another corporate research study, this one conducted in November 1993 and cryptically dubbed "Project Sphinx." Heineken, it turned out, was giving serious thought to a global advertising campaign—meaning that the consumer in Holland, who viewed Heineken in much the same way we view Budweiser (from the standpoints of market share and price), might soon be seeing the same ad as an American, who was being asked to pay a premium for it.

It was singularly the dumbest idea I'd heard from anyone at Heineken, with the possible exception of Heineken Light. It presupposed enough cultural similarities that one message would carry appropriate meaning in every nation. Worse, it just about guaranteed a watering down of the brand's attributes to appeal to the widest range of people, probably to the point of meaninglessness. For instance, part of the study involved testing "concept boards" of global communication possibilities. Among those tested: "Wherever you are, you can always count on Heineken" and "Heineken. For those relaxing moments." (My brother, Christopher, jokingly suggested another theme with global potential: "Heineken. Goes great with cheese.")

The good news Vuyk gave me a few weeks later was that the findings of Project Sphinx had apparently led Heineken to the same conclusion I'd reached without spending a dime on research: that there were enough differences among the cultures of the world to negate any attempt at one global campaign. The bad news was that the research done on our shores in the name of internationalism would instead be used to plan our future Heineken strategy. Which indicated to me that Vuyk felt we needed a new strategy. I was as confused as ever.

I found enlightenment in *The New York Times.* I'd wanted to know why our own management was hell-bent on replacing a winning strategy, and a column in the Sunday business section provided an explanation of sorts. Written by marketing guru Al Ries, the article was titled "Marketers, Stop Your Tinkering" and related the key problem Ries found with the discipline of marketing:

> Each year, hundreds of graduate schools of business turn out thousands of marketing people. When they arrive on the

> scene, these newly minted marketers want to make their mark. So they dismiss their advertising agencies and hire new ones. They revamp the marketing plans . . . they change names, logos, slogans and strategy statements. Welcome to the world of marketing.

Though Ries was speaking of brand-new business school graduates, his words were as clear an explanation of Van Munching & Company's predicament as I had found. He went on:

> Marketing ought to be like flying. It takes great power and the pilot's total concentration to get a jet off the runway. But at 30,000 feet the pilot throttles the engines back to 70 percent of power and puts the autopilot on. It takes tremendous effort to start a new product, too. But once it reaches an optimum market share, a company should throttle back the marketing program and make minor corrections only.
>
> If many marketers were at the jet's controls, though, they would first try 35,000 feet, then 25,000 feet. They would speed up, then slow down the engines, and maybe try a few banking maneuvers. All the while, they would interview passengers for their input.

Ironically, I saw the column because it crossed my desk in an envelope from a press clipping service. Like many companies, we paid to have all newspaper and magazine mentions of us or our brands and company clipped and sent to us. Ries's column came because he mentioned Van Munching, along with companies like Southwest Airlines, the Gap, and Starbucks, as an example of an operation that had managed to be quite successful without any memberships in the American Marketing Association. This, he felt, showed the company's wise lack of reverence for current principles of textbook marketing. In our case, he spoke too soon.

I passed the article on to Vuyk, which wasn't the brightest thing to do, because I highlighted the part about change for change's sake, and he took that as a knock on his initiatives. Which, of course, it was. Vuyk dismissed Ries's point of view and then went on, over the next year, to precipitate every change Ries predicted of a new marketer.

One was an agency change, though he would not be successful in that endeavor until the middle of 1995. The plan first surfaced in the summer of 1994, when he informed me that it was a corporate wish that we separate Heineken and Amstel Light in terms of ad agencies. This put me in an odd position, because even though I honestly thought the edict was stupid (considering the brands' recent success), any attempt I made to protect Warwick would seem personal because of my relationship with Fiore. Oddly, when Vuyk first informed me that a change would have to be made, he said that Amstel Light, the smaller of the two accounts, would be shifted, but within a few weeks he'd decided it would be Heineken instead. My protestation put him in an awkward position, because he had no performance reason for shifting the brand. He started imagining personnel problems at the agency. Suddenly the same people he'd been happy with a few months before weren't "taking direction adequately" or showing "an understanding of our positioning needs."

My protestation—which resulted in the postponement of an agency search—sealed my fate at Van Munching & Company. That, and an interview I gave to a trade magazine, where I was apparently too kind to my father when the interviewer asked about how the company had become so successful. When the magazine arrived at our offices in the mail, Morham came into my office to tell me that he thought I'd laid it on a little thick. When I pointed out that I also talked about the exciting possibilities of new management, he stammered through a restatement of his problem with what I'd said about my father. "It was a bit over the top," he said.

He and Foley boarded a plan that afternoon, bound for a meeting in Holland, where Vuyk already was. The next day I received a terse fax from Vuyk, advising me that I was to give no more interviews until we'd spoken. When he returned, he assured me that he wasn't angry with me; he'd been under orders to send the fax. In fact, he seemed gleeful that I'd been able to so thoroughly piss off Morham, whom Vuyk had little use for. Cynically, Vuyk suggested my mistake had been in challenging the view that the company had been floundering before the new management came to the rescue.

I should have known that, judging from the interviews Foley was giving to the press. Unlike Leo, who'd played Greta Garbo, Foley actively sought out personal publicity. He gave interviews to the leading trade magazines, as well as a number of Irish publications. Most highlighted the changes at the company. To explain those changes, Foley neatly ignored the company's strong growth over the last few year's of Leo's management, and said things such as "Perhaps in recent years, the company was not as forward looking as it should have been. It tended to see Heineken's competitors as solely operating in the import sector. I believe we are competing with every beer in every bar in every state in the country." Eventually his public assessment of his predecessor for the press would get more blunt: "[Van Munching] was riding on the back of its own success."

Vuyk let me know that through my resistance to an agency change, and my lack of diplomacy in restating the successes of the past, I was now being seen as a problem by senior management, himself included. There wouldn't be room in the company, he told me, for someone who couldn't handle change. Especially when there was so much coming.

Yet another global research project was making its presence felt on our shores in the form of revised labeling and packaging for Heineken; the chief change was a filling in of the red star outline that appeared above the Heineken name on the body label. Though this had been suggested to us in the past, it had been rejected by Leo repeatedly, largely because a full red star had less than ideal connotations. First and foremost, the red star was still the symbol for Communism, and as Heineken sold terrifically well to the large Cuban population of the U.S. (especially in south Florida), we didn't feel a great need to conjure up images of Castro. Second, we let corporate know that the red star was already used as a symbol for Macy's and on the packaging of Pellegrino mineral water. If the point of the red star was to have a graphic device to be used along with the black "bow-tie" Heineken logo bar, as corporate indicated it was, we wanted no part of it.

Those concerns had left the company along with Leo. Not only would the new folks at Van Munching embrace the red star, they would, within a year and a half of its arrival, attempt to fashion an ad campaign out of it. But we'll get to that.

I expected another change to come in the form of a new moniker. This thought didn't particularly upset me; truth is, it felt strange seeing the name "Van Munching & Company" used in the press when it was no longer my father's management being reported upon. Knowing that the change was probably inevitable, I tried to repair my team-player image by preparing some advice on what the new name should be. As I was still the public relations director in addition to my advertising duties, I figured Foley would ask. Don't use the name Heineken itself, I would tell him, for a few obvious reasons. First, it's hard to stress the importedness—and justify the higher price—when you say "Heineken, imported by Heineken." It sounds too corporate, like "IBM, imported by IBM."

Second, and much more important, big was out, as any follower of the beer business knew. Miller, after years of trouble with new product introductions, created the Plank Road Brewery label, affixed it to their ice beer (Icehouse, *not* Miller Ice), and grabbed on to the mystique of the micros. They took a page from the Sam Adams playbook: smaller = authentic, authentic = snob appeal, snob appeal = $.

The other piece of advice I had planned on giving Foley was Don't, don't, *don't* call the company Heineken North America, or Heineken USA. When you spend millions on radio advertising, I would tell him, you have to think of your company name in terms of how it sounds as the (legally mandated) tag on your spots. For years people had recognized my last name solely because they'd heard it so many times between songs: "Heineken. Imported by Van Munching &

Company, New York, New York." The danger in putting the words "Heineken" and "USA" in proximity was obvious: you might convince people you're now brewing domestically—Löwenbräu, anyone?—so why should they pay more?

Quite rationally, you're saying, "But it still says 'Imported by.' " Maybe that will help, but why risk it? And this wasn't just about Heineken advertising, remember. Amstel Light spent a fortune on radio as well—a fortune that in the worst-case scenario would be tagged with this: "Amstel Light. Imported by Heineken USA."

The resulting nightmare conversation:

"Hey, Bob, didja hear that? Heineken's brewed here now."

"Really? It doesn't come from, uh, um, Germany anymore?"

"Nope, they just said Heineken USA."

"What a rip-off. I just paid four bucks at Houlihan's for one of those."

My advice was going to be this: Find a Dutch city, or an object equated with Holland, and name the company that. Like "Amsterdam Importers" or "Windmill Importing."

Any advice I would've given became moot early in September, when a new moniker, "Heineken USA," was announced at the national sales meeting; the change would become effective with the start of the new year. Not having been invited to the meeting, I was told later by a secretary. It was a measure of how far I'd fallen in the eyes of Foley, Vuyk, and Morham that none of them had bothered to tell me that after sixty years, my family's name was coming off the door.

But I didn't have time to feel slighted. I was too busy preparing for yet another change—a change to our brand portfolio. We were about to launch Heineken USA's first new product: a line extension for Heineken. Thankfully, it wasn't Heineken Light.

14

A Tale of Two Bocks, and a Red Star Rising

In March 1994 Vuyk had sent me to Boston to attend part of a focus group study on a Heineken-brewed bock beer. Bock is Bavarian in origin and traditionally brewed in the fall from the first malt of the harvest, according to the *Encyclopedia of Beer.* Though the name unquestionably comes from the German word for goat, there is some debate about what it means. Some say it has to do with Capricorn, the zodiac sign that falls around Christmas; others ascribe the name to a legend about a billy goat knocking down the last contestant in a medieval drinking contest.

Heineken Wheat Bock beer, as it was known in the early stages of its American testing, was a mild, sweet-tasting version of the traditional bock, brewed with dark malt. As such, it was not unlike many of the dozens of bocks already coming from American specialty and mainstream brewers, like Rolling Rock Bock.

The March testing included name possibilities; Heineken itself would be the prefix to whatever the ultimate name choice might be. Amber Bock, Red Bock, and Tower Bock were all quickly rejected by members of the groups as too generic or, in the case of Tower Bock, too meaningless. The respondents in Boston initially rejected a fourth possibility, Tarwebok, ridiculing its inherent lack of pronounceability. (Tarwebok got its name from the type of wheat contained in the recipe.) Though they alternately referred to it as "Tar-wee-bok" and "Tar-wuh-bok," the name won out because further focus group conversation saw the testees talk themselves into the notion that it was actually quite a good name, because its foreignness connoted authenticity.

Aside from a brand name that took some selling, other aspects of the testing should have been cause for some concern. In the final report, Heineken Tarwebok seemed to be considered good tasting, but not in the way it should have been. Those who hadn't actually had bock previously noted the product's smoothness; one commented that it was "not too heavy or filling. You could drink a lot of this." Those who had drunk bock, though in the minority, found the product lacking in body and too sweet.

Here's why that was a problem: Heineken USA looked at Tarwebok as a potential credibility builder for Heineken. To combat the Jim Koch–inspired notion that Heineken's size as a brand rendered it somehow less sophisticated than a so-called microbrew, the company would offer Tarwebok. According to the introduction strategy sheet Vuyk gave me shortly after the research was completed, the objective of the launch was not to establish a seasonal brand, but "to strengthen the quality image of the Heineken brand, specifically amongst drinkers of microbrews." In essence, then, we'd failed before we'd started, because the heavy microbrew drinkers were the folks telling us they weren't impressed by the taste of Tarwebok. Oddly, Vuyk looked at the findings and saw no reason to consider reformulating the brand.

Worse, though, we were about to break with common sense and

spend our energies on a brand *not* for its own merits, but as an image booster for our flagship. This suggested a certain lack of faith in the volume potential, and it made developing advertising that much more difficult, because we weren't really mandated with selling the most cases of Tarwebok, we were told to use our budget to impress microbrew drinkers. The two tasks were in some ways diametrically opposed, because, frankly, it was hard to imagine that true microbrew drinkers wouldn't see through the whole thing and ignore the brand. When Portland, Seattle, and Denver—three notoriously weak Heineken markets—showed up on the list of six markets that would receive media support for the Heineken Tarwebok launch, I wondered if we weren't spinning our wheels. Or setting ourselves up for a real image problem if hard-core bock drinkers in those markets *did* try the brand and decreed it unworthy.

Whatever my feeling about the objective of the Heineken Tarwebok introduction, my job was to oversee the creation of advertising support. With a scant $400,000 media budget to cover six markets, it was clear that television and radio were not even options; we would have to rely largely on print and outdoor advertising to bring the brand to the attention of microbrew drinkers. The media discussion was not difficult: all we could afford were specialty publications like *All about Beer* and the *Ale St. News* and alternative newspapers like Denver's *Westword* or Seattle's *The Rocket,* along with some transit advertising (bus and train shelters) in the larger of the six markets.

For a creative message to put in those media, I told the Heineken team at Warwick to think heritage. They needed to convey Heineken Tarwebok's seasonality, quality, and brand lineage in a way that would make it look like the real deal, not just the latest bock to hit the market. They came up with a poster (reducible to magazine ad size) that bore the same piece of copy along the top and bottom, in two different languages: "Oogst van 1994," and its English translation, "Harvest of 1994." The bulk of the poster was made up of an illustration featuring the Heineken Tarwebok bottle lying down in a cluster of wheat stalks.

The style of the illustration was very European 1930s (almost the Germanic style of some recent Löwenbräu print advertising), and coupled with the dramatic block lettering used for the copy, it gave the poster the feel of a painting more than an ad. They'd handled the assignment well.

At least *I* thought so. Phil Dolan, the newly hired Heineken brand manager (Mr. Dish Soap, as I thought of him), liked the design but not the style. At first I thought he had another illustrator in mind. I asked him to explain his reservation. "I think it should be a photograph," he said. I patiently explained that because of our clear edict to reach people to whom authenticity carried a great deal of weight, the classier route of the illustration seemed logical. He thought about it. "I think it should be a photograph," he repeated. He told me that he was recommending to Vuyk that the agency's work be altered to reflect his belief. "We're just going to have to agree to disagree," he told me as he left my office.

I won the battle, partially by stressing my job title and my experience to Vuyk. It really wasn't that hard a sell, but it angered me no end that there would clearly be no deference paid to those of us who'd spent our careers working on the brand by the new brand manager. My brother, Christopher, as he would do many times during 1994, calmed me down with a little levity. "Consider the guy's business background, would you, when you present creative to him," he said. "Wait, I've got it; a campaign he'll love: 'Heineken Tarwebok. You're soaking in it.' "

I lost the next battle, which involved a minor reference in the "launch plan" Dolan was preparing for the sales force. In it, direction was given to position Heineken Tarwebok on supermarket and package store shelves right next to regular Heineken lager. I disagreed, for image reasons. If the object of the exercise was to gain the attention of existing microbrew drinkers, why not position the brand among the micros and specialties, where they were more likely to see it, and (hopefully) more likely to be intrigued by the fact Heineken had a product in their favorite section? Further, wasn't it placement right next to its parent brand—and, possibly, Heineken's other line extension, Special

Dark—only likely to reinforce the notion that Heineken was just another mass producer of beers? Dolan reiterated what he'd said before: we were going to have to agree to disagree. And this time Eric Morham got into the act and declared Dolan's version of the launch plan the final word. We were now officially working at cross purposes: the marketing strategy was designed to boost Heineken's image even at the cost of potential Heineken Tarwebok sales, and the sales strategy was to position Heineken Tarwebok for the most possible exposure—right where it was most likely to draw consumers away from its parent brand.

With our creative and media ready to go by summer's end, we awaited the October arrival of the first Heineken Tarwebok shipment. Knowing that the support (even though it was greater than $2 per case for the 175,000-case equivalent we had ordered, or about four times higher than the Heineken brand's roughly $.50-per-case advertising expenditure) was not going to go very far, we hoped that the press would pick up on Heineken's new bock offering and spread our message a bit further.

The press did become enamored with a small bock introduction that fall; unfortunately it was that of our nemesis, Jim Koch. His Sam Adams Triple Bock was yet another stroke of marketing genius: it was heavy enough to impress the most hard-core micro drinker, it came in corked bottles, and it carried a whopping $100-per-case price tag. In other words, it wasn't just the bock of the month; it had *unique selling propositions.* Because Koch knew that it wasn't enough just to jump on the bandwagon—you have to offer some point of difference—he again managed to get all the press attention he could handle: the brand was written about in national magazines such as *Fortune* and *Newsweek,* and the Samuel Adams myth grew even stronger.

Koch guesstimated his product needs, as Heineken did, but he lowballed. He brewed and aged only thirty thousand cases of Samuel Adams Triple Bock. This not only helped him avoid potential complaints from wholesalers about being pressured to take in too much, it created a sort of scarcity, the sort that makes people believe a product is in demand, that it is "hot." Heineken USA, on the other hand, got wildly optimistic and ordered nearly six times Koch's quantity. As most Heineken distributors already handled a number of specialty brands, and most specialty brands are low-volume sellers, the lack of a unique selling proposition made it tough for them to have any real interest in selling Heineken Tarwebok.

So, for the most part, they didn't. Though the average number of cases shipped to each of the twenty-eight states where Tarwebok was sold in 1994 was only about 6,250, the brand was a stiff. The company wouldn't release final sales figures, but one Heineken USA executive said privately that the company's cost for destroying unsold bottled Heineken Tarwebok and shipping unsold kegs back to Holland ran to $800,000, or twice the total advertising budget for the brand. (The fact that any *kegged* Tarwebok was brought in illustrates a mind-boggling lack of experience. It's extremely rare to find accounts that will take even unknown *domestic* brands on as draft beers, because the commitment is to 15 gallons, rather than the 2.25 gallons involved in stocking a case of twelve-ounce bottles. Why would any bar manager commit a tap line to an unheard-of, expensive, imported specialty?)

Even at a hundred bucks a case, Jim Koch sold out of Samuel Adams Triple Bock.

I suspect my biggest clue that I would not be part of the Heineken USA marketing team much past the launch of Tarwebok came in the form of a private memo from Vuyk to Foley, which was slipped to me by a concerned secretary. In it Vuyk outlined his plan for the next phase of departmental transition, a phase that no longer included an advertising director. That explained why, as my former boss had experienced a few months earlier, I was no longer being given much in the way of things to do. That explained why Vuyk barely even spoke to me anymore. I saw no reason to fight. I used the vague contractual obligation the company had to me to negotiate an exit package in late September 1994.

A few days before I left what was still officially (until January 1, 1995) Van Munching & Company, Vuyk called me into his office. Now that I was leaving of my own volition, he was feeling friendly. He offered one last sketch: a four-paned window, which was meant to help me along the road to self-realization as I sought a new career. When he was done sketching and filling in the panes, I pulled out a pen and began drawing on my pad. I sketched for him the very first truth table I learned in Introductory Logic at college. It was also a four-paned proposition, showing why it makes more sense to believe in God than not to—basically because if He exists and one doesn't believe, there's literally hell to pay, and if He doesn't exist and one believes, it's just a little wasted devotion. Vuyk was perplexed.

"Why did you draw that?" he asked.

"I just felt bad . . . you always have something to draw for me, and I never return the favor," I told him, and smiled. It was awfully childish of me, and it made me feel a whole lot better.

It was also the last time he ever spoke to me.

About two months later my equally assignment-starved brother negotiated a package of his own. The last two Van Munchings were out the door before our name officially came off it.

Which meant we missed the full-blown repositioning of Heineken and Amstel Light.

Actually, Amstel Light's repositioning came first, and it was in the works from the day a brand manager was chosen. (The works experienced a slight bump in the summer of 1994, when the cigarette woman was abruptly replaced by a Russian who'd worked at an office of Procter & Gamble in the former Soviet Union. No beer experience there, either.) As a brand, Amstel Light was confusing to the marketing team; it was the only imported light beer with any real sales volume, and as such there was no clear competitive set for comparison purposes. Measured against what other imported light brands there were, such as Molson Light and Corona Light, Amstel Light was huge. Compared with domestic lights, though, its roughly 350,000 barrels was a drop in the ocean: in 1995 *Impact* put category leader Bud Light at 18 million barrels. In addition to the competitive set problem, the Amstel Light positioning that had been used since the launch (the only light beer that offered imported taste) seemed too esoteric for Vuyk and his people, and they set about to find an approach with broader appeal.

A research project, titled "Qualitative-Diagnostic Research into the Perception and Meaning of Communication Possibilities for Amstel Light," was undertaken in December 1994. The project had three basic goals: to understand the perception and usage of light beer as a category, to understand how Amstel Light was perceived within that context, and to test some possible ad campaigns for Amstel Light. As happens with many research projects, the final report got bogged down in feverishly pitched bouts of ten-cent psychology. The reasons for light beer drinking, for example, were mapped into four quadrants and drawn schematically (where the Repressive/Existential Anxiety-Driven Quadrant bore this legend: "Searching for control over situations through the accepted ritual values of beer").

Among the four types of drinkers the report identified—the open relaxation group, the normatives, the control-seeking group, and the self-assured group—the perception of Amstel Light showed little variance. Most felt that it had more flavor than its domestic competition and correctly identified it as imported and therefore more expensive. Two of the groups called it preppy in nature, another called it "uptown," and the fourth used the word "reputable" to describe it.

Essentially the report found what we'd known for years: people drank for all kinds of reasons, including the "search for control through accepted ritual values" reason—which was more eloquently stated in the *Cheers* theme song, "Where Everybody Knows Your Name"—and people who drank light saw Amstel Light as a fuller-bodied, imported alternative. It struck me as bizarre overkill that to reach these conclusions, the marketing team actually asked focus group respondents what animal Amstel Light would be if Amstel Light were an animal. (Lion and racehorse seemed to be the most common responses, in case you were wondering.)

But whatever was learned relating to the first two objectives of the research was rendered meaningless by the approach to the third. In determining how to communicate a brand personality to consumers, the report identified an overall creative strategy already defined by the marketing team: "To create a brand image that reinforces Amstel Light's cachet and specialness while making it more approachable and fun." My *Random House College Dictionary* defines "accessible" as "easy to approach, enter, speak with, or use." This was exactly what Amstel Light should *not* be, for some pretty obvious reasons. Chiefly, Amstel Light was created to be an *aspirational* version of what is traditionally already seen as an accessible category. Millions had been spent to make Amstel Light be recognized in just the way the respondents had done: as a fuller-bodied, classier, *and more expensive* light. The brand's point of difference, again, its *unique selling proposition,* was what you might call a certain inaccessibility to the average drinker: if you drank Amstel Light, you felt it reflected your decidedly above average taste in things.

The advertising message that was found most promising in the research's report, a campaign with the theme "A light beer for a heavy world," was chosen and produced for airing in spring 1995. With a very off-center (and truly funny) visual style, using quick cuts to show the drudgery of everyday life, the commercial used the following voice-over:

> So there's 365 days in a year, 250 of which you're working for the rent, about 98 whole days of sleeping, another 6 doing things you don't want for someone else who doesn't appreciate it. One day brushing your teeth, 2 days combing your hair, 3 entire days standing in elevators, and 4 days waiting in line at the DMV, which, believe it or not, leaves only 1 measly day to sit back and have a beer. So make it a great-tasting one. And since there's not

> much time left to work out, make it a light. Amstel Light. A light beer for a heavy world.

The spot was clever, eye-catching—and completely generic. Coors Light could've run the same thing, as could Bud Light, Miller Lite, or any other brand, as the only product benefit offered was "great-tasting." The word "imported" didn't come into it at all, as ad critic Bob Garfield pointed out in his *Advertising Age* review of the work:

> It is cool, charming, seriously flawed advertising which bizarrely squanders bona fide, unique attributes such as most marketers in a similar competitive position would sell their mothers' kidneys to own. While personality often, by default, becomes the brand essence, it is of only secondary importance when something more specific and valuable defines the product in the consumer's mind.
>
> Import flavor, for instance.

The marketing team decided that in addition to the new brand personality, Amstel Light was in need of a packaging make-over and perhaps a product reformulation. The new packaging arrived in the fall of 1995. While the basic content of the labeling remained the same, the thin, gold-shadowed white script in which the lowercase word "light" was written was replaced by a bolder, capitalized, and underlined all-white version. The basic red and white of the label, which had been highlighted with gold, now had an infusion of the heavy black favored by domestic draft beers, along with a lot more gold. The six-pack and case carton, which had always been primarily red, now carried an unattractive light yellowish gold as the dominant color. (In other words, Amstel Light outer packaging now faced a problem familiar to the owners of light-colored automobiles: every smudge of dirt, every scratch the packaging received along the distribution chain showed.)

One senior Heineken USA executive, who argued unsuccessfully against the packaging change, repeatedly asked a simple question of the Amstel Light brand team: "When consumers repeatedly tell us that the packaging is one of the biggest selling points the brand has, why would we change it?" No one ever answered him.

Shortly before my departure in October 1994, I overheard the conversation of two of Vuyk's recent hires relating to the sales of Amstel Light. One predicted at least 10 percent annual growth for the brand, "now that there's an actual marketing strategy." The other predicted even more. Amstel Light's growth, which had hovered in the 5 percent range over the previous three years, fell to 2.5 percent in 1995, according to company figures.

I had left the company bearing my name just before the Amstel Light relaunch; my father-in-law left the company bearing his just after. The difference was that I jumped ship . . . and Bob Fiore was pushed.

Fiore's partner of ten years, Wilder Baker, handled the account servicing end of Warwick, Baker & Fiore; Bob handled the creative end. Baker was the preppy WASP from the old school of advertising, the kind of guy who made windy pronouncements about "the client/agency partnership" over expensive steak lunches. Fiore was the feisty Italian who ordered his lunches in from the local deli so he could spend his lunch hour carrying on emotional debates with his staff about which piece of music an ad they were writing should use. Baker was a Yale man; Bob was a guy who grew up on the streets of Brooklyn.

For a time, the odd pairing worked. Baker appealed to clients who were accustomed to the old-boy network, those who liked to have their egos stroked by a well-bred man. (Baker, though he appeared to have little other function in the agency, was apparently adept at stroking.) Fiore appealed to more energetic clients, those who didn't mind being argued with or pushed to see something in a different way. Each one could come to the fore or step into the background depending upon which client they were dealing with. Fiore played front and center with Van Munching & Company under Leo—not because he was my father-in-law, but because he was one of the first ad men my father had ever met who didn't kiss his ass and because he was clearly passionate about his work.

After buying out the retiring John Warwick some years earlier, Baker and Fiore became equal partners. They had an equal say in agency decisions and chose to give a nominal amount of votes to a third person (their chief financial officer, Ron Fierman), to be used if they ever got hopelessly deadlocked on an issue. When this arrangement was set up, Fiore had assumed that he and Baker would do their best to work things out between themselves before going to Fierman. He was wrong.

The partners knew of Vuyk's plan to take one of the brands out of their agency as early as October 1994. Not only had they read the speculation in the advertising trade press that my departure spelled trouble for them; I had flat out told them even before I decided to leave that they would in all likelihood lose the Heineken account. I'd bought them a little time—because I felt the decision to take Heineken away was ridiculous considering the brand's continued strong growth—by appealing to Foley's sense of fairness on my way out the door. (He was so relieved that I had decided to leave quietly that I suspect he'd have agreed to just about anything.)

Once I was no longer the ad director, Baker became more of the point man on the Heineken USA business. As advertising (such as the Amstel Light campaign just described) was more and more shaped by research project than by creative thinking, there wasn't as much need for Fiore's leadership. Perhaps more important, Baker's general acquiescence seemed to suit Foley and Vuyk much better.

So it was Baker, and not Fiore, who had more client contact with the folks at Heineken USA when word came down early in 1995 that an agency review process for Heineken was still very much in the cards. Stunned, Baker looked for a way to hang on to the biggest-spending brand on his agency's roster.

At a meeting in Heineken USA's offices in May 1995, he revealed the lengths to which he would go to keep the Heineken business. When it became clear that a decision had been made, Baker "blurted out that he was making a management change," said George Kahl, Heineken USA's executive vice president. "It was pretty clear he had decided that Fiore's tie to the Van Munching family was a problem for Foley . . . though I sincerely doubt he was right." At the meeting, he told Heineken USA's assembled leadership that Fiore was being replaced.

Problem was, he hadn't yet told Fiore.

In early June Baker asked the still unsuspecting Fiore out for a drink one afternoon. Baker told his partner that he felt the agency hadn't been growing as well as he'd hoped; Bob agreed. Baker said that perhaps the time had come for them to rethink their partnership; Bob agreed. Baker dropped a bomb: Though he assured Bob that he'd been "like a brother," and that his decision was "only business," Baker had already, with Fierman's help, voted Fiore out of his own agency. Bob, the consummate *Godfather* fan, told me later that he was tempted to ask Baker which brother he'd been like . . . Fredo? (For you nonaficionados of *The Godfather,* Fredo was the brother Al Pacino ordered shot in the back of the head.)

Oh, and there was more: Bob's replacement had already been chosen.

Fiore sat stunned while his partner of a decade informed him that he had a week to hammer out a financial settlement with the agency. At the end of that week, Baker was planning on announcing Bob's successor to the press.

Though Bob could've fought his partner legally, it was an option that didn't appeal to him on two levels: first, a lengthy legal skirmish might have destroyed the agency financially, jeopardizing the jobs of many of Bob's close friends. Second, what was really the point? After Baker had shown himself for the man he was, why on earth would Bob want to remain his partner? As he began exit negotiations, Bob found himself torn between two conflicting reactions: great relief that he was extricating himself from such an underhanded partner—quite profitably, to boot—and deep self-recrimination that he hadn't seen it coming. Both reactions gave way to mounting anger as Baker started pressuring him to move his exit along, saying that word was leaking out about Fiore's replacement and he couldn't hold off an announcement much longer. Though Bob didn't participate in that announcement, he was too much of a gentleman to do anything to dampen Baker's moment.

I wasn't.

I was flat out pissed about Baker's treatment of his partner, especially considering the loyalty Bob had shown to him in the time I'd known them. Unbeknownst to Baker, Bob had been approached by a whole group of top Warwick people just a few years before; they'd pleaded with him to take over the agency and oust Baker, whom they argued vehemently was "an empty suit." Bob had dismissed their request out of hand. His loyalty was rewarded with a cowardly betrayal.

Figuring that Baker was timing the announcement of Kevin O'Neill as Fiore's replacement for late in the week, so it would be picked up by the weekly trade magazines, which came out on Monday (any earlier and the daily ad columns would've scooped them and dampened their interest in the story), I had a little time to gather and release some news myself. I leaked the details of the upcoming Heineken agency review to *Adweek,* knowing that it was a much bigger story than a management change at a midsize agency like Warwick. I did it for no other reason than to rob Baker of any positive press coming out of his little "coup." I did it so that instead of waking up on Monday morning and seeing headlines in the trades about his victory in a rigged power struggle, Wilder Baker would have to see headlines about his biggest account loss in years. It was petty of me; it was mean, underhanded, vindictive, and rotten. It was also *incredibly* gratifying.

(A postscript, of sorts: With Fiore gone, the execution of the Amstel Light "A light beer for a heavy world" campaign got stranger and stranger. One sample headline from an Amstel Light magazine ad, post-Fiore: "If olive oil is made from olives and corn oil is made from corn, what is baby oil made from?" In June 1996 Heineken USA pulled that account away from the agency as well.

Baker, who according to a reporter wanted to wait until they'd picked up a new piece of business to officially change the name of the agency, wouldn't get a chance for nearly a year after Fiore's departure . . . when the newly rechristened Warwick Baker O'Neill won the account of a used-car company.)

The agency review meant a postponement of the repositioning of Heineken until 1996. In the meantime, an evolution of the "Just being the best is enough" advertising had been developed by Warwick for 1995, dropping the "no blimp with our name on it" approach in favor of a more direct sociability theme. The spots focused on friendship, positioning Heineken as a brand that reflected the high regard in which the spots' characters held each other. For example, one spot featured a man's reminiscences of his lifelong friend Jake, with whom he'd once dreamed of playing in a rock band. The tag line: "With a friend as good as Jake, shouldn't you have a Heineken?"

Though more contemporary in its approach than previous campaigns, the "With a friend as good as . . ." work still put Heineken on a pedestal, still positioned the brand as something to be aspired to. For the meantime, Heineken had escaped the odd logic that had befallen the Amstel Light brand—the belief that to move more cases of beer, the brand had to widen its appeal by embracing a more generic beer imagery.

Unfortunately, the brand didn't entirely escape some of the more generic ideas in packaging.

Aside from the cans that Leo Jr. snuck past his father in the seventies, Heineken had introduced only one new container in its sixty-plus-year history: the Kingsize bottle, which held 21.6 ounces of beer. First imported in 1992, Heineken Kingsize had a built-in market among ethnic drinkers, where a similar package from Beck's (called the Bomber, which had unfortunate connotations considering Beck's German origin) had from all reports done quite nicely. Though the large-bottle concept had originated with Japanese beers, and had initially been an on-premise item, it had developed into a status symbol among some Hispanics and African Americans. We steered the Heineken Kingsize package toward the off-premise and found a solid market for it in the delis and package stores of major cities.

Part of the allure of the Kingsize was that it held a perceived monetary benefit: it did not cost twice as much as a twelve-ounce bottle, although it held nearly twice as much liquid. (In the New York area, a typical spread might be $1.19 for a twelve-ounce to $1.49 for a Kingsize.) The economies of scale made the Kingsize cheaper for us—the larger bottle wasn't much more expensive than the twelve-ounce to produce, and the higher concentration of liquid to packaging made it more economical to ship—and thus we were able to keep the Kingsize at an attractive price point.

Not so of the seven-ounce packaging introduced in 1995. As Eric Morham had first predicted in 1991 (call it a self-fulfilling prophecy, as he was the new packaging's chief backer when it finally arrived), Heineken jumped on the minibottle craze popularized by domestic brands like Rolling Rock. (Rolling Rock offered a terrific gimmick in bars; their "Bucket of Rocks" consisted of a number of the little seven-ouncers packed in ice in a Rolling Rock–logoed tin bucket.)

For Heineken, seven-ounce packaging had a serious handicap: its pricing. Unlike the Kingsize, which was cheaper to produce and ship on a per-ounce basis than the standard twelve-ounce, the seven-ounce was *more* expensive. More packaging, more weight to ship; there was no way to build in a good profit margin without pushing the pricing to near twelve-ounce levels.

Though gimmicks like Rolling Rock's "Bucket of Rocks" had established the seven-ounce bottle as an on-premises phenomenon, Heineken USA didn't want their minibottle sold in bars. They were afraid that it would draw overly from the (more profitable) standard packaging and reduce the liquid production in Holland. Here's why: Bar managers were likely to use seven-ounce bottles to boost profit, by charging the same price for a seven as for a twelve and discontinuing sales of the twelve. If their average drinker only wanted to shell out for three beers, he'd end up buying twenty-one ounces instead thirty-six. Now Heineken has not only lost volume, but possibly profit as well, because the margins on seven-ounce were not terrific.

So seven-ounce was decreed an off-premise product, where the savings *would* be passed on to the consumer and theoretically result in more quantity bought. What no one at Heineken USA counted on was sticker shock. Rather than bring seven-ounce in in an eight-pack or twelve-pack (which would at least make it more difficult for the average consumer to compare pricing and realize what a premium he was paying for a gimmicky package), the company went the six-pack route. While a standard Heineken six-pack might be priced on the supermarket shelf at $5.79, a six of seven-ounce might be only $.50 less. Not a tough decision for the average person standing in the supermarket aisle. Nearly twice as much liquid for about 10 percent more money. The seven-ounce was a flop of Heineken Tarwebok proportions, adding less than the twelve-ounce equivalent of one hundred thousand cases to Heineken's total of 1995 volume. When it was discontinued at year's end, nearly as much as had been sold throughout the year was still sitting in wholesaler warehouses. A Heineken USA sales executive admitted that the package hadn't reached even 10 percent of its first year's sales projections.

Having failed on two external counts—a line extension and a new package—the marketing team finally turned its attention to the flagship itself, only now without Vuyk at the helm. Vuyk had been fired in spring 1995—something that didn't surprise me, considering that Foley had asked during my exit negotiations if I might stay if Vuyk left—and Foley searched for a replacement, a task he told one employee was "the biggest decision" of his career. At least one of the finalists for Vuyk's VP/marketing job hailed from another beer importer, a sign that Foley might finally be recognizing the benefits of industry experience. It was not to be. Steve Davis hailed from Pepsi.

The Ries column I'd passed to Vuyk over a year earlier would prove to be scarily accurate about Heineken USA: the new folks, though their flagship brand was in terrific health, would take about twenty-four months to change the packaging, the advertising agency, and the marketing strategy.

Wells Rich Greene BDDP, the ad agency that replaced Warwick Baker & Fiore, revealed the final step in the repositioning of the brand early in 1996, with their maiden ad campaign for Heineken.

Actually, it was two campaigns. For about a month in some major cities, posters went up on phone kiosks and at bus shelters featuring a red star on a green background. That was it. No copy, no brand identification. This was called a teaser campaign, as it was meant to generate curiosity and intrigue. The consumer was supposed to wonder what it was for. The belief, at least within the halls of Heineken USA during the early days of the campaign's development, was that the red star could be established as an icon representing Heineken, in the same way the swoosh represented Nike. (Of course, it never occurred to anyone working on the red-star-as-icon project that Nike spent many years and hundreds of millions pushing their distinctive swoosh before ever allowing it to appear alone in an ad.) During the second phase of the campaign, in which sentences were added to posters to heighten curiosity (such as "How I wonder what you are" or "Here's something to look at while you use the phone"), one execution bore the following self-delusional line of copy: "It's not a Nike ad."

Considering the Pepsi background of Steve Davis, the man Foley hired to head up the Heineken USA marketing department, it's perhaps not a surprise that I spied an odd coincidence on a New York City bus one spring day in 1996. Along the side, the bus carried a teaser ad for Heineken: the red star on the green background, but no mention of the brand name. Along the back there was another teaser ad, this one bearing only the familiar circular—and equally wordless—Pepsi logo.

Along with the outdoor, and a similar print campaign, a television teaser ad was produced. In it, viewers saw the side of a building being painted green with a large red star, while "Twinkle Twinkle Little Star" was played on a children's piano. Again, no mention of Heineken, and again, this was meant to be intriguing.

What it ended up being was problematic, for a few reasons. First, the red star was already equated with other things, as I indicated earlier: Macy's, Pellegrino . . . and Communism. Ad critic Bob Garfield related his "overwhelmingly negative visceral reaction" to the spot. *Brandweek* reported the concern of Miami-area wholesalers that the campaign "could antagonize South Florida's Cuban-Americans." The second problem was that a red star on a green background just wasn't particularly intriguing. *Brandweek* beer writer Gerry Khermouch recalled taking an informal poll among associates and friends, asking them, "Gee, who do you think is behind that red star stuff?" Not one of the people he asked showed any interest in the answer.

Interestingly, Heineken USA had had a strong indication that the star was a losing proposition even before the campaign started. In a research project commissioned to test the appeal of Wells Rich's work, the red star wasn't embraced by the respondents, some of whom called it "gimmicky" and the approach "immature." By way of defending the strategy, the project pointed out that "although the star isn't seen as a good symbol because of the different connotations, the building-up idea is attractive to a lot of respondents."

The decision was made to downplay the star-as-icon in the second phase of the 1996 television advertising, which established a completely new personality for Heineken.

Wells Rich prepared their first full-blown Heineken campaign in an unorthodox way. The agency held "Heineken Nights" at bars across the country and, in return for providing the beer, got consumers to agree to have their conversations taped. From the transcripts, the agency fashioned a number of thirty-second ad scripts, which would be rerecorded by actors. The final spots would run the conversations as voice-overs while showing a continuous locational shot; for instance, one featured a neon sign outside a bar while another looked across the top of a bar in a strobe-lit nightclub. Without on-screen actors, the spots were cheap to produce in quantity.

At the beginning of each spot, superimposed words were used to explain the location, like "Lansdowne St., Boston, Jan. 20, 10:04 P.M." (In one of the more blatant instances of client ass kissing I've seen, Wells Rich supered one spot "the Dolan Wedding, East Hampton" to commemorate the impending Long Island nuptials of the Heineken brand manager.) A second super explained the concept behind the campaign: "Their words. Their beer. It's all true." A third provided the sell while a shot of a Heineken bottle flashed on the screen: "True to the original recipe since 1886." Other supers throughout served as humorous or ironic counterpoints to the conversations; in one, the rebuffed advances of an obnoxious jerk in a disco elicited this: "So close that time."

If Heineken USA was attempting to distance itself from the Heineken advertising of the past, it succeeded completely. Aside from the super about being true to the original recipe—which was, in fact, inaccurate, as Heineken had been reformulated a few years earlier to remove the corn—there was neither discussion of the product's benefits nor mention of its number one status. The conversations themselves, though sometimes funny, were not always particularly classy. In one spot, a woman's use of the f-word was bleeped out . . . twice.

The outdoor and print versions of the campaign, where the red star teaser had gotten its first exposure, stuck with the star and added large lines of copy, again supposedly uttered by real people. They ranged from the silly ("I know where Amsterdam is. It's right between Broadway and Columbus") to the vaguely offensive ("What do they call people from Holland . . . Holes?"). At least one attempted to work a little brewing discussion into the campaign, with an odd result. Its quote, "Bottom fermentation . . . that's where the action is," begged the question of whether just the person who uttered it didn't realize that almost all major beer brands are bottom fermented or the folks at the agency/client didn't as well.

The radio campaign, built around alleged phone calls to a 1-800 number set up by Heineken USA, went furthest to dispel any sense that Heineken was an upscale beer. Among the executions: A man recounts his friend's habit of saving food money by eating only grocery store samples; a heavily accented *New Yawkah* talks about the couple she watched break up in a grocery store . . . during which she refers to the product as "Heineken's"; a woman with Valley-girl inflections ("like, totally") recalls a big-mouthed friend ruining a potential double date. Oddly, the words "imported by" had been removed from even the mandatory identification at the end of each spot; now the announcer simply said "Heineken USA, White Plains, New York."

The disparaging remarks test respondents had made about the red star didn't seem to dissuade Davis from sanctioning a catalog full of mostly wearable items, some highlighting Heineken's U.S. Open tennis sponsorship. Once again taking a page from his Pepsi playbook, where brand-logoed items became the centerpiece of the "Pepsi Stuff" program, Davis oversaw the creation of a number of Heineken items, which differed from the Pepsi things mostly in that they didn't actually bear any brand identification. The common traits of the items offered by 1-888-HEINSHOP were their emerald green color (not usually a popular color choice for expensive sweater vests and sweatshirts) and the red star. One radio station executive, sent a box of HEINSHOP items *gratis,* quickly dubbed it the "Fidel Castro gift package."

(The insider, ego-satisfaction aspect of the advertising campaign took a strange twist during the U.S. Open, when a television ad was fashioned around the dearth of Heineken promotional wearables actually seen at the event. In the spot, a man asks a companion, "Where are the bandannas? I mean, everyone loved the bandannas at the distributor's meeting." Aside from being painfully obtuse, and therefore completely meaningless to the average viewer, the spot was notable for the identity of the voice-over actor: Michael Silver, a Wells Rich VP.)

One Heineken USA marketing executive privately labeled the HEINSHOP catalog "a complete disaster. Who did Davis think was going to buy a green canvas director's chair with a red star on it for $42.95?"

For the second time in under two years, *Advertising Age*'s critic Bob Garfield wondered why Heineken USA was so intent on walking away from established, envied brand attributes:

> Nearly as mind boggling [as the fact the Heineken Night guests allowed their words to be used on television] is the idea that Heineken would identify itself with these unhappy, inarticulate, semiliterate, underemployed, sexually frustrated and generally embarrassing characters.

As was the case in the most recent Amstel Light advertising, the word "imported" was nowhere to be found in the new Heineken campaign, which I found more than a little ironic, considering all that had happened at Van Munching & Co./Heineken USA over the last few years. The irony is this: When the company was run by an American and a bunch of beer business lifers, the imagery was all dictated by the brand's status as an import and at times probably erred on the side of foreignness. Now that the company is in the hands of foreigners and marketing men who've just come to the beer business, the imagery couldn't be more domestic.

Change is a constant in business. As a shark will drown if it stops moving forward through the water, a company that does not keep up momentum by making constant small course corrections—and even major course corrections, when they're indicated—will eventually stagnate and fail. The key, of course, is to pay attention to the consumer. In the end, his is the only opinion that matters. When a brand is successful, reactive change is the best way to keep it strong.

*Pro*active change, however, is mostly egotistical and foolish. It says, "I know better than the consumer what he wants." For sixty years Heineken had done quite well in the U.S. with one basic image and one straightforward message: quality and quality. Change was a constant, from the way the company distributed its portfolio of brands to the methods in which it communicated the images of those brands. What *didn't* change over the decades was the general perception that Heineken was a superior beer; its importedness and quality justified its higher price tag. When that perception was threatened, as it was by Jim Koch and others in the late eighties, corrections were made. The brand survived and went on to prosper in the early nineties.

With all due respect to my grandfather, my father, and the hundreds who worked for them over the years, keeping Heineken viable as a brand—indeed, keeping it far and away the largest-selling imported beer—was not brain surgery. It was a task meant for people of common sense, people willing to pay attention to the information they had access to every day, from every bar in every city in the country. It did not require focus groups or management training seminars. It required an ability to learn from experience. More than that, it required experience.

I'm not sure what baffles me more about the folks running Heineken USA. Is it the fact that they spend so much time and effort chasing after researched answers to questions rather than applying common sense or the fact that once they have their answers, they tend to ignore them? The Heineken and Amstel Light campaigns running when they took the reins of the company were subjected to qualitative research even though the word from the field was good and sales of both brands were increasing at a healthy rate. When the research came in and pointed out that the campaigns were very much right for their respective brands, Heineken USA . . . changed them. Tarwebok, a product common sense should have told them was too little, too late, died on the shelf, costing the company hundreds of thousands of dollars. Above the protests of at least one experienced company executive, they brought in Heineken seven-ounce bottles, which failed miserably. Amstel Light, newly repackaged and saddled with a generic beer ad campaign, saw its growth cut in half.

At some point they may wake up to the fact that change for the sake of change doesn't tend to work. Perhaps their first clue came from their own sales and financial reports for the first half of 1996. The percent of growth was fine: Heineken's 9.3 percent advance was still in keeping with the 10 percent annual bumps enjoyed over the last few years of Van Munching & Company's stewardship. It was *where* the growth was coming from—and not coming from—that should have been worrisome. For the first time in memory, *all* growth was coming from outside of the Northeast (traditionally Heineken's largest region, accounting for over 50 percent of the brand's sales). Coupled with two other factors—the whopping 10.6 percent decline in the brand's profitability over the previous year and the big percentage gains by packaging traditionally used in price promotions (like twelve-pack cans)—this suggests that the company was manufacturing growth by price discounting; in other words, forcing product into the marketplace to keep volume numbers up rather than concentrating on building more profitable business.

In the meantime, it seems to be business as usual at Heineken USA, where even the most recent experience has no resonance. Over the course of 1996, the company flirted with a number of ideas for new introductions, including a possible change in Heineken's twelve-ounce bottle—to a long-neck—and an Amstel Bock. After months of debate, they ended the year by announcing an even worse idea; Amstel Beer. How else to more efficiently cannibalize Heineken and damage the stature of Amstel Light? And, if the reports that Amstel will be brewed in Canada (so that they can price it lower than their other brands) are proved correct, Heineken USA will have hit the trifecta of inane business thinking: Not only will they have introduced a European-style lager to compete with Heineken, not only will they have introduced a flagship that will immediately negate the benefits Amstel Light enjoyed as a stand-alone light beer brand, they will also have managed to reduce their margins in the bargain.

Part Five

Dispatches from the Front

15

The Search for the Next Big Thing, II: Dry Ice in the 'Hood

If the dawn of the micro age caused some concern among importers, it created abject panic for the marketers of superpremium domestic beers. Imports had spent the first half of the eighties pushing higher-priced domestic brews down toward a state of insignificance; micros and contract brews threatened them with extinction.

Michelob, 66.2 percent of the superpremium category in 1988, had the most to worry about. It had already lost 46 percent of its sales in the previous eight years, from 8 million barrels in 1980 to 4.3 in 1988. The halls of Anheuser-Busch headquarters were abuzz with three words: "What to do?"

The chief problem for Michelob, according to one executive there at the time, was its lack of what marketers call a unique selling proposition—there was no particular reason for consumers to spend the extra money for it. "Here you have a superpremium brand that has no taste difference; it was all marketing . . . you know, the funny-shaped bottle." (Michelob's brown bottle featured a neck that went from the bottle's widest point to its mouth in a straight line, unlike the traditional curved-shoulder, straight-necked bottle.) As funny-shaped bottles (and cans) were now common, it was clear by 1988 that without a substantial price drop, the salvation of the Michelob franchise lay in the brand's taste.

As Miller had done three years earlier (coming up with the successful Miller Genuine Draft), Anheuser-Busch looked to Japan for inspiration.

Less than two years earlier the Japanese beer market had been electrified by the introduction of something called dry beer; by 1988 it had captured fully one-third of all beer sales there. Dry beer was sharper in taste than traditional lager and carried less aftertaste. To create it, Japanese brewers had developed a technique of brewing longer at lower temperatures, which allowed more of the malt and rice to be converted into fermentable sugar. Dry was a cousin of light beer, in the sense that more fermentable sugar meant fewer calories and more alcohol. In Japan the "more alcohol" end of the equation provided the segment with its selling proposition: dry beer meant more kick.

In adapting dry beer for U.S. purposes, Anheuser-Busch shied away from the kick and leaned on the "sharper taste, less aftertaste" end of the equation. A-B had altered the dry-brewing process to avoid producing a beer with a higher alcoholic content. Consequently, when Michelob Dry was introduced in 1988, the average consumer had no clue as to what product benefit the name "dry" promised. Where light beer had clearly meant fewer calories, and draft beer had meant (whether it was marketing hype or not) on-tap taste in a bottle, dry had no clear connotation; taste claims were so common among beers within every segment that they were not paid much attention to. Miller, according to Jerome Schmutte, its director of strategic planning at the time, wasn't about to follow Anheuser-Busch into a category that consumers didn't understand. "[In Japan] the consumer said, 'If I buy a dry beer—this [they'd get more alcohol].' In this country the consumer said, 'If I buy a dry beer—what?' " Though Miller kept tabs on Michelob Dry's sales, the company was unconvinced the brand would do well.

But if Michelob Dry didn't have a clear selling point, it did have something else going for it: it tasted good. Though it didn't have the higher alcoholic content of traditional dry beers, Michelob Dry was smoother for the reduced sugar content and not so bitter in what little aftertaste it had. It was the perfect brand to grow slowly, through word of mouth. In 1989, its first full year of sales, it posted 1.5 million barrels; it was already 40 percent the size of its parent brand, whose sales had fallen to 3.8 million barrels. Though it was a hit on a small scale, Michelob Dry was unmistakably a hit.

For Anheuser-Busch, Michelob Dry was the first successful product introduction they'd had since the Beer Wars began that wasn't a copy of something someone else had done first, like light beer. August Busch's team of analysts were thrilled with the victory. Too thrilled. They wanted to squeeze some more volume from the segment, and quickly.

Jack MacDonough, a marketing vice president for Anheuser-Busch at the time, recalled the internal debate that developed over introducing a dry brand for the flagship. "There were a lot of people worried that this Michelob Dry was such a success that Coors Dry would come out, and Miller Dry would come out. [They said] let's come out with Bud Dry. And I said, if you want to make a bigger success out of this, if you want to protect yourself on a premium rather than superpremium price, drop the price of Michelob Dry. People love it, drop the price and it'll go through the roof."

The problem, MacDonough said, was the company analysts. Budweiser had had a bad summer in 1988, and to put the best face on the flagship's sales problems, the company had taken to referring to the percentage growth of the Budweiser *family* of brands, which included anything bearing the Bud name—such as the surging Bud Light. The analysts, along with Jerry Ritter, Anheuser-Busch's head of finance, favored leaving Michelob Dry where it was, pricewise, and creating Bud Dry, which would boost their precious Bud family volume. *And,* Ritter explained to MacDonough, the analysts would be upset with the company if it came in second with a premium-priced, flagship product. (In fact, Coors would announce a western launch of Coors Dry in 1991.) August placed his twenty-five-year-old son, August IV, in the brand manager spot and unleashed Bud Dry Draft. His decision to entrust a major Budweiser product to an untested brand manager, even though it was his offspring, would have serious ramifications for the company three years later, from a personnel standpoint.

MacDonough's fear was that the new product would destroy Michelob Dry, because Anheuser-Busch's distributors would say, in essence, "Hey, I have Bud Dry to push . . . now I'm going to make some real sales." He was also afraid that August Busch's plan to introduce the Budweiser version as Bud Dry Draft was only going to confuse consumers, because they equated draft brands with clear glass bottles, which the new product would not be packaged in. He was quickly proven correct on his initial fear. From Michelob Dry's high of 1.5 million barrels in 1989, it fell to 1.1 million in 1990, Bud Dry Draft's first full year on the market.

A cynic might say that the first sign the dry category as a whole was in trouble came at about the same time Michelob Dry started sinking. Analyst Robert Weinberg, the same former Anheuser-Busch executive who'd dubbed light beer "a fraud, it's people rationalizing," suggested to *Beverage Dynamics,* an industry trade magazine, how far-sighted his former company was with its introduction of Bud Dry: "Many brewers, who are now out of business, put themselves out of business by not realizing the importance of new products."

The second sign came in the advertising Anheuser-Busch approved for Bud Dry Draft. A humorous collection of unanswerable questions about the nature of life, the campaign's tag line was "Why ask Why? Try Bud Dry." By joking their way around it, but never answering, they highlighted the very problem Miller Brewing was afraid of:

consumers were asking what the point of dry beer was. The Bud Dry Draft ads seemed to say, "Don't ask." (In a wickedly funny parody, *Saturday Night Live* would skewer meaningless product extensions with a beer commercial of its own, for a fictional brand named Bud Gay.)

The third sign came in the form of the commanding share Anheuser-Busch held of the category. Though Coors came out with two drys of its own in 1991, Keystone Dry and Coors Dry, and Heileman had weighed in with at least four dry brands by as early as 1988, the joint Bud Dry/Michelob Dry share never dipped below 81 percent. What this meant was that no one else thought enough of the category to make a concerted effort to get into the fray: Coors never brought Coors Dry national, and Miller never got into the category at all.

Their mistrust of the potential was well placed: Bud Dry Draft's first full year was also its best, at 3.2 million barrels in sales. It declined steadily after that, as did the category. The 3.2 million it posted in 1990 accounted for just under 70 percent of the category's sales; in 1994 Bud Dry Draft's 1.2 million barrel gave it 75 percent of all dry beers sold.

Back at Anheuser-Busch headquarters in St. Louis, some of the very analysts who'd pressured August Busch and Jerry Ritter into backing a dry for Budweiser reacted the way MacDonough'd predicted they would: "You idiots, you've destroyed your Michelob Dry business."

Anheuser-Busch's hopes for dry to become a viable segment of the marketplace were understandable, if a bit on the wishful side. Growth in the major beer categories was all but nonexistent by 1990. Over the previous five years popular-priced brands had dipped as a category by 3.4 percent, premiums had lost 21 percent, and superpremiums stepped off the cliff with a whopping 46 percent decline. Of the major domestic beer categories tracked by *Impact Databank,* only two grew in that time. The first category was light beer, which was dominated by the Big Three. (In 1990 Miller Lite led the category with shipments of

19.9 million barrels, followed by a Bud Light with 11.8 million barrels and Coors Light with 11.6 million. The largest non–Big Three brand, Stroh's Old Milwaukee Light, sold 1.9 million barrels that year.)

The other domestic category showing growth was something that is sometimes referred to as "headache beer" for its ability to inflict a serious hangover. For marketers, though, malt liquor was a headache in a different way.

The term "malt liquor" connotes nothing except additional alcohol content; malt liquor is merely lager brewed (often cheaply) to be stronger. It is a name made necessary by the fact that some states will not allow beer with an alcoholic content greater than 5.5 percent by volume to be called beer. Like light beer and the Japanese version of dry beer, malt liquor is made by converting unfermentable dextrins to fermentable sugars, increasing the alcohol and decreasing the flavor that would result from the dextrins. As a style of beer, the recently published *Encyclopedia of Beer* described malt liquor as "an unseemly, poorly balanced product at best and may be described as basically light beer with high alcohol."

In other words, malt liquor is to beer what Thunderbird is to wine.

That analogy can conjure up a very specific racial image, and for good reason. As cheap wines are known as the drink of choice for the destitute (what not-so-polite society calls "winos"), malt liquors have long been identified with inner-city poverty. Thanks to the marketing efforts of a few brewers, they would become identified more specifically with black inner-city poverty.

One of the fastest-growing malt liquors in 1991 was Olde English "800," brewed by Pabst. Olde English had virtually created the higher-strength beer category in the sixties. The authors of the *Encyclopedia of Beer* claim that its alcoholic content was as high as 8.3 percent, 66 percent stronger than a full-bodied imported lager such as Heineken. Olde English overtook Stroh's Schlitz Malt Liquor and Heileman's Colt 45 in 1991 to lead the malt liquor category with sales of 1.7 million barrels.

Read that last sentence again and note an amazing fact: Unlike every other category in the domestic beer business, not one of the top three sellers in the malt liquor category came from the production lines of Anheuser-Busch, Miller, and Coors.

For a time, the reluctance of the Big Three to enter the malt liquor ring was based on the belief that there was nothing to be gained from it. Unlike light or dry, malt liquor was not a category Anheuser-Busch, Miller, or Coors could own by way of parenthood; malt liquor had been around long before the start of the Beer Wars in the mid-seventies. Of more importance, it was perfectly well serviced by established brands like Colt 45 and Schlitz Malt Liquor. As early as 1980 those two brands made up nearly 62 percent of the malt liquor market; add in then number three Olde English "800," and the share climbed past 83 percent.

Still, the segment was growing, and industry leaders couldn't stay away forever. Miller, bowing to repeated requests from distributors to add a malt liquor to its portfolio, launched a brand called Magnum in 1981, without much in the way of marketing support. Magnum never managed to reach higher than a 3 percent market share. With a mound of research that showed the typical malt liquor drinker as a young man who will eventually change over to beer as he gets older, they realized that there was little or no potential to build meaningful brand loyalty. Building and maintaining share in the segment, in other words, would involve a constant infusion of advertising dollars, to recruit new drinkers to replace those who had moved on. After the quick success of Lite, such an uphill battle in a segment that in 1980 constituted only 5.5 percent of all beer sales just didn't seem worth it.

Anheuser-Busch, still smarting over the public relations problems caused by the launch of Chelsea in 1978, didn't launch a malt liquor until 1985. As they hadn't liked being accused of pushing "training beer" to children, they were clearly uncomfortable with being seen as promoting a high-alcohol product in the inner city. If their distributors hadn't pleaded for years for a malt liquor, it's doubtful that Anheuser-Busch would ever have brewed one. Though their market share would reach 9 percent by 1990, Anheuser-Busch's King Cobra immediately ran up against the same problem Miller had foreseen: there was no way to build a following for a brand when the segment's consumers were constantly changing.

Because Magnum and King Cobra made up such a small percentage of their respective parents' sales volume, and the downside of failure was minimal, both Miller and Anheuser-Busch tried a different tack to raise the sales of their malt liquors; they dropped their prices. In doing so, they value-classified the segment and made it increasingly difficult for the makers of the leading brands to make any money. From 1988 to 1991 the average price for a premium brand such as Budweiser or Miller Genuine Draft rose from $2.95 to $3.40 per six-pack. The average import went from $5.05 a six-pack to $5.45. Malt liquor prices stayed dead flat, at $2.85.

As I said, it didn't matter much to Anheuser-Busch and Miller if their brands failed, but for smaller companies like the ailing G. Heileman, which produced Colt 45, and McKenzie River, which marketed a brand named St. Ides, the flat pricing hurt badly. Attempts to recruit new malt liquor drinkers would take on an air of desperation . . . and exploitation.

McKenzie River was run by Minott Wessinger, son of Fred Wessinger, the man who introduced the world to Olde English "800" in the sixties. The younger Wessinger found himself locked in a battle with the brand his father started; perhaps "turf war" is a better way of putting it, considering the methods St. Ides and Olde English would use to reach each other's customers.

Neither brand masked its appeal to inner-city youth. Olde English ran advertising in 1991 referring to itself with the slang expression "8 ball," which any city cop can tell you is a reference to an eighth of an ounce of drugs. Wessinger had hired rap star Ice Cube in 1990 to come up with radio commercials for St. Ides, at least one of which directly took on Olde English in unflattering terms: "Forget eight ball, that beer makes you hurl [vomit]." Both brands covertly played up their alcohol content in their advertising, as did most of their competitors. Olde

English ran billboards declaring "It's the Power," while rival Schlitz Red Bull referred to itself in its point-of-sale materials as "the Real Power!" St. Ides used promotional materials to declare "It'll blow you away" and "No. 1 strongest malt." In case any of its consumers missed the point, another rapper hired by McKenzie River sang the following in a St. Ides radio ad: "Too cold to hold/Bold like Smith & Wesson/ One quart and my whole thought's hiphop related/Write a rhyme and my pen's intoxicated."

St. Ides in particular drew the ire of public-interest groups in major cities, and state legislatures across the country, for the lengths it was willing to go to reach young blacks. An organization called the Citywide Coalition Against Alcohol Billboards protested in August 1991 in front of a suburban Chicago office complex where the actual brewer of St. Ides, G. Heileman, had an office. (Like Samuel Adams, St. Ides was contract brewed.) That same year the Oregon Liquor Control Commission banned the brand's posters on the grounds that they appeared to be gang related and aimed at underage drinkers. The gang-related imagery centered largely around St. Ides spokes-rapper Ice Cube, who appeared, often with a can of St. Ides in hand, in the 1991 film about gang violence, *Boyz N the Hood*. In one St. Ides spot Ice Cube rapped the line "Pour a little out on the curb for my homies," which *The Washington Post* called "[a reference] to the gang ritual in which liquor is poured to honor gang members who are in jail, or more often, as a memorial to gang members who have been killed."

New York State Attorney General Robert Abrams, early in 1992, announced that McKenzie River had agreed to stop running ads for St. Ides that claimed the brand increased male sexual prowess. (One of the lyrics in question: "[Get] your girl in the mood quicker, and get your jimmy thicker with St. Ides malt liquor.")

For the BATF, the action by local government agencies was an embarrassment, because it made the agency look as though it wasn't doing its job in policing the beer industry. Power claims in packaging and advertising had long been forbidden by agency rules, as had the use of disparaging comments, such as St. Ide's assertion that

Olde English "makes you hurl." Why hadn't the BATF been the first to step in?

Well, three reasons. First, the BATF approved all beer packaging in advance, but not advertising. Second, the advertising for malt liquor was not exactly mainstream in its exposure; one wonders how many BATF employees were listening to the same radio stations as young, inner-city blacks or doing their shopping in the inner-city bodegas where point-of-sale material for malt liquors was usually posted. Third, the agency really *wasn't* doing its job. For years within the malt liquor category, covert strength claims and strength imagery had been central to marketing. The blue bull charging through walls for Schlitz Malt Liquor was only one of the more well-known incarnations of that fact.

It took a public outcry over a new malt liquor in 1991 to make the agency start enforcing its own rules. G. Heileman, already the brewer of its own Colt 45 and McKenzie River's St. Ides, got BATF approval early in the year on another high-alcohol product to be marketed in the inner city: PowerMaster. For urban activists concerned about the targeting of disadvantaged blacks by breweries, PowerMaster was the lightning rod. The name not only had the strength claim in it; it was also vaguely racist for its use of the word "master." Even Heileman's fellow brewers wilted under the heat that PowerMaster was drawing to the industry. Anheuser-Busch executive and Beer Institute chairman Patrick Stokes wrote in June to Heileman's president, Thomas J. Rattigan, to ask the brewer to rethink its strategy with PowerMaster.

Amid a major public outcry, caused largely by the media attention created by a *Wall Street Journal* article on the brand, the BATF did an about-face and revoked its approval of PowerMaster's label shortly after Anheuser-Busch's letter arrived at Heileman. PowerMaster was pulled from the market, and a chastened BATF finally went after other brewers making claims about the strength of their products. A year later the brand formerly known as PowerMaster was repackaged and reintroduced . . . as Colt 45 Premium. The BATF approved it.

Though Heileman continued to brew St. Ides, it lost another contract-brewed malt liquor a year after PowerMaster was derailed, this time thanks to an act of Congress. Crazy Horse malt liquor, brewed under contract by Heileman and marketed by an outfit named Hornell Brewing, of Brooklyn, New York, drew fire from Native American groups, concerned that its packaging (a whiskey-shaped clear glass quart bottle that revealed the whiskeylike coloring of the product) and Sioux name made light of—or worse, encouraged—the historical problem Native Americans have had with alcohol. In April 1992 then Surgeon General Antonia Novello spoke publicly against the brand. In May Hornell agreed to alter the packaging but drew the line at changing the name. In September the U.S. Senate took the dramatic step of passing an amendment to an appropriations bill, already passed by the House, barring Hornell from selling the brand at all.

Though the public was outraged by the lengths marketers would go to sell malt liquor, one brewing executive blamed the incursion of Anheuser-Busch and Miller into the category and the downward pricing spiral they created when they discounted their brands. The executive suggested that the folks exploiting gang imagery and Native American drinking problems weren't being callous as much as they were acting out of desperation to stay in business: "The person [marketing] Crazy Horse wasn't a marketer; he was interested in staying alive." Though malt liquor survived the intense scrutiny by the BATF and others and continued to pick up market share as a category—it rose 27 percent between 1991 and 1994—the margins remain so low and the public relations risks so high that Anheuser-Busch and Miller continue to downplay their own malt liquor brands. Coors, which briefly introduced a brand called Turbo 1000 in 1988, hasn't been back in the category since.

One of the MBAs recruited by August Busch III in the late seventies would put a name to the next arena the big boys could look to for growth in 1991: the world.

Jack MacDonough, whose concerns about Bud Dry Draft were ignored, was named executive vice president/marketing for Anheuser-Busch International in 1991. He'd joined the company in 1977, after a stint as marketing manager at General Mills that included the launch of granola bars. MacDonough was credited with bringing the aging Budweiser brand back into the consciousness of younger drinkers in the early eighties through more targeted advertising and media placement; and he pioneered what *Business Week* called "an ultra-aggressive style that became known in the industry as guerrilla marketing." As an example, the magazine cited MacDonough's foxy countermove following Schlitz's acquisition of the sponsorship rights to the 1980 Winter Olympics: Budweiser advertising over the two months leading up to the start of the games featured the U.S. bobsled team, giving the appearance Anheuser-Busch was the sponsor instead of Schlitz.

Whether MacDonough's 1991 promotion to executive VP/international marketing was by way of apologizing for not heeding his council on dry, or whether it was a way to make room for August IV on the domestic side of the business, it radically changed the fortunes of Anheuser-Busch's nearest competitor.

MacDonough made an interesting discovery as his new position opened his eyes to the rest of the world, and it was this: Domination here doesn't necessarily translate into domination everywhere. "I was horrified to discover that the world wanted an American beer, and it didn't have to be Budweiser. It was disturbing to find that Budweiser had no edge as a brand [outside the U.S.]." In fact, what he found was that on an international level, Miller had a leg up: Philip Morris. With its tremendous network of international businesses, the ability of the cigarette maker to hit the ground running in many foreign countries was unmatched, as were its intelligence capabilities, as the importation of the draft beer concept had shown. Further, MacDonough found, August Busch III was seen around the globe as something of a controlling personality, which made some players hesitant to get into business with him.

At the same time he was seeing the potential problems of August's perception on a global scale, MacDonough was dealing with similar problems with his boss on a more local level. As in interoffice. In 1992, after fifteen years of service to the company—years that with his help saw the company's market share rise over 21 percent—it was increasingly clear to the forty-eight-year-old MacDonough and everyone else in the St. Louis office of Anheuser-Busch who the next president of the company would be: August Busch IV, or "the Fourth," as he was known. For MacDonough, who'd gotten his MBA at Stanford and cut his teeth at General Mills while the Fourth was a toddler, the twenty-eight-year-old's quick ascension must have been galling. MacDonough had spearheaded the successful repositioning of the franchise brand; the Fourth had presided over the failure of Bud Dry Draft. Worse, as one Anheuser-Busch executive present at the time said, the father-son relationship was dangerous to those on the perimeter. "They had a weird thing going on; almost a rivalry. Those who were aligned with III were not in favor with the boy, and somewhat vice versa."

It's not surprising, then, that MacDonough walked into August III's office in September 1992 to tell his boss that he was leaving the company. What *was* surprising, considering the all-out animosity the Beer Wars had generated among the large brewers, was his destination: Miller Brewing. The story made the rounds that in that meeting, August asked MacDonough what he could do to keep him at Anheuser-Busch. "Adopt me," MacDonough supposedly replied. Later MacDonough laughed at that piece of lore, recalling his fear at having to tell the most powerful man in the beer business that he was leaving to head up the competition: "When I was explaining what I was doing, I was afraid of death. I don't think I would have been so cavalier."

MacDonough went to Miller Brewing as president and chief operating officer, taking with him, as a former colleague lamented to *Business Week,* "the innermost secrets of Anheuser-Busch." He also took with him the unique perspective of a former blood rival; he had no illusions about his new company's shortcomings. From a profitability standpoint, Miller was in terrible shape: on a per-case basis, its profits ran at about one-third of Anheuser-Busch's. From a market-share standpoint,

Miller had stood within one percentage point of 22 percent since 1980, while Anheuser-Busch had gone steadily upward from 28.5 percent to 44.8 percent in the same time frame.

To trim overhead from the company and increase its profitability, MacDonough reorganized the sales structure, cutting back on the number of regional offices and giving each one more autonomy in terms of local marketing. In other words, a decision on pricing in Des Moines, which might have taken weeks to reach through the old way of operating at Miller, could now be reached locally within a few days. He also focused on improving relations with distributors, which had been strained in recent years by what some wholesalers saw as a lack of personal attention from the company.

Two of MacDonough's chief operating principles were speed and synergy. He believed that for Miller to get back on track, it would have to show an ability to react quickly to new ideas in the marketplace, and it would have to use the business relationships it was developing with brewers around the world to help it scout out new products (as it had already done with draft beer and A-B had done with dry). Though he wouldn't admit it, many believed MacDonough wanted to be faster and smarter so that he could show the world August Busch III had made a grave mistake in picking blood over experience.

Credit, then, MacDonough's need to show up his former employer with the arrival of ice beer in 1993.

MacDonough and Miller jumped on the latest foreign beer sensation, Canada's ice beer, early in 1993, "not because we thought it would work, but because we wanted to demonstrate that this new Miller bureaucracy wouldn't slow things down." Miller had just acquired Molson USA, the renamed Martlet, and it owned a 20 percent share of Molson Canada. To demonstrate a growing sophistication in the area of new products, Miller took the nontraditional route: rather than coming up with Miller Ice, they convinced Molson to develop a self-named version of their wildly successful Canadian Ice, which along with an ice beer from Labatt's had captured 10 percent of the Canadian beer market in a matter of months. Molson Ice debuted in test markets in August.

Perhaps out of respect for MacDonough's savvy as a marketer, Anheuser-Busch strayed from their usual MO and didn't bother with denigration or attempts at regulation. They went straight to replication: Bud Ice Draft hit some western states just a few months after Molson Ice.

Theoretically, ice beer comes from a much more easily understood set of brewing techniques than light beer, so-called bottled draft, or dry beer. Though there is no one way to brew ice beer, the common denominator in most techniques involves the cooling of beer at lower-than-normal temperatures, followed by the removal of the resulting ice crystals. Since water freezes before alcohol, filtering out the ice crystals increases the concentration of alcohol, leaving the brewer with a stronger beer.

I say "theoretically," because, as it had done with dry, Anheuser-Busch managed to co-opt a segment name without actually brewing a beer that fit within that segment's intended definition. Ice Draft from Budweiser was made with a process similar to that of many other ice beers, with one notable exception: after ice crystals formed, they were allowed to melt right back into the beer, resulting in a beer of no greater alcoholic content than traditional lager. And no clear product benefit. And no clear difference from any other beer.

But it had the Budweiser name; in fact, the original Ice Draft from the Budweiser name was quickly jettisoned in favor of a more predictable handle. On any given store shelf in 1994, it was possible to find Bud, Bud Light, Bud Dry, and newly rechristened Bud Ice. Of course, with dry beer on its deathbed in 1994, only six years after a splashy introduction, the beer industry analysts wondered if ice wasn't just the next fad to be hyped and then dropped. Anheuser-Busch's avoidance of making real ice beer didn't make for much confidence.

But the marketplace held signs that ice beer had a bit more substance as a category. For starters, shipments of ice beer in 1994—its first full year as a segment—reached an astonishing 8.2 million barrels, compared with dry's high of 4.6 million barrels in 1990. Perhaps even more encouraging for the segment was the fact that, unlike dry, where the leading brand in the category's peak year held a 72.7 percent market share, the top brand held only one-quarter of the market. Three additional brands held double-digit market share in 1994, including an import, Molson Ice. In fact, in 1994 Molson Ice was in a dead heat with Corona for the import category's number two spot.

In addition, ice beer held the attention of every major brewer, as dry had failed to do. Coors introduced something called Artic Ice in 1994; the misspelling, though it played into the cutesy tag line ("Party with an Arty"), was attributed by the brewery to their inability to get a trademark on the correctly spelled Arctic Ice. G. Heileman, which had attached the dry name to four of its brands, had seven ice beers by the end of the category's first full year. Pabst introduced four ices, including the bizarrely cross-pollinated Olde English "800" Ice.

Miller, though it had introduced the category to America through the importation of Molson Ice, took an odd route toward further ice extensions. Perhaps predictably, it beefed up its by then moribund Lite beer with the introduction of Miller Lite Ice, but it didn't extend either of its premium brands, High Life or Genuine Draft, with ice versions. Instead it used the category to test a theory it had about the nature of line extensions.

The general assumption of beer marketers had been that line extensions were the way to go when entering a new category. The use of an established brand name like Bud, Miller, or even Old Style gave each new category immediate credibility, or at least immediate consumer interest. But with that name-induced interest came a few drawbacks.

Line extensions proved to be expensive propositions, because the line names they carried necessitated serious marketing support. How do you introduce a Bud Dry and not spend a lot of money behind it? When your franchise name is at stake, you can't let your wholesalers or consumers think you're not 1,000 percent behind a new brand. Cannibalization presents another huge problem for line extensions: If you're marketing Bud Ice to typical premium lager drinkers, who's your most likely consumer? A Bud drinker, who's already shown a liking for Budweiser products. You've effectively robbed Peter to pay Paul. The problem is even more pronounced once a number of line extensions have been established under a flagship's banner: if Miller had done a Miller Ice, it might well have been damaging to Miller Genuine Draft, a cold-filtered product.

A third problem with line extensions, when you're a huge brewer like Anheuser-Busch or Miller, is that some consumers will have preconceived notions about anything you sell. "We have research," said MacDonough of the phenomenon, "that says 30 percent of [consumers] will not buy an Anheuser-Busch product, and another 30 percent will not buy a Miller product. They think that all [products brewed by a particular brewery] taste the same, and [their] mind is closed." Some of that, surely, was caused by the publicity generated by microbrews and contract beers like Sam Adams: the smaller-is-better line that Jim Koch and his ilk were using against imports had to be even more damaging to the big boys. If Miller's research was accurate, it meant that negative feelings toward giant domestic breweries dropped the potential market for a line extension by a full third.

Which is why Miller Brewing created something called the Plank Road Brewery to introduce Icehouse. Named for the brewery Frederick Miller bought in 1855 from the Best brothers, Plank Road didn't actually exist as a separate entity; Icehouse came off the same production lines as Miller High Life and Miller Lite Ice. As such, Icehouse enjoyed all the benefits of being a Miller brand—the cost-efficiencies of mass production and real distribution clout—without any of the potential drawbacks associated with being *called* a Miller brand.

Icehouse was a modest hit; even without the Miller name, it racked up full-year sales almost equal to those of the much more familiar-sounding Miller Lite Ice. Though Bud Ice beat both for the top spot on the ice sales list in 1994, their combined share, along with that of Molson Ice, made Miller the largest shipper of ice beers in the country, with a 48.2 percent share of the market. Anheuser-Busch, with Bud Ice and Bud Ice Light, held a 28.7 percent share.

Miller's ability to brag about dominating the ice beer segment would be short-lived. In 1995, only its second full year in existence, the segment dropped off by 17 percent to 6.8 million barrels. The most interesting theory on the cause of that rapid decline came from Pete Coors, who said the fate of ice beers had been determined from the start by Anheuser-Busch, wittingly or not. The problem, Coors said, was that the folks in St. Louis had poisoned the consumer pool: "They came out with a brand that had absolutely no product differentiation. [Though] they touted it as being ice beer, there wasn't anything special about it. Our friends in St. Louis killed the ice category." His point was this: When an industry leader invests heavily enough in a brand to take the lead position in a new category, that brand is going to shape the perceptions of a number of people about the category as a whole. In the case of Bud Ice, the brand didn't taste that much different from regular Bud, and the segment was written off by many as hype.

Though ice beer doesn't appear to be a category with much of a shelf life, and dry beer is all but dead, they've managed to play a dramatic role in the future of the domestic beer industry. For one major player, the lessons learned during the reign of fad products would lead to a dramatic change in business philosophy—a change that some believe could have positioned it to close in on Anheuser-Busch's lead. For another major player, the lessons ignored would lead to a series of increasingly costly blunders that have put its future in question.

For Anheuser-Busch, which had presided over the life and (imminent) death of two new categories in the span of seven years, there was only one lesson in the disappointing trajectory of the ice category: "Maybe we should have denigrated and regulated, first."

16

The Empire Strikes Back . . . Sort Of

The earth's first ice age wiped out a bunch of dinosaurs. The second one revealed a few.

The lumbering giants who dove into the ice beer category probably couldn't help themselves. They'd seen light change the face of the beer business, so they'd chased nearly every possible successor to the "hot new thing" mantle, with increasingly disappointing results. Why should ice have been any different?

Like the separated criminals in "the Prisoner's Dilemma" (discussed in the introduction), ice beer was yet another example of how fear of what the other fellow would do drove the Big Three brewers to a needlessly harsh outcome. Just look at the numbers.

In 1994, ice beer's first full year on the

market, Anheuser-Busch spent $31.5 million to advertise Bud Ice. The category leader, they sold 2.2 million barrels of the stuff, which put their per-barrel spending at $14, compared with the $2.50 per barrel they spent to advertise Budweiser. Coors put a whooping $31 behind every barrel of Artic Ice (and sold a measly one-eleventh of Bud Ice's volume), compared with $4.80 per barrel for Coors Light. Even Miller, the most thrifty of the three in the ice category, managed to spend $8.25 per barrel on Icehouse, while they spent $3.75 per barrel on Lite.

But for all the investment spending in 1994, the category languished in 1995; though Icehouse remained flat at 1.5 million barrels, big spender Bud Ice fell 27 percent to 1.6 million barrels. Clearly something was wrong with the way the big boys were approaching new segments, beer and otherwise. Low-alcohol hadn't worked; wine coolers were a disaster. Dry had withered quickly, and Ice—the splashiest starter of the lot—looked to be doing the same.

More troubling, though, the flagship brands of each of the Big Three were in serious decline. From 1990 to 1994, ice's first full year, Budweiser's average annual compound growth rate was -5 percent, Miller High Life's was -5.8 percent, and Coors Banquet's was a scary -15.9 percent. Though light brands were still growing well in some cases—most notably Bud Light and Anheuser-Busch's popular-priced Natural Light—as a category they were flattening out in volume. The desperate spending behind ice was understandable; with the traditional premium brands on the wane, and the light brigade slowing, no one seemed terribly sure how to get back on the growth track.

To hedge their bets on the latest new category, two of the Big Three were readying alternative approaches to that very problem in 1993, even as ice beer was being introduced. Though those approaches were wildly different, Miller and Coors would find some clear similarity in their next new product introductions.

My father was in his last year at Van Munching & Company when I showed him a blurb in a marketing magazine that said Miller was testing something called Miller Clear. He just shook his head and laughed. "Wacky business you're leaving," I told him.

"And not a moment too soon," he replied.

Miller Clear was just that: a beer with no color. Which, even more than dry beer, provoked one question: Why? What was the product benefit in lack of color? It seemed to be difference for the sake of difference. Oddly enough, though, even as business writers and fellow brewers snickered over what seemed to be the dumbest idea to reach the shelf in a long time, Miller Clear was testing very well. At least at first.

According to Miller president Jack MacDonough, Miller Clear's test markets showed two general responses to the brand. The first came immediately, and it was strong curiosity. Drinkers were intrigued and eager to try the stuff. Initial trial was so strong, in fact, that MacDonough very nearly rolled the brand nationally. But the second response stopped him long enough to wait and see how the repeat business was going to develop. There wasn't much to see.

"You'd go into a test market and walk into a bar and watch people drinking Miller Clear—and they'd all try it—and then the person who likes the taste of Clear gets laughed at by his buddy," recalled MacDonough. The first reaction may have been curiosity, but the second reaction was scorn. "[So] he says, 'I like the taste, but I can't stand the ridicule of my buddy here.' " Unfortunately for MacDonough and Miller, the company had spent an estimated $12 to $15 million to develop and test the brand and its advertising before realizing they had a brand that consumers would be made fun of for drinking.

Actually, unfortunate is not the way to describe the failure of Miller Clear. It prompted the company to rethink its new product launch strategy, which may have been the best thing that happened to Miller Brewing since Lite. Miller Clear forced the company to extend the internal debate it was having about the negative perceptions of its relative size as a brewer—the debate that fathered the Plank Road Brewery—to include a discussion about its bloated new product strategy. Something called "momentum marketing" was born.

Or at least rechristened. So-called momentum marketing was little more than applied common sense; it was a return to product-focused testing rather than strategy-focused testing. Where in a more traditional new product test, a number of markets might be saturated with advertising for a new brand, and pumped full of the brand itself, momentum marketing involved no advertising and an extremely limited number of bars within an extremely limited number of markets. Momentum marketing meant finding out if anyone was actually interested in the stuff independent of marketing hype. Once the test was completed, a successful brand could be rolled out slowly, building on its own word of mouth rather than the megadollar advertising that usually accompanied a major beer brand launch.

Here's how it worked: Testers hung out in accounts (bars) featuring a new product, noting the comments and social interaction of patrons drinking the brand. They'd note whether consumers tended to stop at one bottle of the new stuff or ordered another. They'd ask questions of both the bartenders and the customers that same evening, and they'd follow up those questions at a later date, to keep track of not only repeat business, but how brand perceptions developed over a little bit of time. They asked consumers if they'd recommended the brand to anyone else or had it recommended to them by anyone else. This kind of testing was relatively cheap—momentum tests cost around $500,000, rather than several million—and offered a sharper product focus. It also allowed a bit more privacy from the prying eyes of competitors, because it involved no advertising. Best of all, its relatively tiny cost meant a new brand didn't have to have mammoth volume to be financially successful.

With its new momentum marketing strategy, Miller brewing turned its new Plank Road entity into something of a skunk works. Reduced costs and the lack of worry about harming the Miller name meant brewers were freer to experiment; not so much was riding on each new brand introduction. For every successful launch, like the specialty-positioned Red Dog, there was something that never made it out of test, like a lime-flavored beer named Citro; but now the mistakes weren't so costly. *Impact* noted that in 1994, though most of Miller's major brands were down in terms of volume, new products had helped boost its overall volume by 2.6 percent.

The best sign for Miller that the Plank Road Brewery and momentum marketing were smart moves came in the September 19, 1994, issue of *Fortune,* when August Busch IV felt the need to weigh in on the subject. "Our system is set up to brew big brands," he said. "Our competition can't compete with big brands. That's why they've had to introduce lots of little brands." Never mind that the Fourth had neatly ignored the fact that the so-called big brands were mostly not doing so well. Denigration had begun. Regulation and replication couldn't be far behind.

Having taken a respectable step forward with its Plank Road strategy, Miller turned its attention in 1996 to its actual "Miller" brands, Miller Genuine Draft and Miller High Life. In doing so, it took three huge steps back. The same men who had developed Plank Road after paying careful attention to the mood of America's beer drinkers inexplicably returned to the vacuum of theoretical marketing for their next introduction, Miller Beer.

The Theory: Miller brands suffered from the lack of what a marketing executive there called a "vertical brand structure." That is, unlike Bud Light, Bud Dry, Bud Ice, and so on, which sprang from good ol' Bud, Miller Genuine Draft and Miller High Life didn't actually serve as extensions of anything called Miller. They were mired in what the exec called a "horizontal brand structure." Miller Beer, launched early in 1996 with an estimated $50 to $80 million in marketing support, was meant to change all that.

The Reality: The first person at Miller to use the phrase "vertical brand structure" should have been thrown out of an office window, charts, graphs, and all. It's hard to say who greeted the launch of Miller Beer—quickly dubbed "Miller Miller" by the competition—with *less* enthusiasm, Miller distributors or actual consumers. At a time when flagship brands from each of the major brewers were in serious and steady decline, Miller had the breathtakingly bad sense to *launch* a flagship. By year's end, estimates put the brand's market share at something under 1 percent, or at most one-twentieth the size of (the still declining) Budweiser.

Coors, meanwhile, had taken a radically different approach to the problem of declining beer volume. In a manner of speaking, it walked away from the beer business.

This was a two-step process, brought about by Pete Coors's belief that he needed outside help because, as he told *Fortune,* he "wasn't smart enough to know what to do." In 1993 he hired a new president, W. Leo Kiely III, who hailed from Frito-Lay. From his corn-chip days, Kiely brought more of a focus on in-store merchandising, or making a bigger impression on consumers right at the point at which they were spending money. As had worked so well for Van Munching and for the Boston Beer Company, Kiely also insisted that his sales force get more involved with the retail trade by making some sales calls themselves. That was smart.

And Kiely brought something else from his corn-chip days: a reverence for gimmickry. He quickly identified within Coors's new products division a potential vehicle for incremental growth, a vehicle so far removed from traditional beer that it could not easily be copied by the much larger competition. That turned out to be not so smart.

Zima Clearmalt was born of the belief that some beer drinkers didn't really much like the taste of beer. This was not a difficult belief to hold, considering the success of the lightest of the light beers and the popularity of stuffing a lime wedge into bottles of Corona. If, went the thinking at Coors, we can make something from malt that doesn't taste like beer but has some alcohol and fizz to it, something refreshing, we will have provided these people with an alternative they could be comfortable drinking. Think of it as sort of a cousin to wine coolers.

Better still, think of Zima Clearmalt as sort of a descendant of the disastrous Colorado Chiller, Coors's previous malt-based cooler. Lord knows Coors should have.

Backed by an advertising campaign that called it "Zomething Different," Zima really wasn't. It was a clear, malt-based cooler, something *Impact* was comfortable classifying along with Gallo's Bartles & Jaymes and Seagram's Coolers as a "Low-Alcohol Refresher." However different Coors wanted people to believe Zima may have been, the reality was that the company—at a time when it most needed to focus on its Coors Banquet and Coors Light brands—was putting its efforts behind a return to a small-volume category that had been at best stagnant for over half a decade.

And those efforts were formidable, if completely misguided. Though it was available only in part of the country in 1993, Coors spent $12 million behind Zima, which amounted to half of all money spent in the category. That worked out to better than $2 per each nine-liter case of product sold. The next year their spending better than tripled to $38 million, which accounted for 94 percent of the category's media expenditures. More important, though, that $38 million accounted for nearly one-third of Coors's total ad budget. The brand catapulted to the number one spot on the low alcohol refresher list with sales of 16.5 million cases. So all the spending worked . . . if you consider spending a third of your budget on a brand that peaks at 6.4 percent of your total volume working.

Like Miller Clear, Zima had one thing going for it. People were curious. They were willing to try the brand. The question was, were they going to come back for more in sufficient numbers to make the investment worth it? By early 1995 Coors had an answer: a resounding "No." *Fortune* magazine attributed the lack of repeat business to the fact that "people [didn't] like the stuff very much." In fact, *Fortune* said, an informal poll found the taste of Zima compared to "tonic water, antifreeze, and crushed SweetTart candies mixed with skunked Molson." As at least one pithy respondent put it, "Zima zucks." As the drop-off from the previous year's numbers approached the 50 percent mark, Kiely and his management team led a very odd charge: they line extended. In May of 1995, Coors rolled out Zima Gold, a "bold, rugged" version of Zima, with the beer color added in. Almost no one bought it. Pete Coors later called it "a stupid mistake. . . . I'm still kicking myself 'cause I knew it would be dumb, and I still let it happen." Zima Gold was pulled from the market by summer's end.

Its parent brand ended 1995 back in third place in the low-alcohol refresher category, with a 48 percent decline to just over 8.5 million cases. And, thanks in part to all the attention the company lavished on Zima and Zima Gold, Coors saw sales of Coors Light go flat (while competitors Bud Light and Miller Lite rose 10 percent and 2 percent respectively) and sales of Coors Banquet drop another 13 percent.

Coors had made a fundamental mistake: it took its eyes off established brands just when they needed the most attention. While the dire predictions of its competitors—one Miller executive opined that Coors wouldn't be around in a meaningful way in five years—may have been infused with wishful thinking, the generally held belief in the beer business was that the company had squandered some real potential for Coors Light and Coors Banquet while chasing after a silly gimmick. Even its own distribution chain seemed disenchanted with the company, as evinced in a *Brandweek* story from March of 1996: "Wholesalers [at Coors's annual sales convention] were enthusiastic about Coors's new-product news: that there wouldn't be any. . . ." Unlike Miller, which had settled on a reasonably inexpensive new product strategy that seemed rooted in reality, Coors faced an uncertain future with no apparent strategy at all.

At Anheuser-Busch's 1996 sales meeting, it was as if wholesalers were seeing a ghost: the ghost of Gussie Busch. More than two decades after wresting control of the brewery from him, August III was sounding more like his old man than ever before. Using the size of his brands as a very big stick, Three-Sticks told his wholesalers in no uncertain terms that they were to put their efforts behind his brands and his alone. This was not convention-stage rhetoric; he made it clear he wanted every non-Anheuser-Busch brand out of every wholesale operation that handled Anheuser-Busch brands. Since about half of his wholesalers did substantial business with solid-margin brands like Heineken and Samuel Adams, there was a lot of hand-wringing at the New Orleans meeting site.

August III had been growing increasingly frustrated with the attention being paid to brands like Samuel Adams, not only by his wholesalers, but by consumers. More than that, he seemed frustrated that Jim Koch was perceived as a real brewer and his brand was generally considered as somehow more authentic than Budweiser. For a man who'd spent much of his career agonizing over brewing capacity investments, it was galling that a competitor who had others make his beer should be more highly regarded.

The first sign that Jim Koch was at the forefront of August III's thoughts came in 1994, when Anheuser-Busch put out a press release announcing a "distribution alliance" with one of Koch's biggest competitors, Washington state's Redhook Ale Brewery. "That was not a press release," Koch told *Inc.*, "That was a declaration of war." Koch couldn't help himself; he had to sarcastically christen Anheuser-Busch's new partnership: "You know, just when you think things are going pretty well, along comes 'Budhook,' " he said, adding, "[I'm going to] go home and rent the second movie in the *Star Wars* trilogy. I forget how it ends and whether the good guys win." The title of the film Koch referred to: *The Empire Strikes Back.*

But if August III was fixated on Koch in 1994, he seemed positively obsessed with him following an incident in late 1995. What is undisputed is that while on a Hawaiian vacation in December, August III was angered to discover the relative lack of attention his brands were receiving from his own wholesaler, who also carried Samuel Adams and Heineken. The stories coming out of the islands, though completely unsubstantiated, struck fear across the distribution chain.

In one, August III allegedly found an account so loaded up with the import and the contract brew that he bought a case of Heineken, drove it to the wholesaler's office, threw it onto the floor, and said, "You're going to rue the day you paid more attention to somebody else's brand."

In another story making the rounds, he found a Samuel Adams banner up at the wholesaler, and he made an executive there read it aloud. "The Best Beer in America," the fellow stammered.

"Do you *really* believe that Samuel Adams is the best beer in America?" Busch is supposed to have asked him icily.

When the frightened man said, "No," August Busch III made him take down the banner.

Back to what is known: Within days, a crew of Anheuser-Busch merchandisers arrived on the island, plastering accounts with signage and giving the brand the attention that August III so clearly felt it had been lacking. Koch confirmed that for at least the month of January, his salesman on the islands wasn't even allowed to accompany wholesaler salesmen on account calls.

Filled with a renewed competitive zeal, August III launched into his familiar three-stage pattern, but this time with no space between the denigrate and regulate stages. By January 1996 Anheuser-Busch had prepared promotional materials to alert consumers about the hype they were being subjected to by the little guys . . . and by one big guy posing as a little guy through the Plank Road Brewery. A-B used table tents (those small, cardboard ads set on bar and restaurant tabletops like inverted V's) to knock their competitors. "Do you know where your beer comes from?" read one, which challenged drinkers to correctly identify the actual brewers behind brands like Samuel Adams, Red Dog, and Pete's Wicked Ale. The brewery followed that theme in scratch-off game cards that offered a free Bud to the consumer who could correctly identify each brew's source.

The materials sprang from the belief that "50 percent of the consumers go haywire when they find out [that Plank Road] is not a real brewery," as the Fourth told *Business Week.* (To which MacDonough shot back, "The only people annoyed are at Anheuser-Busch. The consumer doesn't care.") Experience, of course, showed MacDonough to be right; that Samuel Adams Boston Lager wasn't brewed in Boston had been an open secret for years, and Anheuser-Busch would have killed to have that brand's average annual growth rate: 61 percent between 1990 and 1994.

Nevertheless, Anheuser-Busch broadened its attack to the legislative front by filing a complaint with BATF just as its new point of sale was hitting accounts. The complaint sought to punish rival brewers for misleading consumers through their labeling. For example, the complaint cited language on the label of Pete's Wicked Ale describing the beer as being brewed "one batch at a time." True enough, said Anheuser-Busch, but misleading, because those batches were a whopping 400 barrels each, and they were brewed not at some small brewery, but at the giant Stroh Brewery, where Stroh's and Old Milwaukee were also made. The complaint also cited Jim Koch's (discontinued) small-batch claim on Samuel Adams labels, as well as the lack of Miller Brewing identification on Plank Road products. (It was highly unlikely that the BATF would rule against Plank Road, as existing guidelines required only the city of origin to appear on the label, not the name of the brewer itself.)

Eventually, Anheuser-Busch would get around to directly knocking Sam Adams in its advertising. Late in 1996, A-B ran radio ads in which an actor playing Boston Beer's Jim Koch is visited by the ghost of Samuel Adams, who takes him to task for not being honest about where his brands are brewed. The *real* Koch cheekily responded with radio ads thanking Anheuser-Busch for pointing out that it was Samuel Adams's expensive ingredients that made the brand special, not the location of its breweries.

Though the BATF complaint and the eventual ghost of Sam Adams ads were designed to make the competition look bad, they had an ironic, boomerang effect on the world's largest brewer: they highlighted, more than anything the contract brewers had done or said, the relative size of Anheuser-Busch. The brewer of Budweiser was now acting exactly like the Goliath it had been accused of being. *Brandweek* pointed out that "the nation's largest brewer [was] trying to legally squash competitors," and *The Wall Street Journal* quoted Jim Koch accusing Anheuser-Busch of "trying to strangle the baby while it's in the cradle."

Those sentiments were shared by many of the wholesalers sitting in the convention hall in New Orleans in March 1996, as they listened to Anheuser-Busch executives warn them that they'd better give "total commitment." The rationale went like this: We at Anheuser-Busch have jettisoned most of our other businesses to concentrate our efforts on beer, and therefore you the wholesaler should concentrate your efforts on us. The problem was, the rationale was nonsense. Anheuser-Busch *had* spent the last year selling off its St. Louis Cardinal baseball team, closing the doors on its Eagle Snacks unit, and spinning off its Campbell Taggert baking unit, but it had done so because the first two were money losers and the third was only marginally profitable at best. Had any of them been strongly in the black—like the Busch Gardens and Sea World theme parks the brewery held on to—would Anheuser-Busch have divested itself, so that it could concentrate on beer? Not likely. Why then, the wholesalers at the convention must have wondered, should we get rid of *profitable* side brands?

More important, though, why should wholesalers jettison *growing*, profitable side brands, when Budweiser itself was in steady decline? While they spent the New Orleans convention hearing a lot about mutual commitment, what they really wanted to know was what August Busch IV, Anheuser-Busch's vice president for brand management, was going to do about the company's sinking flagship.

Their first clue should have been his hairstyle.

Sometime in early 1996 the Fourth abandoned the classic, serious, slicked-back wet look of his father's hair for a more current, George Clooney look. Like the handsome television star, young August took out the grease, had his hair cut very short, and wore it with little bangs combed straight down on his forehead. Very cutting edge. Very modern.

Unfortunately, his hair sense extended retroactively to his advertising sense. In 1995 the Fourth had decided that what the King of Beers really needed was an up-to-date, humorous approach. Suddenly the beer that had been positioned in sort of a masculine way, the beer that was literally pushed as a reward for a hard day's work ("For all you do, this Bud's for you"), was being advertised with partying ants and croaking bullfrogs. It was as if he thought that because Bud Light was still growing, its positioning must therefore be right for Bud. As one rival ad agency executive told *Brandweek,* "The Bud you and I grew up with is a man's beer: very masculine, full of proud manhood. Now they're saying, 'Screw that. Let's make 'em laugh.' "

If the Fourth was looking for bullfrogs and ants to lift Budweiser from its multiyear slump, he failed. The brand's volume descent actually steepened; down 3.9 percent in 1994, it fell off 4.3 percent in 1995.

The Fourth's failures with Bud Dry, Bud Ice, and—so far—the flagship brand itself underscored the real concern among many of the wholesalers, and many industry watchers, about the future of Anheuser-Busch. Such was the strength of the brewer that almost no one would speak for the record about the Buschs III and IV; but privately, almost everyone I spoke to while writing this book said the same thing: The Fourth ain't the Third. One executive at a competitor said that, as had been indicated by MacDonough's departure as well as the more recent departures of other longtime Anheuser-Busch MBAs, the inevitability of the son's rise has kept the company from attracting, or keeping, great marketing minds. But more to the point, said some, the father's workaholism and respect for applied business theory were not mirrored in the son. As one former Anheuser-Busch executive said, only half-jokingly, "Auggie surrounded himself with [Wharton professor] Ackoff and a bunch of MBAs; his kid's closest adviser is a guy he met at a bar night." That, more than anything else, might explain the ants and the bullfrogs. It would also explain the trepidation so many Anheuser-Busch wholesalers feel about the day August III decides to retire.

In the meantime, though, Anheuser-Busch was in no immediate danger of losing its top spot, or even much market share, to any of its competitors. With its market share hovering around 45 percent, or nearly double number two Miller's, it would have to do something disastrous—like, say, Zima—to seriously hurt itself. That wasn't likely to happen as long as the company followed its pattern of waiting for someone else to innovate and then swooping in with its financial clout to corner the market on whatever the innovation was. (After the original light beer's five-year head start, Bud Light overtook Miller Lite in 1994.)

That pattern would extend to the specialty segment, as first seen in the brewery's "distribution alliance" with Redhook. A number of new products were planned or launched by the brewer in 1995 and 1996, many of them regionals aimed at the "local pride" element of specialty popularity. (Ironically, considering Anheuser-Busch's BATF complaint, the brewer's Texas-only ZiegenBock label carried the Anheuser-Busch name in letters so small that one beer writer noted that consumers needed "to really squint" to see it.) With August III still at the helm, and still full of competitive fire, no one was going to sneak up on the King of Beers.

Many attribute the current, humbled state of most of the beer mega-brands to something marketers call "product cycles." To me, this is a little like believing in astrology: Whatever happens is inevitable—it's dictated by forces beyond my control—so therefore, I don't have to take the blame when things go badly. In other words, it's a cop-out.

Rather, I suspect that megabrands like Budweiser, the now declining Miller Genuine Draft, and maybe even Coors Light are guilty of a lack of faith in themselves. Their marketers believed more in the vagaries of the marketplace than in the attributes of the brands, and they changed their marketing plans in ways that made what would have been short-term dips into longer-term chasms. If my father had panicked when Corona took off and aimed his advertising squarely at the party-hearty crowd stuffing limes into their beer, I suspect Heineken really would have dropped to number two or worse.

What's a product cycle, anyway? Coke's been around forever; the only time it's been threatened is when it was stupid enough to think it needed reformulation. Once it came back to reality, it went right back up to number one. Last time I checked, Mercedes-Benz was still considered to be one of the best carmakers in the world. Why? *Because it stuck to established core values.* It knew what it was, and it didn't try to be the carmaker for hipsters.

It is telling, I think, that the man who most upsets the president of the largest brewer in the world is the man who most understands the importance of clearly defined brand attributes. Rather than thinking about ways to stifle the success of Jim Koch, August Busch III might better spend his time wondering why his son is turning Budweiser into a generic, good-time brand.

And rather than wondering how a bunch of little brewers managed to paint Anheuser-Busch, Miller, and Coors as something less than serious brewers, he might reflect upon the last two decades in the industry he's presided over. Come on, Mr. Busch; did you really expect consumers to hold in high regard the companies that gave us LA beer, dry beer, and ice beer? Did you really think that drinkers would take the creators of Spuds MacKenzie, Bud Bowl, and beer-toting ants *seriously*?

Afterword

Losing the Romance

Twenty years after a few wildly successful brewers put dozens of their old, tiny brethren out of business, dozens of their new, tiny brethren have them more than a little bit edgy. This is not nearly as ironic as it is inevitable, considering the way in which Anheuser-Busch, Miller, and Coors have handled their respective successes.

Like the song says, don't it always seem to go, that you don't know what you've got 'til it's gone? For the Big Three, the heady growth that followed the introduction of light beer in the mid-seventies is gone, and it doesn't look to be coming back anytime soon. And there's a very simple reason for it: they bought into their own hype.

When light beer came along, it was an honest-to-God revolution in the brewing industry. It was a new product with a distinct and coveted selling proposition—two or three, even. It catered to those who didn't want such heavy flavor, and it catered to those who were watching their weight. It was less filling, *and* it tasted great.

Unfortunately, its makers mistook the sizzle for the steak and believed that—more than just cleverly launching and then supporting a product people desired—they had *manufactured* that desire themselves. The marketers in their offices took on more importance than the salesmen in the trade, and growth became something that the big boys believed could be mapped out in a boardroom rather than something that had to be won bar by bar, city by city.

And for a time, the cynical marketing machine that churned out silly promotions and even sillier new categories worked: everyone likes a little hype. The problem with hype, of course, is that it almost inevitably leads to backlash. First it's just a few people wondering what all the fuss is about. Soon enough, though, Toto is pulling back the curtain and revealing the Wizard for the foolish old man in the topcoat that he really is. (In this evening's performance, the role of Toto has been played by Jim Koch.)

The other problem with hype is that it clouds thinking. Caught up in a frenzy of spending, obsessed with the notion that every new product or campaign must be bigger, brighter, and bolder than anything that has gone before, the Big Three (and most of their competitors) broke some or all of the following rules . . . let's call them "the Eleven Basic Laws of Beer Marketing." (Though they're certainly applicable to other categories as well.)

Start with a good product:

Elemental, to be sure, but you'd be surprised. . . . The quickest kiss of death is to market something you already know in your gut isn't very good. Forget the test scores for a minute and ask yourself, Do I believe in the product? Gablinger's low-calorie beer was awful . . . and it failed. Coors's Colorado Chiller, about which one Coors executive quipped, "Less chilling . . . tastes like shit," failed miserably. Miller's Matilda Bay wine cooler was not only bad, it wasn't remotely like what people understood the category to be, and it failed, too. Zima, well . . . Zima *zucks,* and no matter how much of its total budget Coors sinks into this loser, it will never do enough business to justify the money being spent on it. All of these failures would have been avoidable had the companies involved been a little more honest with themselves.

Beware of small changes in quality; they can add up to disaster:

Schlitz, convinced that consumers wouldn't be able to tell, cheapened its ingredients, shortened its brewing time, and tried to artificially protect its product from the adverse effects such cost savings had on shelf life. Before all this, Schlitz rivaled Budweiser. As a result of it, Schlitz rivaled . . . well, just about no one. Meanwhile, Gussie Busch resisted the advice of those who suggested he didn't need to spend so much to make his beer, and his beer has stayed far and away number one in sales for *forty* years.

(Maybe this rule should be "Beware cost-efficiency experts," as it isn't just the actual quality of the product that counts; it's everything that contributes to a product's image. There are always ways to save money on packaging, advertising, and quality control. Those ways often belong under the heading Brand Suicide.)

Know who your customers are, and speak to them in your advertising:

Miller High Life languished pre–Philip Morris, largely because its image was almost diametrically opposed to that of most beers. The little-girl-sitting-in-the-moon logo and the "champagne of bottled beers" tag line didn't make sense for the largely blue-color constituency for brew; once they changed it to the "Miller time" ode to the workingman, the brand was revived. The marketers of Gablinger's, the first light beer, were not only guilty of breaking the first rule (by marketing a lousy product), they also broke this one by using their advertising dollars to essentially scold their most likely consumers. Not a smart way to convince people to buy a leisure product.

Protect your flagship:

Mom always said, "The most valuable thing you've got is your good name," and she was right. The positive images people associate with a brand name are priceless, and the quickest way to lose customers is to debase those images. Lowering quality, obviously, is one way of debasing them . . . and so is over-line extending. Budweiser has very possibly overextended its brand name with Bud Light, Bud Dry, and Bud Ice. Where does that leave regular Bud? (The question proves the problem: Is the original Bud now thought of as "regular" or, worse still, "plain"?)

The folks at Miller have recently shown some awareness of the damage done to their name by a sloppy handling of it: in their case, unlike Anheuser-Busch's, no one is quite sure what their line extensions are extensions *of.* They've got three major beer lines—Lite Beer from Miller, Miller Genuine Draft, and Miller High Life—which until 1996 didn't actually *extend* from anything called Miller Beer. (Showing awareness of a problem doesn't guarantee that proper steps are taken to defuse it, though: one has to wonder if the hype surrounding the recent launch of Miller Beer doesn't just feed into the backlash against megabrands . . . a backlash Miller itself acknowledged by creating its Plank Road Brewery.)

One other way to risk a flagship's image is by decentralizing it, or putting it in the hands of a diverse, and geographically separated, group of caretakers. This is the "too many cooks" problem, and it means that the imagery a brand puts out becomes subject to the taste levels of a number of individuals, instead of being agreed upon centrally. When I first learned of the regional sales and marketing structure Heineken USA was putting into place, I quietly pointed out to the marketing director that one of the four new caretakers of our brands' image had once allowed that he thought there was nothing wrong with Heineken T-shirts bearing this slogan: "Grab a Heiney." A few months later my fears were borne out when the same man had to be cautioned that a series of Heineken-sponsored "wet T-shirts nights" going on in his region was not a terrific idea.

Don't be seduced by the other guy's market:

A brand cannot be all things to all people, and in attempting to do so, it only winds up diluting its sales message to the point of meaninglessness. August Busch IV apparently decided in 1995 that if hip, funny commercials were working for Bud Light, there might as well be hip, funny commercials for Budweiser itself. Problem is, Budweiser hasn't ever been perceived as a hip, funny brand, so its sales slide continues. The marketers at Heineken USA, despite a strong indication that consumers considered Amstel Light a step up from other light beers in terms of quality and sophistication, thought the brand needed to be made more "accessible." In creating a generic ad campaign for Amstel Light—one that they hoped would appeal to drinkers of more mainstream (and less expensive) lights—they managed to cut the brand's growth in half.

Don't sacrifice existing customers for new ones:

In his book *Managing Brand Equity,* marketing professor David Aaker points out the folly of tying growth efforts mostly to the attraction of new customers. Aaker notes that once a brand is established, appealing to new customers is largely expensive and inefficient (because people who don't use your brand already aren't very likely to pay attention to your advertising message) especially when compared to keeping your current customer base loyal. Current customers—satisfied ones—will do your recruiting for you, through their example.

Michael Silver, the man in charge of the Heineken account at the brand's ad agency, Wells Rich Greene BDDP, lamented to *New York* magazine in August 1996 that "the problem with the young is that their beer consumption is high but they have no loyalty." He was, as anyone with any beer-selling experience knows, correct in this. So why on earth did he let Heineken's advertising message abandon its more established drinkership to chase after the fickle young? And why didn't it occur to anyone at either the agency or Heineken USA that Heineken's already considerable following existed *precisely because of* the maturity and class orientation of its previous advertising imagery? The answer to the first question, I would guess, is that Silver broke the previous rule, the one about being seduced by the other guy's market. The answer to the second question, to be blunt, is that this is what you get when your brand is managed by a group of people with no experience in your industry. Of course, beer probably isn't the only industry in which the allure of potential growth seems to blind folks to common sense.

Protect your pricing, and let your image justify it:

When he launched Samuel Adams Boston Lager, Jim Koch knew that charging a premium price would create a certain snob appeal. In the beer business, where there really aren't *that* many differences among brands, cost is one of the only ways to signal to the consumer that your product is better than the other guy's. (In the related liquor category, Chivas Regal's sales soared when it raised its price dramatically, even though the product was unchanged.)

That having been said, a higher price has to be bolstered by some claim that has resonance with the consumer; just saying "Hey, we're better than the other guy" won't cut it, as *everyone* says that. Koch supported his higher price by pointing out that Sam Adams was not only "craft brewed," but it was also voted "America's best beer." Heineken, aside from touting the fact it came from Europe, noted that it was "America's number one-selling imported beer."

I use the phrase "protect your pricing" for a simple reason: pricing is part of a brand's image, and that image needs protection. The lowering of pricing, though it can be done temporarily (and sparingly) as part of a promotion, can in time endanger the image of the brand by making the consumer believe it isn't really worth its usual price. The image of an entire beer category became cheapened when Anheuser-Busch and Miller both dropped the prices of their respective malt-liquor brands as a last-ditch attempt to boost sales.

Use research sparingly:

Though it's tempting to cover one's tail with extensive focus group testing, most of what qualifies as qualitative research rarely seems to disagree with good old applied common sense. When it does disagree, it tends to be because no matter how sophisticated testers claim to be, the research setting is unnatural, and (gasp!) subjects aren't always honest. (Typical focus group response: "Oh, *I'm* never swayed by advertising." This is what is known as self-delusion.) Qualitative research *can* tell you when an ad campaign is a complete, unmitigated disaster, but I submit that if you can't figure that out for yourself, you're in the wrong business.

Also, qualitative research has a deadening effect on creativity. Here is every copywriter's worst nightmare: The carefully worded gem they've just produced after months of work is rejected because a couple of twenty-eight-year-old stockbrokers at a focus group trashed it . . . probably for no other reason than to have something to say to the tester.

Quantitative research, done by an outside supplier, can be very helpful but, again, is often not necessary. Too many companies don't rely on the information they have at their fingertips every day—the stuff generated by their distribution system, their accounting department, and especially their sales force. By sifting through internally generated material, most marketers should be able to build a solid, unbiased picture of who's buying their brand and why.

Don't change for the sake of change:

As marketing guru Al Ries pointed out, marketers who've just come into a company can't seem to resist the temptation to put their own stamp on things by changing everything in sight. This is at best arrogant and at worst deadly to the brands involved.

I recently asked the public relations guy at Heineken USA why Amstel Light's packaging had been changed so dramatically *before* any decisions had been made about the direction of the brand's marketing. "You know how people like to look busy," he replied. I relate that story for two reasons. The first, obviously, is that it illustrates the point. The second is that it gives a little insight into *why* new marketers change everything: like the PR guy just quoted, who was hired *after* the Amstel Light packaging change was in place, marketers feel the overwhelming need to criticize what has come before them, so they can make a name for themselves by spearheading some *new* direction. This is because there seems to be less and less job longevity among marketers; the guy selling soda pop this year might be selling beer next year and feminine hygiene products the year after that. I suspect that the marketer of today is afraid to go to an interview for the next job and say, "Well, I've spent the last few years as a caretaker for a brand image created before I arrived on the scene."

Perhaps part of the problem is that so much exciting (and constantly changing) advertising comes out of categories where product change is inevitable, even necessary. Sneakers (sorry, *cross-trainers*) need replacing, and companies like Nike and Reebok pour hundreds of millions of dollars into introducing the "latest thing," whether it's a pump, or a new Velcro strap, or some weird green gel meant to support your arch better. Their products are constantly updated (and almost infinitely varied) and so is their marketing. Personal computers have built-in obsolescence, not to mention an incredibly diverse set of uses and users, so their marketing is by necessity all over the board.

What many beer marketers fail to realize is that beer isn't particularly exciting and is certainly not known for using the words "new" and "improved" in its marketing vocabulary. Budweiser has been essentially the same for over one hundred years; Jim Koch touts Sam Adams's generations-old recipe. Brand loyalty in the beer business comes because consumers like the notion they can count on their brand to always taste the same. Too much change in a brand's marketing message, then, is *dangerous* because it can convince a brand loyalist that the brand *itself* is somehow changed, or carries with it a new set of images that are at odds with the reasons the user picked it up in the first place. (Not to overly beat up on August Busch IV's frog commercials for Budweiser, but they stand as a perfect example of this.)

This rule goes hand in hand with the next rule:

Beware advertising agencies bearing "bold new ideas":

There is a basic tension between the advertising industry and the beer industry, and it is, simply put, *change*. Think about it: for an agency to win a new client, it must almost always convince that client that it has come up with a better (read: different) way of peddling the client's wares. Even with existing clients, agencies seem to feel that it's not enough to say, "Hey, your message is spot on; you should keep pushing the same theme with only minor creative variations," which, of course, is *exactly* what many clients should do. Agencies make their money by selling *continuous* change, which is often at odds with the best interests of their clients.

Quick: Why did Lite Beer from Miller, after years of successful Lite All-Star advertising, completely jettison not only the execution, but also the spectacularly effective "tastes great/less filling" positioning for the instantly forgettable "It's it and that's that" campaign? Stumped? You're not alone. My suspicion is that marketers at Miller got bored and let the folks comedian Jerry Seinfeld derides as "ad wizards" talk them into something new.

And finally . . .

Don't lose the romance:

Brands like Samuel Adams and Pete's Wicked have enjoyed a good run for exactly the reason Starbucks Coffee has found success in recent years: the big boys lost the romance of the product. Beer—like coffee—is a ritual. Beer is pleasure. Like most pleasures, it is taken very seriously by the people who use it.

More than anything, though, beer is a badge. Jim Koch and his brigade of upstart brewers made shinier, more attractive badges, and they took them just seriously enough.

Knowing that inevitably each one will put some serious money behind the microbrew path to future growth, the real question facing Anheuser-Busch, Miller, and Coors right now is this: Once that path bears a little fruit, can they resist temptation to return to form? Or will we one day turn on our television sets to see bikini-clad women serving Bud Micro to a dog?

A NOTE ABOUT NUMBERS

Except where otherwise noted, all sales figures and advertising expenditures quoted in *Beer Blast* come from *Impact Databank*. Of all of the numbers gathering done in the beer business, it's been my experience over the years that *Impact* does the most thorough and consistent job, thanks in large part to the Herculean efforts of its director of research, Frank C. Walters.

It bears noting that Frank's job is made difficult by the fact that the numbers brewers and importers report to him every year are not always truthful or consistent: It should come as no great surprise to the business reader that some companies inflate their numbers by providing shipment figures (which include distributor inventory) rather than actual sales figures (what the distributor has actually sold to the trade.) In addition, when a company refuses to release figures, Frank has to estimate based on whatever data he can find. And, of course, sometimes companies simply fib. For these reasons, *Impact* figures are a somewhat fluid thing; they have a tendency to adjust slightly as more complete information comes Frank's way.

Where possible, I have endeavored to use the most complete *Impact* figures available, understanding that while they may still be slightly inaccurate, they are not so much so that the sales volume or ad spending rankings of brands, brewers, and importers is inaccurately portrayed.

In the instances where *Impact*'s Heineken volume numbers were incorrect (because my father, knowing that some of his competitors sharply overstated theirs, refused to release his own and appear to be condoning the process), I have still used *Impact* figures, for the sake of consistency.

NOTES

The following abbreviations appear throughout the notes: MBA *for* Modern Brewery Age, NYT *for* New York Times, PD *for* St. Louis Post-Dispatch, *and* WSJ *for* Wall Street Journal.

Chapter 1. The Philly Keg Party, Billy Carter's Near Miss, and Al Capone's Bathtub: A Brief History of Beer in the U.S.

In preparing an admittedly whirlwind tour through roughly 350 years of beer in America, I relied chiefly on the following books:

Anderson, Will. *The Beer Book.* Princeton: Pyne Press, 1973.

Anderson, Will. *From Beer to Eternity.* Stephen Green Press, 1987.

Finch, Christopher. *A Connoisseur's Guide to the World's Best Beer.* New York: Abbeville Press Publishers, 1989.

Hernon, Peter, and Ganey, Terry. *Under the Influence: The Unauthorized Story of the Anheuser-Busch Dynasty.* New York: Simon & Schuster, 1991.

Jackson, Michael, ed. *The World Guide to Beer.* New York: Exeter Books, 1982.

Rhodes, Christine P., ed. *The Encyclopedia of Beer.* New York: Henry Holt & Company, 1995.

Yenne, Bill. *Beers of North America.* Gallery Books, 1986.

The discussion of Philip Morris's purchase of Miller Brewing is drawn largely from Richard Kluger's terrific (and exhaustive) look at the American tobacco industry, *Ashes to Ashes,* published by Knopf, 1996.

page 15 "so inferior [that] St. Louis": "The King of Beer," by Gerald Holland, *American Mercury Magazine,* Oct. 1929.

page 17 The new cap extended: Hine, Thomas, *The Total Package.* Little, Brown, 1995, p. 74.

page 18 The first push toward: Kobler, John, *Ardent Spirits: The Rise and Fall of Prohibition.* New York: DaCapo Press, 1993, p. 90.

page 19 thanks to tinkering by: Ibid., p. 207.

page 21 van Munching had convinced: van der Werf, J., ed. *Heineken History.* Self-published by Heineken, N.V., 1992, p. 257.

page 25 he managed to bring in beer from . . . Java: Ibid., p. 259.

page 25 The Dutch government forbade: Ibid., p. 260.

Chapter 2. "Let There Be Lite"

Except where noted in the text, the story of light beer's beginnings, including Miller's launch of Lite and the creation of the Lite advertising campaign, comes from the following sources:

Anderson, *From Beer to Eternity.*

Deford, Frank. *Lite Reading.* Penguin Books, Ltd., 1984.

Hernon and Ganey, *Under the Influence.*

Kluger, *Ashes to Ashes.*

The discussion of Anheuser-Busch's somewhat rocky transition between the Gussie era and the reign of August III is drawn largely from Hernon and Ganey's *Under the Influence,* in addition to the following:

"August Busch Brews up a New Spirit in St. Louis," by Thomas O'Hanlon, *Fortune,* Jan. 15, 1979.

"Get 'Em Before They Get You," by Seth Lubove, *Forbes,* July 31, 1995.

"We Missed the Boat . . . We Were Unsmarted," by Robert J. Flaherty, *Forbes,* Aug. 7, 1978.

page 30 "god-awful . . . so metallic": Interview, George Kahl.

page 31 "You'd walk into a bar": Ibid.

page 35 "I don't want to hear": quoted in Hernon and Ganey, *Under the Influence,* p. 229.

page 36 "Anheuser-Busch was a $700 million": Quoted in "Sports and Suds," by William Oscar Johnson, *Sports Illustrated,* Aug. 8, 1988.

page 37 "Three-Sticks": Interview, George Kahl.

page 40 For ninety-five days: *WSJ,* June 7, 1976.

page 40 "It was the first time": Quoted in Flaherty, "We Missed the Boat. . . ."

Chapter 3. Number Two Schlitz Its Wrists

page 42 He boasted openly: *PD,* Aug. 12, 1979.

page 42 the thinking behind it: Interview, Jack MacDonough.

page 43 For lager beer, age is everything: Duddington, C. L., *The Plain Man's Guide to Beer.* London: Pelham Books, 1974, p. 137.

page 43 Schlitz made a change in the foam stabilizer: Aaker, David, *Managing Brand Equity.* New York: Free Press, 1991, pp. 82–83.

page 44 Uihlein had taken out an option: *PD,* Aug. 12, 1979.

page 44 the waters of the Merrimack: Ibid.

page 44 Budweiser sales dropped: Ibid.

page 44 by 1977 they'd finally: "Getting Schlitz Back on Track," by Charles G. Burck, *Fortune,* April 24, 1978.

page 45 "menacing [that the] approach": Ibid.

page 45 largely using information: Interview, not for attribution.

page 45 installing G. Gordon Liddy: Liddy, G. Gordon, *Will: The Autobiography of G. Gordon Liddy,* New York: St. Martin's Press, 1980.

page 45 They were largely right: Interview, Bob Maxwell

page 46 "questionable payments": Quoted in Hernon and Ganey, *Under the Influence,* p. 243.

page 46 "Go make a case against Schlitz": Interview, Bob Maxwell.

page 46 "Uihlein's approach to BATF's: Burke, "Getting Schlitz. . . ."

page 46 "denigrate, regulate, and replicate": Interview, Gerry Khermouch.

page 47 "The whole light . . . tastes awful": Quoted in *PD,* Aug. 12, 1979.

page 47 who still did consulting: Interview, Jack MacDonough.

page 47 "too damn long": Quoted in Flaherty, "We Missed the Boat. . . ."

page 47 "A lot of people think Miller": Quoted in O'Hanlon, "August Busch Brews up. . . ."

page 47 "we were simply unsmarted": Quoted in Flaherty. "We Missed the Boat. . . ."

page 47 from a prestrike $30 million: Ibid.

page 47 "arrogant and complacent": Ibid.

page 48 "This business is now": Quoted in O'Hanlon, "August Busch Brews up. . . ."

page 48 had a rug made with: *PD,* Aug. 12, 1979.

page 48 something called "Gussie Beer": *PD,* Sept. 28, 1978.

page 48 Miller went after G. Heileman: *PD,* Aug. 12, 1979.
page 48 "We seriously doubt that consumers": Quoted in *PD,* Feb. 1, 1979.

Chapter 4. The Regulatory Waltz

There are two main sources for the story of the public relations licking Löwenbräu took at the hands of Anheuser-Busch. The first is an article that appeared in the July 8 issue of *The New Republic,* "Frothing and Foaming," by Eliot Marshall, which details the differences between the imported and domestic versions of the brand, as well as the curious BATF rule that prohibits beer-ingredient labeling. The second is an interview with Bob Maxwell, the former deputy assistant director of the BATF, wherein he explained the bureau's reason for its labeling rule, as well as Löwenbräu's circuitous route to comeuppance.

page 54 That version of Anheuser-Busch's: *PD,* March 23, 1979.
page 54 Miller would lose this game, too: Hernon and Ganey, *Under the Influence,* p. 319.
page 54 "This is how we would": Quoted in *PD,* Aug. 12, 1979.
page 55 brewers discovered an enzyme: "Light On," by Rona Gindin, *Cheers,* July/August 1995.
page 56 Miller withdrew from the group: Hernon and Ganey, *Under the Influence,* p. 320.
page 56 "What's wrong with this beer?": Quoted in *PD,* Aug. 12, 1979.
page 56 "hysterically anti-gun": Ibid.
page 56 "a marksman and an avid hunter": Ibid.
page 57 "adult soft drink": "Felled By a Head of Foam," by Thomas O'Hanlon, *Fortune,* Jan. 15, 1979.
page 58 simply buy 7UP: *PD,* Aug. 13, 1979.

Chapter 5. Take Me out to the Beer Game

The fight for sports media-buying supremacy between Anheuser-Busch and Miller is explained thoroughly in "Sports and Suds," by William Oscar Johnson, which appeared in *Sports Illustrated* on August 8, 1988. In expanding on Johnson's telling, I relied on Hernon and Ganey's *Under the Influence,* Deford's *Lite Reading,* and an extensive interview with Jack MacDonough, who explained the morale problems at Anheuser-Busch following Gussie Busch's slashing of the marketing department, as well as shedding light on the problems spectacular volume growth were causing A-B during the seventies. Specific quotes from those sources are endnoted below.

As Anheuser-Busch declined to cooperate with the writing of this book, the basic recounting of the theme of the "*Bud* Light" commercials comes from the author's memory—with a number of phone calls to friends and industry figures to back up that memory. Chalk it up to the effectiveness of the campaign, along with the massive budget behind it, that *everyone* seems to have some memory of it.

page 62 The statistics go: Johnson, "Sports and Suds."
page 63 "the proper drink . . .": Ibid.
page 64 An economics professor: Marshall, "Frothing and Foaming."
page 64 $69 a share . . . to a low of $18: Hernon and Ganey, *Under the Influence,* p. 321.
page 65 "We told you so": Interview, Jack MacDonough.
page 65 "looked at us like we had just": Quoted in Johnson, "Sports and Suds."
page 66 "That book was about five or six": Quoted in Hernon and Ganey, *Under the Influence,* pp. 325–326.
page 68 "the greatest defection since Solzhenitsyn": Quoted in Deford, *Lite Reading,* p. 10.
page 68 "freaked out": Quoted in Johnson, "Sports and Suds."

Chapter 6. The Wisconsin Hare and the Rocky Mountain Tortoise

Tracing the ever-expanding Heileman empire was possible in large part due to the "Special Report" on the beer business published annually by *Modern Brewery Age.* The rise of Coors and its eventual, endless PR struggle are both chronicled in Robert J. Burgess's *Silver Bullets,* published by St. Martin's Press in 1993. The information found in these sources was backed up by other industry publications and fleshed out through interviews with a number of participants and writers, most notably Pete Coors and Joe Fuentes from Coors, and Terri Allen, who for many years authored the *Modern Brewery Age* annual reports.

page 72 "It's like elephants dancing on gnats": Quoted in *PD,* Aug. 13, 1979.
page 73 Anheuser-Busch was paying: *MBA,* Feb. 25, 1974.
page 76 "price classified": By 1989 the management of G. Heileman had come to acknowledge the problem with discounting. Then president Murray S. Cutbush told *Liquor Store* in March 1989, "We as a company do not believe in price discounting because we think it ends up cheapening your brand."
page 78 forced to publicly sell: Phone interview, Joe Fuentes.
page 80 "the intellectual capacity to succeed": *The Rocky Mountain News,* as quoted in Burgess, *Silver Bullets,* p. 17.
page 81 "I've been doing some figuring": Quoted in Burgess, *Silver Bullets,* pp. 133–134.

Chapter 7. The Search for the Next Big Thing

In describing the rapid movement from one trend to the next—from low alcohol to nonalcoholic, from wine coolers to "draft in a bottle"—I relied heavily on the *Modern Brewery Age* annual reports for some sense of chronology and *Impact Databank* to keep up with the sheer breadth of offerings in those segments. In addition, Susan Gurevitz's piece in the August 19, 1985, issue of *Adweek,* "Low Alcohol Beer Struggles for Glass Distinction," put the problems faced by the category into perspective.

The strange story of Masters III is detailed in Burgess's *Silver Bullets,* as is Coors's response (or lack thereof) to Miller's encroachment on their "cold-filtered" turf.

Michael Crete and Stuart Bewley's tremendous success with California Cooler is recounted from a *Nation's Business* article from Oct. 1985: "How They Became the Kings of Coolers," by Richard Steven Street. An understanding of the genesis of that segment came from another *Adweek* story, "Cooler Makers Thirsting for a Winter Windfall," by Sarah Stiansen, Dec. 2, 1985.

Susan Henderson at Miller Brewing provided copies of the pamphlets used by both Anheuser-Busch and Miller to "educate" bartenders about draft beer in a bottle. A BATF official who wished to remain nameless explained why the bureau felt the need to get into the fray.

page 85 sales at half a million barrels: *Beer Marketer's Insights,* quoted in *Adweek,* Aug. 19, 1985.
page 85 "We've come to the conclusion": Quoted in *Adweek,* Aug. 19, 1985.
page 85 a number of countries tax beverages: Interview, Jerome F. Schmutte.
page 90 "That's not going to work, because": Interview, Jack MacDonough.
page 91 The first product, launched: *Adweek,* Oct. 7, 1985.
page 91 when Ginny suggested to her husband: Interview, not for attribution.
page 92 "a horrendous idea": Interview, Jack MacDonough.
page 92 "I didn't say . . .": Ibid.
page 94 "This draft thing . . .": Interview, Jerome F. Schmutte.
page 97 "a routine analysis": *WSJ,* Oct. 5, 1988.
page 97 "The best barometer . . .": Ibid.
page 98 "At Miller, we innovate . . .": *WSJ,* April 2, 1991.

Chapter 8. Honey Tree Evil Eye Is a Bitch

Anheuser-Busch's fight with Soho Natural Soda and August Busch IV's brush with the law are both detailed in Hernon and Ganey's *Under the Influence. Modern Brewery Age* was invaluable in explaining, again with its annual "Special Report," both the issue of alcohol equivalency and the push by advocacy groups to severely restrict (or ban) beer advertising.

The Spuds MacKenzie saga comes chiefly from William Oscar Johnson's "Sports and Suds" and Barbara Lippert's "With Spuds for Bud, It's a Dog's Light with Real Bite," which ran in *Adweek's Marketing Week* on June 29, 1987.

page 99 bested by $1.25 million: *MBA,* Feb. 25, 1985.
page 99 "A-B required or induced": Ibid.
page 100 Anheuser-Busch countered Collier's: *MBA,* March 14, 1988.
page 100 "They think by this kind of hardball": Quoted in *PD,* May 7, 1987.
page 103 "contributing to the problem": Quoted in *MBA,* March 17, 1986.
page 104 "technically correct": Ibid.
page 104 "Trojan horse intended to": Ibid.
page 104 "underscores the need": Ibid.
page 105 "the brilliance of this campaign": *Adweek's Marketing Week,* June 29, 1987.
page 105 she had to endure: *Movieline,* 1996.
page 106 "Some guy in our Chicago": Quoted in Johnson, "Sports and Suds."
page 106 "targeting youthful drinkers": Quoted in *MBA,* March 14, 1988.
page 107 featuring Spuds as Santa: *Adweek,* Dec. 14, 1987.
page 107 "actually in treatment": *Newsweek,* quoting from *Rolling Stone* interview with Clapton, Sept. 26, 1988.
page 108 **Government Warning**: Content of warning label as reported in *MBA,* March 13, 1989.
page 110 "Like it or not . . . beer ads": Quoted in *MBA,* March 1991.
page 110 "lower on the educational ladder": Ibid.
page 111 "When I go home tonight": Quoted in *NYT,* Dec. 24, 1989.
page 111 "If we continue on the same track": Quoted from the text of Peter Coors's speech to the California Beer & Wine Wholesalers, made available by Coors Brewing.
page 112 "unite under a banner": Ibid.

Chapter 9. Show Us Your Badge

As should be obvious, much of the material in chapters 9 through 14 comes from my family's and my own experience in the beer business. In re-creating the rise of the imported beer segment, I spoke extensively with former Van Munching & Company employees, current and former imported beer wholesalers, and Gerald Regan and Pete Fearon, two men who led the Molson efforts during the seventies and eighties.

Direct quotes, where they appear in relating the inner workings of Van Munching & Company, were either heard by me or repeated to me by the persons who heard them.

page 128 a study of consumer attitudes: "Consumer Evaluations of Brand Extensions," by David A. Aaker and Kevin Lane Keller, *Journal of Marketing,* vol. 54, Jan. 1990.

page 129 "a metallic red background": "Matters of Import," by Paul B. Brown, *Inc.,* Oct. 1988.

Chapter 10. Mexican Soda Pop

Marvin Kimmel and George Kahl were especially helpful in explaining the unique problems created for suppliers by transshipping. Quotations from advertisements are taken directly from videotaped copies of the ads.

page 134 "very light, airy": Klein, Bob, *The Beer Lover's Rating Guide,* New York: Workman Publishing, 1995, p. 92.

page 135 "These guys absolutely were not geniuses": Interview, not for attribution.

page 136 one Corona distributor . . . had thirty-five: *Los Angeles Times,* July 28, 1987.

page 136 "free of any contamination": Ibid.

page 139 *doubled,* from $.28 to: Bloomberg Financial Markets.

page 139 "has its finger in the dike": "Heineken Holland Beer, Its Influence Slipping, Is Skating on Thin Ice," by Fran Brock, *Adweek's Marketing Week,* Nov. 16, 1987.

page 139 "Heineken has simply gotten too big": Ibid.

page 140 "For years Heineken has been": "Beer Blunder," by Claire Poole, *Forbes,* Feb. 8, 1988.

page 141 "later this year . . . nothing will keep": Ibid.

page 141 "When the market changes": Ibid.

page 142 "a trendy brew": Ibid.

Chapter 11. Sam Adams: Brewer, Patriot, Pain in the Ass

Quotations from Samuel Adams Boston Lager advertising came directly from either copies of the print ads or transcripts of the radio ads prepared by SSC&B/Lintas, Van Munching & Company's advertising agency through the first few years of Sam Adams's rise.

page 149 founded on $400,000 in 1985: *WSJ,* Aug. 18, 1987.

page 149 If Julia Child brings her: Koch would make this argument in the *WSJ,* April 15, 1996.

page 151 Chivas Regal, whose sales soared: Aaker, *Managing Brand Equity,* pp. 99–100.

page 153 "the Schlitz of Europe": Quoted in *San Juan,* June/July 1983.

page 154 "If what I said was untrue": Quoted in *Adweek,* June 8, 1987.

page 154 "I spent six months making sure": Quoted in the *Cambridge Chronicle,* Oct. 9, 1986.

page 155 "If I were wrong, do you think": Quoted in an Associated Press story, run in the *Bridgeport Post,* July 13, 1986.

page 155 "I don't think any of us": Quoted in "Beer Wars, Round Two," by Mark Starr, *Newsweek,* June 9, 1986.

page 156 "I do wish we had been able": Letter from Richard M. Smith to Leo Van Munching Jr., Aug. 8, 1986.

page 159 "people like to know some dirty": Quoted in Starr, "Beer Wars, Round Two."

page 159 "I read an interview": Letter from Skip Miller to Philip Van Munching, Aug. 28, 1986.

page 160 if the rumors were to be believed: The complaints by small brewers about Koch's alleged "buying" of the award are mentioned in the *WSJ,* Dec. 31, 1995.

page 161 the association didn't eliminate: In the Dec. 31, 1995, *WSJ,* Charles Papazian, the president of the Association of Brewers, said the prize was discontinued in part because of the complaints about Koch.

page 162 [The] beer is currently: "Good for What Ales You," by Harold J. Bauld, *Boston* magazine, June 1986.

page 162 "serious problems": Quoted in "Beer Wars," by Kevin R. Convey, *Boston* magazine, June 1988.

page 163 "I am very offended": Ibid.

page 165 we got word . . . that Koch's lawyer: Letter from H. John Campaign, of Graham, Campaign & McCarthy, to Rob Stevens, of Heineken's U.S. office.

Chapter 12. Heineken Light, Heineken Chunky Style

page 177 the tax increase enacted: *MBA,* March 1991.

page 177 European brands were the hardest hit: *Impact Databank,* 1992 edition.

page 179 "Americans tend to segment": "A Market Structure Study of the U.S. Beer Category," a research project prepared by the Patrick Group, New York, for Heineken B.V., June 15, 1992, p. 8.

page 179 "Budweiser is still the 'standard' ": Ibid., p. 6.

page 179 "It is inconceivable to most": Ibid., p. 14.

page 185 his numbers . . . doubled those: *New York Daily News,* Sept. 1, 1993.

Chapter 13. Beerbarians at the Gate

page 196 "aging" and "no labor turnover": "Presentation of Key Issues to Executive Board," presented by Michael Foley to Heineken B.V., July 13, 1994.

page 196 "It was so disheartening": Interview, not for attribution.

page 197 "on both emotional and rational levels": "Qualitative Research on Advertising for Heineken and Amstel Light," a research project prepared by Research International, New York, for Heineken B.V., June 1992, p. 3.

page 197 "a clear, on-target message": Qualitative Research on 3 Television Commercials," a research project prepared by the B/R/S Group, New York, for Heineken B.V., Van Munching & Company, and Warwick Baker & Fiore, March 1994, p. 19.

page 197 "excellent fit with [the] brand image": Ibid., p. 20.

page 199 "Wherever you are" and "Heineken. For those": "Project Sphinx: U.S. Research on Global Positioning Concepts for Heineken," a research project prepared by the B/R/S Group, New York, for Heineken B.V., Nov. 1993.

page 199 Each year, hundreds of: "Marketers, Stop Your Tinkering" by Al Ries, *NYT,* June 19, 1994.

page 200 Marketing ought to be like flying: Ibid.

page 202 "Perhaps in recent years": Quoted in "Business 100 1994," *Irish America* magazine, 1994.

page 202 "was riding on the back": Quoted in *MBA,* July 10, 1995.

Chapter 14. A Tale of Two Bocks, and a Red Star Rising

page 205 brewed in the fall: Rhodes, ed., *The Encyclopedia of Beer,* p. 95.

page 206 "not too heavy or filling": "Tarwebok: A Qualitative Look at U.S. Potential," a research study prepared by the B/R/S Group, New York, for Heineken B.V. and Van Munching & Company, April 1994, p. 23.

page 212 "Searching for control": "Qualitative-Diagnostic Research into the Perception and Meaning of Communication Possibilities for Amstel Light," a research project prepared by Censydiam USA for Van Munching & Company, Dec. 8, 1994, p. 8.

page 213 "To create a brand image": Ibid., p. 3.

page 214 It is cool, charming: "Amstel's new personality ignores its import importance," by Bob Garfield, *Advertising Age,* May 15, 1995.

page 220 might be $1.19: Interview, George Kahl.

page 221 on the . . . shelf at $5.79: Ibid.

page 221 adding less than . . . 100,000 cases: Interview, not for attribution.

page 223 "overwhelmingly negative": Interview, Bob Garfield.

page 223 "could antagonize": *Brandweek,* March 4, 1996.

page 223 "Gee, who do you think": Interview, Gerry Khermouch.

page 223 "gimmicky" and "immature": From a research project prepared by Censydiam USA for Heineken USA (exact title and date unknown), p. 121.

page 223 "although the star": Ibid.

page 225 "Fidel Castro gift package": Interview, not for attribution.

page 225 the identity of the voice-over: *NYT,* Sept. 26, 1996.

page 225 "a complete disaster": Interview, not for attribution.

page 226 Nearly as mind boggling: "Heineken Nights, Embarrassing Daze," by Bob Garfield, *Advertising Age,* April 29, 1996, p. 51.

page 228 Heineken's 9.3 percent advance: From an internal memo, Heineken USA, July 1, 1996.

page 228 *all* growth was coming: Ibid.

page 228 10.6 percent decline in the brand's profitability: "Heineken USA Inc. Financial Management Report," distributed internally, dated July 10, 1996.

Chapter 15. The Search for the Next Big Thing, II: Dry Ice in the 'Hood

page 232 "Here you have a superpremium": Interview, not for attribution.

page 232 it had captured fully one-third: *MBA,* March 13, 1989.

page 232 Japanese brewers had developed: "My Beer Is Dry Beer," by Cheryl Ursin, *Cheers,* March/April 1992.

page 232 A-B had altered the dry-brewing: Interview, not for attribution.

page 233 "the consumer said, 'If I buy' ": Interview, Jerome Schmutte.

page 233 "There were a lot of people worried": Interview, Jack MacDonough.

page 234 August placed his twenty-five-year-old son: Ibid.

page 234 "a fraud, it's people rationalizing": Quoted in *PD,* Aug. 12, 1979.

page 234 "Many brewers, who are now out of business": Quoted in *Beverage Dynamics,* Sept. 1990.

page 235 "You idiots, you've destroyed": Interview, Jack MacDonough.

page 236 malt liquor is made by converting: Rhodes, ed., *The Encyclopedia of Beer,* p. 312.

page 236 "an unseemly, poorly balanced": Ibid.

page 236 as high as 8.3 percent, 66 percent stronger: Ibid., p. 313.

page 237 the belief that there was nothing: Interview, Jerome Schmutte.

page 238 "8 ball": *WSJ,* July 1, 1991.

page 238 "Forget eight ball, that beer": Ibid.

page 239 "It's the Power": Ibid.

page 239 "the Real Power!": Ibid.

page 239 "It'll blow you away" and "No. 1 strongest malt": Ibid.

page 239 "Too cold to hold": Quoted in *Washington Post,* Sept. 4, 1991.

page 239 protested in August 1991: *Chicago Tribune,* Aug. 22, 1991.

page 239 banned the brand's posters: *MBA,* March 1992.

page 239 "Pour a little out on the curb": Quoted in *Washington Post,* Sept. 4, 1991.

page 239 Robert Abrams . . . announced: *NYT,* Feb. 27, 1992.

page 239 "[Get] your girl in the mood": Quoted in *WSJ,* March 9, 1992.

page 240 Patrick Stokes wrote in June: *WSJ,* July 1, 1991.

page 240 The BATF approved it: *Los Angeles Times,* May 12, 1992.

page 241 Antonia Novello spoke publicly: *WSJ,* April 22, 1992.

page 241 "The person [marketing] Crazy Horse": Interview, not for attribution.

page 242 "an ultra-aggressive style": "Now It's Jack MacDonough Time," by Julia Flynn, *Business Week,* Dec. 7, 1992.

page 242 "I was horrified to discover": Interview, Jack MacDonough.

page 243 "They had a weird thing going on": Interview, not for attribution.

page 243 "When I was explaining": Interview, Jack MacDonough.

page 243 "the innermost secrets": Quoted in Flynn, "Now, It's Jack MacDonough Time."

page 244 "not because we thought": Interview, Jack MacDonough.

page 245 the common denominator in most techniques: Rhodes, ed., *The Encyclopedia of Beer,* p. 263.

page 245 they were allowed to melt: Interview, not for attribution. (This was confirmed by Anheuser-Busch's two main rivals, Pete Coors of Coors Brewing and Jack MacDonough of Miller Brewing.)

page 246 the cutesy tag line . . . was attributed: "Cold Spell," by Paul Lukas, *New York,* Feb. 26, 1996.

page 247 "We have research": Interview, Jack MacDonough.

page 248 "They came out with a brand": Interview, Pete Coors.

Chapter 16. The Empire Strikes Back . . . Sort Of

page 251 "You'd go into a test market": Interview, Jack MacDonough.

page 251 had spent an estimated $12 to $15 million: The June 6, 1994, edition of *USA Today* put the figure at $12 million, and the Feb. 12, 1996, edition of *Brandweek* put it at $15 million.

page 251 "momentum marketing": *WSJ,* June 24, 1994.

page 253 "Our system is set up": Quoted in "A Whole New Ball Game in Beer," by Patricia Sellers, *Fortune,* Sept. 19, 1994.

page 254 "wasn't smart enough": Ibid.

page 254 the belief that some beer drinkers: Interview, Pete Coors.

page 255 "people [didn't] like the stuff": Sellers, "A Whole New. . . ."

page 256 "a stupid mistake": Interview, Pete Coors.

page 256 "Wholesalers . . . were enthusiastic": *Brandweek,* March 18, 1996.

page 257 "That was not a press release": Quoted in "Brewed Awakening," *Inc.,* Oct. 1994.

page 258 for at least the month: Interview, Jim Koch.

page 258 "Do you know where your beer": Interview, Jack MacDonough.

page 258 followed that theme in scratch-off: *WSJ,* April 15, 1996.

page 258 "50 percent of the consumers go haywire": Quoted in "From the Microbrewers Who Brought You Bud, Coors . . ." by Richard A. Melcher, *Business Week,* April 24, 1995.

page 258 "The only people annoyed": Ibid.

page 259 filing a complaint with BATF: *WSJ,* April 15, 1996.

page 259 "the nation's largest brewer": *Brandweek,* April 8, 1996.

page 260 "trying to strangle the baby": Quoted in *WSJ,* April 15, 1996.

page 260 "total commitment": Quoted in *Brandweek,* March 18, 1996.

page 260 selling off its St. Louis Cardinal: "How the Eagle Became Extinct," by Richard A. Melcher, *Business Week,* March 4, 1996.

page 260 a more current, George Clooney look: If you don't believe me, check out the cover photo of August IV on the April 8, 1996, issue of *Brandweek.* In an unfortunate coincidence, another cover story that ran in an adjacent column (this one about Rogaine) carried an oddly appropriate headline, considering it appeared alongside Busch IV's new 'do: "Hair Today."

page 261 "The Bud you and I grew up with": Quoted in "Recrowning the King of Beers," by Gerry Khermouch, *Brandweek,* April 8, 1986.

page 261 "Auggie surrounded himself": Interview, not for attribution.

page 262 "to really squint": Khermouch, "Recrowning the King of Beers."

Afterword: Losing the Romance

page 267 "Less chilling . . . tastes like shit": Quoted in Burgess, *Silver Bullets,* p. 38.

page 269 the folly of tying growth efforts: Aaker, *Managing Brand Equity.*

page 269 "the problem with the young": Quoted in "Beer Hall Push," by Alex Williams, *New York,* Aug. 26, 1996.

page 270 Chivas Regal's sales soared: Aaker, *Managing Brand Equity,* pp. 99–100.

INDEX

A

B

C

I

J

K

L

M

N

O

P

Q

R

S

Z

About the Author

PHILIP VAN MUNCHING, a writer living in New York City, received his journalism degree from Northwestern University. The third generation to enter the beer business (and the first American-born), he spent a decade at Van Munching & Company, Inc., importer of Heineken Beer, holding several posts, including director of advertising. Preceding his stint at Van Munching & Company, he spent twenty-two years across the breakfast table from the most successful man ever in the imported beer business, absorbing lessons in history, marketing philosophy, and the importance of sitting up straight. Van Munching's political and social commentary has appeared on the op-ed pages of *The New York Times* and the *Chicago Tribune.* He and his wife, Christina, have two daughters.

To the great disappointment of most of his friends and acquaintances, he can no longer get free beer.